Yale University

College Hymnal for Divine Service

at Yale College in the Battell Chapel

Yale University

College Hymnal for Divine Service
at Yale College in the Battell Chapel

ISBN/EAN: 9783337370893

Printed in Europe, USA, Canada, Australia, Japan

Cover: Foto ©Lupo / pixelio.de

More available books at **www.hansebooks.com**

The College Hymnal

FOR DIVINE SERVICE

AT

YALE COLLEGE

IN THE

BATTELL CHAPEL

NEW YORK
HENRY HOLT AND COMPANY
1877

Table of Subjects

FOR THE LORD'S DAY	1–44
FOR MORNING AND EVENING	45–67
GOD THE CREATOR	68–108
OUR LORD JESUS CHRIST	109–161
THE HOLY SPIRIT	162–179
REDEMPTION	180–225
THE CHURCH	226–240
THE LORD'S SUPPER	241–255
REPENTANCE	256–281
CHRISTIAN JOY AND HOPE	282–395
CHRISTIAN DUTY AND TRIAL	396–447
TIME, DEATH, AND JUDGMENT	448–482
HEAVEN	483–511

For the Lord's Day

1 *"Enter into His gates with thanksgiving."* [OLD HUNDRED

WITH one consent, let all the earth
  To God their cheerful voices raise;
Glad homage pay, with awful mirth,
  And sing before Him songs of praise :—

2 Convinced that He is God alone,
    From whom both we and all proceed;
  We, whom He chooses for His own,
    The flock that He vouchsafes to feed.

3 O enter then His temple gate,
    Thence to His courts devoutly press;
  And still your grateful hymns repeat,
    And still His name with praises bless.

4 For He's the Lord—supremely good,
    His mercy is for ever sure;
  His truth, which always firmly stood,
    To endless ages shall endure.
                              Tate and Brady

2 *"God, even our own God, shall bless us."* [RETREAT

COMMAND Thy blessing from above,
  O God! on all assembled here;
Behold us with a Father's love,
  While we look up with filial fear.

For the Lord's Day

 2 Command Thy blessing, Jesus! Lord!
  May we Thy true disciples be;
 Speak to each heart the mighty word,
  Say to the weakest, 'Follow me.'

 3 Command Thy blessing in this hour,
  Spirit of truth! and fill this place
 With humbling and with healing power,
  With smiting and with quickening grace.

 4 O Thou, our Maker, Saviour, Guide,
  One true eternal God confest!
 Whom Thou hast joined let none divide,
  None dare to curse whom Thou hast blest.
James Montgomery

3 *"This is the day which the Lord hath made."* [SCHUMANN

 THIS day at Thy creating word
 First o'er the earth the light was poured:
 O Lord, this day upon us shine,
 And fill our souls with light divine.

 2 This day the Lord, for sinners slain,
 In might victorious rose again:
 O Jesus, may we raised be
 From death of sin to life in Thee.

 3 This day the Holy Spirit came
 With fiery tongues of cloven flame:
 O Spirit, fill our hearts this day
 With grace to hear, and grace to pray.

 4 O day of light, and life, and grace,
 From earthly toils sweet resting-place!
 Thy hallowed hours, best gift of love,
 Give we again to God above.
William Walsham How

4   [FEDERAL STREET

"That Christ may dwell in your hearts by faith."

Come, dearest Lord, descend and dwell
   By faith and love in every breast;
Then shall we know, and taste, and feel
   The joys that cannot be exprest.

2 Come fill our hearts with inward strength,
   Make our enlarged souls possess,
And learn the height, and breadth, and length
   Of Thine unmeasurable grace.

3 Now to the God whose power can do
   More than our thoughts or wishes know,
Be everlasting honors done
   By all the church, through Christ His Son.
                              Isaac Watts

5   *"The gift of the Holy Ghost."*   [LATOUR

Spirit of truth! on this Thy day,
   To Thee for help we cry,
To guide us through the dreary way
   Of dark mortality.

2 We ask not, Lord, Thy cloven flame,
   Or tongues of various tone;
But long Thy praises to proclaim
   With fervor in our own.

3 No heavenly harpings soothe our ear,
   No mystic dreams we share;
Yet hope to feel Thy comfort near,
   And bless Thee in our prayer.

4 When tongues shall cease, and power decay,
   And knowledge empty prove,
Do Thou Thy trembling servants stay,
   With faith, with hope, with love.
                              Reginald Heber

For the Lord's Day

[DARWELL

6 *"How amiable are Thy tabernacles, O Lord of Hosts."*

  Lord of the worlds above,
   How pleasant and how fair
  The dwellings of Thy love,
   Thine earthly temples are!
To Thine abode | With warm desires
My heart aspires, | To see my God.

  2 O happy souls, that pray
   Where God appoints to hear!
  O happy men, that pay
   Their constant service there!
They praise Thee still; | That love the way
And happy they | To Zion's hill.

  3 They go from strength to strength,
   Through this dark vale of tears,
  Till each arrives at length,
   Till each in heaven appears.
O glorious seat, | Shall thither bring
When God our King | Our willing feet!
         Isaac Watts

7 *"God be merciful unto us, and bless us."* [RETREAT

 O God, whose presence glows in all
  Within, around us, and above!
 Thy word we bless, Thy name we call,
  Whose word is truth, whose name is love.

2 That truth be with the heart believed
  Of all who seek this sacred place;
 With power proclaimed, in peace received,
  Our spirits' light, Thy Spirit's grace.

3 That love its holy influence pour,
  To keep us meek, and make us free,
 And throw its binding blessing more
  Round each with all, and all with Thee.

4 Direct and guard the youthful strength,
   Devoted to Thy Son this day;
   And give Thy word full course at length
   O'er man's defects and time's decay.

5 Send down its angel to our side;
   Send in its calm upon the breast;
   For we would know no other guide,
   And we can need no other rest.

   Nathaniel Langdon Frothingham

[WOODSTOCK

8 *"In Thy fear will I worship toward Thy holy temple."*

   LORD, in the morning Thou shalt hear
   My voice ascending high;
   To Thee will I direct my prayer,
   To Thee lift up mine eye:—

2 Up to the hills where Christ is gone,
   To plead for all His saints,
   Presenting at His Father's throne
   Our songs and our complaints.

3 Thou art a God, before whose sight
   The wicked shall not stand;
   Sinners shall ne'er be Thy delight,
   Nor dwell at Thy right hand.

4 But to Thy house will I resort,
   To taste Thy mercies there;
   I will frequent Thy holy court,
   And worship in Thy fear.

5 O may Thy Spirit guide my feet
   In ways of righteousness!
   Make every path of duty straight,
   And plain before my face.

   Isaac Watts

For the Lord's Day

9 [GERMAN TE DEUM
"Blessed is He that cometh in the name of the Lord."

HOSANNA to the living Lord!
Hosanna to the incarnate Word!
To Christ, Creator, Saviour, King,
Let earth, let heaven, Hosanna sing.

2 Hosanna, Lord! Thine angels cry;
Hosanna, Lord! Thy saints reply:
Above, beneath us, and around,
The dead and living swell the sound.

3 O Saviour! with protecting care,
Return to this Thy house of prayer:
Assembled in Thy sacred name,
Here we Thy parting promise claim.

4 But, chiefest, in our cleansed breast,
Eternal! bid Thy Spirit rest,
And make our secret soul to be
A temple pure, and worthy Thee!

5 So, in the last and dreadful day,
When earth and heaven shall melt away,
Thy flock, redeemed from sinful stain,
Shall swell the sound of praise again.

Reginald Heber

10 [DARMSTADT
"O Thou that hearest prayer, unto Thee shall all flesh come."

PRAISE waits in Zion, Lord, for Thee;
 There shall our vows be paid:
Thou hast an ear when sinners pray;
 All flesh shall seek Thine aid.

2 Lord, our iniquities prevail,
 But pardoning grace is Thine,
And Thou wilt grant us power and skill
 To conquer every sin.

3 In answering what Thy church requests
   Thy truth and terror shine;
   And works of dreadful righteousness
   Fulfill Thy kind design.

4 Thus shall the wondering nations see
   The Lord is good and just;
   And distant islands fly to Thee,
   And make Thy name their trust.

Isaac Watts

11   "*In Thee, O Lord, do I hope.*"   [MENDELSSOHN

Come, Thou desire of all Thy saints,
   Our humble strains attend,
While, with our praises and complaints,
   Low at Thy feet we bend.

2 How should our songs, like those above,
   With warm devotion rise!
  How should our souls, on wings of love,
   Mount upward to the skies!

3 Come, Lord, Thy love alone can raise
   In us the heavenly flame;
  Then shall our lips resound Thy praise,
   Our hearts adore Thy name.

4 Dear Saviour, let Thy glory shine,
   And fill Thy dwellings here,
  Till life, and love, and joy divine
   A heaven on earth appear.

5 Then shall our hearts enraptured say,—
   Come, great Redeemer, come,
  And bring the bright, the glorious day,
   That calls Thy children home.

Anne Steele

For the Lord's Day

12   *"Those that seek Me early shall find Me."*   [HENDON

  LORD! we come before Thee now:
  At Thy feet we humbly bow;
  O, do not our suit disdain;
  Shall we seek Thee, Lord, in vain?

2 Lord! on Thee our souls depend;
  In compassion, now descend;
  Fill our hearts with Thy rich grace;
  Tune our lips to sing Thy praise.

3 In Thine own appointed way,
  Now we seek Thee, here we stay;
  Lord, we know not how to go,
  Till a blessing Thou bestow.

4 Send some message from Thy word,
  That may joy and peace afford;
  Let Thy Spirit now impart
  Full salvation to each heart.
                    William Hammond

13   *"In Thy light shall we see light."*   [KLEIN

  MORN of morns, and day of days!
  Beauteous were thy new-born rays:
  Brighter yet from death's dark prison,
  Christ, the Light of lights, is risen.

2 He commanded, and His word
  Death and the dread chaos heard;
  O shall we, more deaf than they,
  In the chains of darkness stay?

3 Unto hearts in slumber weak,
  Let the heavenly trumpet speak;
  And a newer walk express
  Their new life to righteousness.

4 Grant us this, and with us be,
O Thou Fount of charity,
Thou who dost the Spirit give,
Bidding the dead letter live.

5 Glory to the Father, Son,
And to Thee, O Holy One,
By whose quickening breath divine
Our dull spirits burn and shine.
Isaac Williams

14   "*Now is Christ risen from the dead.*"   [TEMA

THE day of resurrection!
   Earth, tell it out abroad!
The Passover of gladness!
   The Passover of God!
From death to life eternal,
   From this world to the sky,
Our Christ hath brought us over,
   With hymns of victory.

2 Our hearts be pure from evil,
   That we may see aright
The Lord in rays eternal
   Of resurrection-light:
And, listening to His accents,
   May hear, so calm and plain,
His own All Hail,—and hearing,
   May raise the victor strain!

3 Now let the heavens be joyful!
   Let earth her song begin!
Let the round world keep triumph,
   And all that is therein:
Invisible and visible
   Their notes let all things blend,
For Christ the Lord hath risen,—
   Our Joy that hath no end.
John Mason Neale

15 "*Return unto thy rest, O my soul.*" [TEMA

O DAY of rest and gladness,
　O day of joy and light,
O balm of care and sadness,
　Most beautiful, most bright;
On thee the high and lowly,
　Through ages joined in tune,
Sing, Holy, Holy, Holy,
　To the great God Triune.

2 On thee, at the creation,
　　The light first had its birth;
　On thee for our salvation
　　Christ rose from depths of earth;
　On thee our Lord victorious
　　The Spirit sent from heaven;
　And thus on thee most glorious
　　A triple light was given.

3 To-day on weary nations
　　The heavenly manna falls;
　To holy convocations
　　The silver trumpet calls,
　Where gospel-light is glowing
　　With pure and radiant beams,
　And living water flowing
　　With soul-refreshing streams.

4 New graces ever gaining
　　From this our day of rest,
　We reach the rest remaining
　　To spirits of the blest;
　To Holy Ghost be praises,
　　To Father and to Son;
　The church her voice upraises
　　To Thee, blest Three in One.

　　　　　　Christopher Wordsworth

For the Lord's Day

[WOODSTOCK

16 *"Herein is My Father glorified, that ye bear much fruit."*

O God! by whom the seed is given,
  By whom the harvest blest;
Whose word, like manna showered from heaven,
  Is planted in our breast.

2 Preserve it from the passing feet,
  And plunderers of the air,
The sultry sun's intenser heat,
  And thorns of worldly care.

3 Though buried deep, or thinly strown,
  Do Thou Thy grace supply;
The hope in earthly furrows sown
  Shall ripen in the sky!   *Reginald Heber*

[UNION

17 *"If ye know these things, happy are ye if ye do them."*

I love the volume of Thy word;
What light and joy those leaves afford
  To souls benighted and distrest!
Thy precepts guide my doubtful way,
Thy fear forbids my feet to stray,
  Thy promise leads my heart to rest.

2 Thy threatenings wake my slumbering eyes,
And warn me where my danger lies;
  But 'tis Thy blessed gospel, Lord,
That makes my guilty conscience clean,
Converts my soul, subdues my sin,
  And gives a free but large reward.

3 Who knows the errors of his thoughts?
My God, forgive my secret faults,
  And from presumptuous sins restrain:
Accept my poor attempts of praise,
That I have read Thy book of grace,
  And book of nature, not in vain.
          Isaac Watts

For the Lord's Day

[ZEPHYR

18 *"They that wait upon the Lord shall renew their strength."*

How pleasant, how divinely fair,
O Lord of hosts, Thy dwellings are!
With long desire my spirit faints
To meet the assemblies of Thy saints.

2 My flesh would rest in Thine abode,
My panting heart cries out for God;
My God, my King, why should I be
So far from all my joys and Thee!

3 Blest are the saints who sit on high
Around Thy throne of majesty;
Thy brightest glories shine above,
And all their work is praise and love.

4 Blest are the souls that find a place
Within the temple of Thy grace;
There they behold Thy gentler rays,
And seek Thy face, and learn Thy praise.

5 Blest are the men whose hearts are set
To find the way to Zion's gate:
God is their strength; and through the road
They lean upon their helper, God.

6 Cheerful they walk with growing strength,
Till all shall meet in heaven at length;
Till all before Thy face appear,
And join in nobler worship there.

Isaac Watts

[ZANESVILLE

19 *"A day in Thy courts is better than a thousand."*

BLEST day of God, most calm, most bright,
 The first and best of days,
The laborer's rest, the saint's delight,
 A day of joy and praise!

2 My Saviour's face did make thee shine,
    His rising did thee raise:
  This made thee heavenly and divine
    Beyond the common days.

3 The first-fruits oft a blessing prove
    To all the sheaves behind;
  And they the day of Christ that love
    A happy week shall find.

4 This day I must with God appear,
    For, Lord, the day is Thine;
  O help me spend it in Thy fear,
    Then shall the day be mine.
                            John Mason

20   "*The Lord loveth the gates of Zion.*"   [LATOUR

  ARISE, O King of grace! arise,
    And enter to Thy rest;
  Lo! Thy church waits with longing eyes,
    Thus to be owned and blest.

2 Enter with all Thy glorious train,
    Thy Spirit and Thy word;
  All that the ark did once contain
    Could no such grace afford.

3 Here, mighty God! accept our vows,
    Here let Thy praise be spread;
  Bless the provisions of Thy house,
    And fill Thy poor with bread.

4 Here let the Son of David reign,
    Let God's Anointed shine;
  Justice and truth His court maintain,
    With love and power divine.
                            Isaac Watts

For the Lord's Day

21   *"Thy Word is a lamp unto my feet."*   [HAYDN

THE starry firmament on high,
And all the glories of the sky,
Yet shine not to Thy praise, O Lord,
So brightly as Thy written word;
The hopes that holy word supplies,
Its truths divine, and precepts wise,
In each a heavenly beam I see,
And every beam conducts to Thee.

2 When, taught by painful proof to know
That all is vanity below,
The sinner roams from comfort far,
And looks in vain for sun or star;
Soft gleaming then those lights divine
Through all the cheerless darkness shine,
And sweetly to the ravished eye
Disclose the Day-spring from on high.

3 The heart, in sensual fetters bound,
And barren as the wintry ground,
Confesses, Lord, Thy quickening ray;
Thy word can charm the spell away;
With genial influence can beguile
The frozen wilderness to smile;
Bid living waters o'er it flow,
And all be paradise below.

4 Almighty Lord, the sun shall fail,
The moon forget her nightly tale,
And deepest silence hush on high
The radiant chorus of the sky;
But, fixed for everlasting years,
Unmoved amid the wreck of spheres,
Thy word shall shine in cloudless day,
When heaven and earth have past away.
                              Sir Robert Grant

For the Lord's Day

[SPANISH HYMN

22 *"Blessed are they that dwell in Thy house."*

PLEASANT are Thy courts above,
In the land of light and love;
Pleasant are Thy courts below,
In this land of sin and woe.
O, my spirit longs and faints
For the converse of Thy saints,
For the brightness of Thy face,
For Thy fulness, God of grace!

2 Happy birds that sing and fly
Round Thy altars, O Most High!
Happier souls that find a rest
In a Heavenly Father's breast!
Like the wandering dove, that found
No repose on earth around,
They can to their ark repair,
And enjoy it ever there.

3 Happy souls! their praises flow
Even in this vale of woe;
Waters in the desert rise,
Manna feeds them from the skies:
On they go from strength to strength,
Till they reach Thy throne at length,
At Thy feet adoring fall,
Who hast led them safe through all.

4 Lord! be mine this prize to win!
Guide me through a world of sin!
Keep me by Thy saving grace;
Give me at Thy side a place:
Sun and Shield alike Thou art;
Guide and guard my erring heart!
Grace and glory flow from Thee;
Shower, O shower them, Lord, on me!

Henry Francis Lyte

23 *"There remaineth a rest to the people of God."* [ZEPHYR

 Lord of the Sabbath! hear our vows,
 On this Thy day, in this Thy house;
 And own as grateful sacrifice
 The songs which from the desert rise.

2 Thine earthly Sabbaths, Lord, we love;
 But there's a nobler rest above;
 To that our laboring souls aspire
 With ardent pangs of strong desire.

3 No more fatigue, no more distress,
 Nor sin nor hell shall reach the place;
 No groans to mingle with the songs
 Which warble from immortal tongues.

4 No rude alarms of raging foes;
 No cares to break the long repose;
 No midnight shade, no clouded sun,
 But sacred, high, eternal noon.

5 O long-expected day, begin!
 Dawn on these realms of woe and sin!
 Fain would we leave this weary road,
 And sleep in death, to rest with God!
      Philip Doddridge

24 *"Surely the Lord is in this place."* [GERMAN TE DEUM

Lo! God is here! Let us adore,
 And own, how dreadful is this place!
Let all within us feel His power,
 And silent bow before His face!
Who know His power, His grace who prove,
Serve Him with awe, with reverence love.

2 Lo! God is here! Him day and night
    United choirs of angels sing:
   To Him, enthroned above all hight,
    Heaven's hosts their noblest praises bring:
   Disdain not, Lord, our meaner song,
   Who praise Thee with a stammering tongue!

3 Gladly the toys of earth we leave,
    Wealth, pleasure, fame, for Thee alone:
   To Thee our will, soul, flesh, we give;
    O take, O seal them for Thine own!
   Thou art the God! Thou art the Lord!
   Be Thou by all Thy works adored!
                                John Wesley

25   [JESUS, MEIN LEBEN
   "The foundation of God standeth sure."

CHRIST is made the sure foundation,
    Christ the Head and Corner-stone,
Chosen of the Lord, and precious,
    Binding all the church in one,
Holy Zion's help for ever,
    And her confidence alone.

2 To this temple, where we call Thee,
    Come, O Lord of hosts, to-day:
   With Thy wonted loving-kindness,
    Hear Thy servants as they pray;
   And Thy fullest benediction
    Shed within its walls alway.

3 Here vouchsafe to all Thy servants
    What they ask of Thee to gain,
   What they gain from Thee for ever
    With the blessed to retain,
   And hereafter in Thy glory
    Evermore with Thee to reign.
                            John Mason Neale

For the Lord's Day

26   "*Thou wilt keep him in perfect peace, whose*   [NEWTON
             mind is stayed on Thee."

SAFELY through another week,
   God has brought us on our way;
Let us now a blessing seek,
   Waiting in His courts to-day:
Day of all the week the best,
Emblem of eternal rest.

2 While we pray for pardoning grace,
     Through the dear Redeemer's name,
   Show Thy reconciled face—
     Shine away our sin and shame;
   From our worldly care set free,
   May we rest this day in Thee.

3 Here we come Thy name to praise;
     May we feel Thy presence near:
   May Thy glory meet our eyes,
     While we in Thy house appear:
   Here afford us, Lord, a taste
   Of our everlasting rest.

4 May the gospel's joyful sound
     Wake our minds to raptures new;
   Let Thy victories abound,—
     Unrepenting souls subdue;
   Thus may all our Sabbaths prove,
   Till we rest in Thee above.
                              John Newton

27   "*My soul thirsteth for Thee.*"   [LANESBORO'

EARLY, my God, without delay,
   I haste to seek Thy face;
My thirsty spirit faints away,
   Without Thy cheering grace.

2 So pilgrims on the scorching sand,
    Beneath a burning sky,
  Long for a cooling stream at hand,
    And they must drink or die.

3 I've seen Thy glory and Thy power
    Through all Thy temple shine:
  My God, repeat that heavenly hour,
    That vision so divine.

4 Not all the blessings of a feast
    Can please my soul so well,
  As when Thy richer grace I taste,
    And in Thy presence dwell.

5 Not life itself, with all its joys,
    Can my best passions move,
  Or raise so high my cheerful voice,
    As Thy forgiving love.

6 Thus till my last expiring day,
    I'll bless my God and King;
  Thus will I lift my hands to pray,
    And tune my lips to sing.
                                Isaac Watts

28 *"Where two or three are gathered together in* [FOUNTAIN
      My name, there am I in the midst of them."

  JESUS, we look to Thee,
    Thy promised presence claim:
  Thou in the midst of us shalt be,
    Assembled in Thy name.

2 Thy name salvation is,
    Which here we come to prove;
  Thy name is life, and health, and peace,
    And everlasting love.

3 We meet, the grace to take
   Which Thou hast freely given;
  We meet on earth for Thy dear sake,
   That we may meet in heaven.

4 Present we know Thou art,
   But O, Thyself reveal;
  Now, Lord, let every bounding heart
   The mighty comfort feel.

5 O might Thy quickening voice
   The death of sin remove;
  And bid our inmost souls rejoice
   In hope of perfect love.
                      Charles Wesley

29   *"Every one that asketh, receiveth."* [RETREAT

Jesus, where'er Thy people meet,
There they behold Thy mercy-seat;
Where'er they seek Thee, Thou art found,
And every place is hallowed ground.

2 For Thou, within no walls confined,
  Inhabitest the humble mind;
  Such ever bring Thee where they come,
  And going take Thee to their home.

3 Dear Shepherd of Thy chosen few,
  Thy former mercies here renew;
  Here to our waiting hearts proclaim
  The sweetness of Thy saving Name.

4 Here may we prove the power of prayer
  To strengthen faith and sweeten care,
  To teach our faint desires to rise,
  And bring all Heaven before our eyes.

For the Lord's Day

5 Lord, we are few, but Thou art near;
Nor short Thine arm, nor deaf Thine ear;
O rend the heavens, come quickly down,
And make a thousand hearts Thine own!
William Cowper

[ADVENT EVENING HYMN
30 *"Great is the Lord, and greatly to be praised."*

SING to the Lord a joyful song,
  Lift up your hearts, your voices raise;
To us His gracious gifts belong,
  To Him our songs of love and praise.

2 For life and love, for rest and food,
  For daily help and nightly care,
Sing to the Lord, for He is good,
  And praise His name, for it is fair.

3 For strength to those who on Him wait,
  His truth to prove, His will to do,
Praise ye our God, for He is great;
  Trust in His name, for it is true.

4 For joys untold that daily move
  Round those who love His sweet employ,
Sing to our God, for He is love;
  Exalt His name, for it is joy.

5 For life below, with all its bliss,
  And for that life, more pure and high,
That inner life, which over this
  Shall ever shine, and never die:

6 Sing to the Lord of heaven and earth
  Whom angels serve and saints adore,
The Father, Son, and Holy Ghost,
  To whom be praise for evermore.
John Samuel Bewley Monsell

For the Lord's Day

[HAMDEN

31 *"He will fulfill the desire of them that fear Him."*

In Thy name, O Lord! assembling,
    We Thy people now draw near:
Teach us to rejoice with trembling;
    Speak, and let Thy servants hear;
      Hear with meekness,
Hear Thy word with godly fear.

2 While our days on earth are lengthened,
    May we give them, Lord, to Thee:
Cheered by hope, and daily strengthened,
    May we run, nor weary be,
      Till Thy glory
Without cloud in heaven we see.

3 There, in worship purer, sweeter,
    All Thy people shall adore;
Tasting of enjoyment greater
    Than they could conceive before;
      Full enjoyment,—
Full, and pure, for evermore.

Thomas Kelly

[HENDON

32 *"And God said, Let there be light: and there was light."*

On this day, the first of days,
God the Father's name we praise;
Who, creation's Lord and Spring,
Did the world from darkness bring.

2 On this day the Eternal Son
Over death His triumph won;
On this day the Spirit came
With His gifts of living flame.

3 O that fervent love to-day
May in every heart have sway,
Teaching us to praise aright
God the Source of life and light.

4 Father, who did fashion me
  Image of Thyself to be,
  Fill me with Thy love divine,
  Let my every thought be Thine.

5 Holy Jesus, may I be
  Dead and buried here with Thee;
  And, by love inflamed, arise
  Unto Thee a sacrifice.

6 Thou who dost all gifts impart,
  Shine, sweet Spirit, in my heart;
  Best of gifts Thyself bestow;
  Make me burn Thy love to know.
                    Sir Henry Williams Baker

[EFFEN
33 "*The law of the Lord is perfect, converting the soul.*"
  GOD, in the gospel of His Son,
  Makes His eternal counsels known;
  'Tis here His richest mercy shines,
  And truth is drawn in fairest lines.

2 Here sinners of a humble frame
  May taste His grace and learn His name;
  May read in characters of blood,
  The wisdom, power, and grace of God.

3 Here faith reveals to mortal eyes
  A brighter world beyond the skies;
  Here shines the light which guides our way
  From earth to realms of endless day.

4 O grant us grace, Almighty Lord,
  To read and mark Thy holy word;
  Its truth with meekness to receive,
  And by its holy precepts live.
                    Benjamin Beddome

For the Lord's Day

34   *"The Lord is risen indeed."*   [CALVARY

CHRIST the Lord is risen to-day,
Sons of men and angels say;
Raise your joys and triumphs high,
Sing, ye heavens, and earth reply.

2 Love's redeeming work is done,
Fought the fight, the battle won:
Lo! our Sun's eclipse is o'er;
Lo! He sets in blood no more.

3 Vain the stone, the watch, the seal;
Christ hath burst the gates of hell!
Death in vain forbids His rise;
Christ hath opened Paradise!

4 Lives again our glorious King:
Where, O Death, is now thy sting?
Once He died, our souls to save:
Where thy victory, O Grave?

5 Soar we now where Christ has led,
Following our exalted Head;
Made like Him, like Him we rise;
Ours the cross, the grave, the skies.
                            Charles Wesley

35 *"The grace of God that bringeth salvation."* [CAPERNAUM

SOVEREIGN and transforming Grace,
    We invoke Thy quickening power;
Reign the spirit of this place,
    Bless the purpose of this hour.

2 To the anxious soul impart
    Hope all other hopes above;
Stir the dull and hardened heart
    With a longing and a love.

3 Give the struggling peace for strife;
    Give the doubting light for gloom;
    Speed the living into life;
    Warn the dying of their doom.

4 Work in all, in all renew,
    Day by day, the life divine;
    All our wills to Thee subdue,
    All our hearts to Thee incline.
                    Frederic Henry Hedge

36   *"In the Spirit on the Lord's day."*   [LISBON

THIS is the day of light:
    Let there be light to-day;
    O Day-spring, rise upon our night,
    And chase its gloom away.

2 This is the day of rest:
    Our failing strength renew;
    On weary brain and troubled breast
    Shed Thou Thy freshening dew.

3 This is the day of peace:
    Thy peace our spirits fill;
    Bid Thou the blasts of discord cease,
    The waves of strife be still.

4 This is the day of prayer;
    Let earth to heaven draw near;
    Lift up our hearts to seek Thee there,
    Come down to meet us here.

5 This is the first of days:
    Send forth Thy quickening breath,
    And wake dead souls to love and praise,
    O Vanquisher of death!
                    John Ellerton

37   "*Walk as children of light.*"   [MIDNIGHT

AGAIN the Lord of Life and Light
  Awakes the kindling ray,
Unseals the eyelids of the morn,
  And pours increasing day.

2 O what a night was that which wrapt
  The heathen world in gloom!
O what a sun, which broke this day
  Triumphant from the tomb!

3 This day be grateful homage paid,
  And loud hosannas sung;
Let gladness dwell in every heart,
  And praise on every tongue.

4 Ten thousand differing lips shall join
  To hail this welcome morn,
Which scatters blessings from its wings
  To nations yet unborn.

5 The powers of darkness leagued in vain
  To bind His soul in death;
He shook their kingdom, when He fell,
  With His expiring breath.

6 And now His conquering chariot wheels
  Ascend the lofty skies;
While broke beneath His powerful cross
  Death's iron scepter lies.

7 To Thee, my Saviour and my King,
  Glad homage let me give;
And stand prepared like Thee to die,
  With Thee that I may live!

Anna Lætitia Barbauld

38   *"The Lord is my strength and song, and is become my salvation."*   [DARMSTADT

This is the day the Lord hath made,
    He calls the hours His own;
Let heaven rejoice, let earth be glad,
    And praise surround the throne.

2 To-day He rose and left the dead,
    And Satan's empire fell;
To-day the saints His triumph spread,
    And all His wonders tell.

3 Hosanna to the anointed King,
    To David's holy Son;
Help us, O Lord; descend, and bring
    Salvation from Thy throne.

4 Blest be the Lord, who comes to men
    With messages of grace;
Who comes, in God His Father's name,
    To save our sinful race.

5 Hosanna in the highest strains
    The church on earth can raise;
The highest heavens in which He reigns,
    Shall give Him nobler praise.
                  Isaac Watts

39   [ADVENT EVENING HYMN
"This is the generation of them that seek Him."

O Thou, to whom, in ancient time,
    The lyre of Hebrew bards was strung,
Whom kings adored in song sublime,
    And prophets praised with glowing tongue!

2 Not now on Zion's hight alone
    The favored worshiper may dwell,
Nor where, at sultry noon, Thy Son
    Sat weary by the patriarch's well.

3 From every place below the skies,
    The grateful song, the fervent prayer,
The incense of the heart, may rise
    To heaven, and find acceptance there.

4 O Thou, to whom, in ancient time,
    The lyre of prophet bards was strung!
To Thee, at last, in every clime,
    Shall temples rise, and praise be sung.
                        John Pierpont

40 [MENDELSSOHN
"*The entrance of Thy words giveth light.*"

THE Spirit breathes upon the word,
    And brings the truth to sight;
Precepts and promises afford
    A sanctifying light.

2 A glory gilds the sacred page,
    Majestic, like the sun;
It gives a light to every age,
    It gives, but borrows none.

3 The hand that gave it, still supplies
    The gracious light and heat;
Its truths upon the nations rise,
    They rise but never set.

4 Let everlasting thanks be Thine,
    For such a bright display,
As makes a world of darkness shine
    With beams of heavenly day.

5 My soul rejoices to pursue
    The steps of Him I love,
Till glory breaks upon my view
    In brighter worlds above.
                        William Cowper

For the Lord's Day

41 *"Thy kingdom come; Thy will be done."* [BADEA

Lord, at this closing hour,
  Establish every heart
Upon Thy word of truth and power,
  To keep us when we part.

2 Peace to our brethren give;
  Fill all our hearts with love;
In faith and patience may we live,
  And seek our rest above.

3 Through changes, bright or drear,
  We would Thy will pursue;
And toil to spread Thy kingdom here,
  Till we its glory view.

4 To God, the Only Wise,
  In every age adored,
Let glory from the church arise
  Through Jesus Christ our Lord.
                    Eleazar Thompson Fitch

42   [PLEYEL'S HYMN

Now may He who from the dead
  Brought the Shepherd of the sheep,
Jesus Christ, our King and Head,
  All our souls in safety keep.

2 May He teach us to fulfill
    What is pleasing in His sight;
  Make us perfect in His will,
    And preserve us day and night!

3 To that dear Redeemer's praise,
    Who the covenant sealed with blood,
  Let our hearts and voices raise
    Loud thanksgivings to our God.
                       John Newton

43 [Dismission

Lord, dismiss us with Thy blessing,
 Fill our hearts with joy and peace;
Let us each, Thy love possessing,
 Triumph in redeeming grace;
  O refresh us,
 Traveling through this wilderness.

2 Thanks we give, and adoration,
 For Thy gospel's joyful sound;
May the fruits of Thy salvation
 In our hearts and lives abound;
  May Thy presence
 With us evermore be found.

3 So, whene'er the signal's given
 Us from earth to call away,
Borne on angels' wings to heaven,
 Glad the summons to obey,
  May we ever
 Reign with Christ in endless day.
Walter Shirley

44 [Burney

Dismiss us with Thy blessing, Lord;
Help us to feed upon Thy word;
All that has been amiss forgive,
And let Thy truth within us live.

2 Though we are guilty, Thou art good;
Wash all our works in Jesus' blood;
Give every fettered soul release,
And bid us all depart in peace.
Joseph Hart

For Morning and Evening

45   "*On Thee do I wait all the day.*"   [POTSDAM

THRICE happy souls, who born of heaven
   While yet they sojourn here,
Thus all their days begin with God,
   And spend them in His fear!

2 Mid hourly cares, may love present
   Its incense to Thy throne;
And, while the world our hands employs,
   Our hearts be Thine alone!

3 When to laborious duties called,
   Or by temptations tried,
We'll seek the shelter of Thy wings,
   And in Thy strength confide.

4 As different scenes of life arise,
   Our grateful hearts would be
With Thee, amid the social band,
   In solitude with Thee.

5 At night, we lean our weary heads
   On Thy paternal breast;
And safely folded in Thine arms,
   Resign our powers to rest.

6 In solid, pure delights like these,
   Let all my days be past;
Nor shall I then impatient wish,
   Nor shall I fear, the last.

Philip Doddridge

46   *"He that keepeth thee will not slumber."*   [WARE

Up to the hills I lift mine eyes,
The eternal hills beyond the skies;
Thence all her help my soul derives,
There my Almighty Refuge lives.

2 He lives, the Everlasting God,
That built the world, that spread the flood;
The heavens with all their hosts He made,
And the dark regions of the dead.

3 He guides our feet, He guards our way;
His morning smiles bless all the day;
He spreads the evening veil, and keeps
The silent hours while Israel sleeps.

4 Should earth and hell with malice burn,
Still thou shalt go, and still return,
Safe in the Lord; His heavenly care
Defends thy life from every snare.

5 On thee foul spirits have no power;
And, in thy last departing hour,
Angels, that trace the airy road,
Shall bear thee homeward to thy God.

Isaac Watts

47   *"The Lord is my portion."*   [TALLIS' EVENING HYMN

My God, how endless is Thy love!
   Thy gifts are every evening new;
And morning mercies from above
   Gently distill like early dew.

2 Thou spread'st the curtains of the night,
   Great Guardian of my sleeping hours;
Thy sovereign word restores the light,
   And quickens all my drowsy powers.

3 I yield my powers to Thy command;
  To Thee I consecrate my days;
  Perpetual blessings from Thine hand
  Demand perpetual songs of praise.

Isaac Watts

48 *"In all thy ways acknowledge Him."* [SEYMOUR

As the sun doth daily rise
Brightening all the morning skies,
So to Thee with one accord
Lift we up our hearts, O Lord!

2 Thou by whom all things are fed,
  Give us for the day our bread;
  Strength unto our souls afford
  From the Bread of Heaven, Lord!

3 Be our Guard in sin and strife;
  Be the Leader of our life;
  While we daily search Thy word,
  Wisdom true impart, O Lord!

4 When the hours are dark and drear,
  When the tempter lurketh near,
  By Thy strengthening grace outpoured
  Save the tempted ones, O Lord!

5 Praise we with the heavenly host
  Father, Son, and Holy Ghost;
  Thee would we with one accord
  Praise and magnify, O Lord!

Horatio, Earl Nelson

[BARNBY

49 *"My voice shalt Thou hear in the morning, O Lord."*

AWAKE, my soul, and with the sun
Thy daily stage of duty run;
Shake off dull sloth, and joyful rise
To pay thy morning sacrifice.

2 Thy precious time misspent redeem;
Each present day thy last esteem;
Improve thy talent with due care;
For the great day thyself prepare.

3 In conversation be sincere;
Keep conscience as the noontide clear;
Think how All-seeing God thy ways
And all thy secret thoughts surveys.

4 By influence of the light divine
Let thy own light to others shine;
Reflect all heaven's propitious rays,
In ardent love and cheerful praise.

5 Wake and lift up thyself, my heart,
And with the angels bear thy part,
Who, all night long, unwearied sing
High praise to the Eternal King.

6 Lord, I my vows to Thee renew;
Disperse my sins as morning dew;
Guard my first springs of thought and will,
And with Thyself my spirit fill.

7 Direct, control, suggest, this day,
All I design, or do, or say;
That all my powers, with all their might,
In Thy sole glory may unite.

8 Praise God, from whom all blessings flow;
Praise Him, all creatures here below!
Praise Him above, ye heavenly host;
Praise Father, Son, and Holy Ghost!

Thomas Ken

50 *"In Thy light shall we see light."* [ALL SAINTS

O JESUS, Lord of heavenly grace,
Thou brightness of Thy Father's face,
Thou Fountain of eternal light,
Whose beams disperse the shades of night!

2 Come, holy Sun of heavenly love,
Shower down Thy radiance from above,
And to our inward hearts convey
The Holy Spirit's cloudless ray!

3 So we the Father's help will claim,
And sing the Father's glorious name;
And His almighty grace implore,
That we may stand, to fall no more.

4 May He our actions deign to bless,
And loose the bonds of wickedness;
From sudden falls our feet defend,
And grant us patience to the end.

5 May faith, deep rooted in the soul,
Subdue our flesh, our minds control;
May guile depart, and discord cease,
And all within be joy and peace!

6 O Christ! with each returning morn
Thine image to our hearts is borne;
O may we ever clearly see
Our Saviour and our God in Thee!

John Chandler

51 *"I have set the Lord always before me."* [BARNBY

FORTH in Thy Name, O Lord, I go,
My daily labor to pursue,
Thee, only Thee, resolved to know
In all I think, or speak, or do.

2 The task Thy wisdom hath assigned
 O let me cheerfully fulfill;
 In all my works Thy presence find,
 And prove Thine acceptable will.

3 Thee may I set at my right hand,
 Whose eyes mine inmost substance see,
 And labor on at Thy command,
 And offer all my works to Thee.

4 Give me to bear Thy easy yoke,
 And every moment watch and pray;
 And still to things eternal look,
 And hasten to Thy glorious day.

5 For Thee delightfully employ
 Whate'er Thy bounteous grace hath given,
 And run my course with even joy,
 And closely walk with Thee to heaven.
                                Charles Wesley

[HARMONY GROVE
52 *"I will go in the strength of the Lord God."*

AGAIN the daylight fills the sky;
We lift our hearts to God on high,
That He, in all we do or say,
Would keep us free from harm to-day;

2 Would guard our hearts and tongues from
   strife;
 Would shield from anger's din our life;
 From all ill sights would turn our eyes,
 And close our ears from vanities;

3 Would keep our inmost conscience pure;
 Our souls from folly would secure;
 Would bid us check the pride of sense
 With due and holy abstinence.

4 So we, when this new day is gone,
And shades of night are drawing on,
With conscience by the world unstained
Shall praise His name for victory gained.

5 All praise to God the Father be;
All praise, Eternal Son, to Thee;
Whom with the Spirit we adore
For ever and for evermore.
John Mason Neale

53   *"Order my steps in Thy word."*   [ST. GEORGE

Now that the day-star glimmers bright
  We suppliantly pray
That He, the uncreated Light,
  May guide us on our way.

2 No sinful word, nor deed of wrong,
  Nor thoughts that idly rove;
But simple truth be on our tongue,
  And in our hearts be love.

3 And, while the hours in order flow,
  O Christ, securely fence
Our gates, beleaguered by the foe,—
  The gate of every sense.

4 And grant that to Thine honor, Lord,
  Our daily toil may tend;
That we begin it at Thy word,
  And in Thy favor end.

5 To God the Father glory be,
  And to His Only Son,
And to the Spirit, One and Three,
  While endless ages run.
John Henry Newman

54 *"Unto you that fear My Name shall the [ROSEFIELD
Sun of righteousness arise."*

Christ, whose glory fills the skies,
    Christ, the true, the only Light,
Sun of rightcousness, arise,
    Triumph o'er the shades of night;
Day-Spring from on high, be near!
Day-Star, in my heart appear!

2 Dark and cheerless is the morn,
    Unaccompanied by Thee;
Joyless is the day's return,
    Till Thy mercy's beams I see;—
Till they inward light impart,
Glad my eyes and warm my heart.

3 Visit, then, this soul of mine;
    Pierce the gloom of sin and grief;
Fill me, radiant Sun divine;
    Scatter all my unbelief;
More and more Thyself display,
Shining to the perfect day!
                  Charles Wesley

                                        [EFFEN
55 *"His compassions fail not: they are new every morning."*

O timely happy, timely wise,
Hearts that with rising morn arise!
Eyes that the beam celestial view,
Which evermore makes all things new!

2 New every morning is the love
Our wakening and uprising prove,
Through sleep and darkness safely brought,
Restored to life, and power, and thought.

3 New mercies, each returning day,
Hover around us while we pray;
New perils past, new sins forgiven,
New thoughts of God, new hopes of heaven.

4 If, on our daily course, our mind
    Be set to hallow all we find,
    New treasures still, of countless price,
    God will provide for sacrifice.

5 The trivial round, the common task,
    Will furnish all we ought to ask;
    Room to deny ourselves; a road
    To bring us, daily, nearer God.

6 Seek we no more: content with these,
    Let present rapture, comfort, ease,
    As Heaven shall bid them, come and go;
    The secret this of rest below.

7 Only, O Lord, in Thy dear love
    Fit us for perfect rest above;
    And help us, this and every day,
    To live more nearly as we pray!
                                John Keble

56   "*All my springs are in Thee.*"   [ALL SAINTS

O GOD of truth, O Lord of might,
Who orderest time and change aright,
Brightening the morn with golden gleams,
Kindling the noon-day's fiery beams;

2 Quench Thou in us the flames of strife,
    From passion's heat preserve our life,
    Our bodies keep from perils free,
    And give our souls' true peace in Thee.

3 Almighty Father, hear our cry,
    Through Jesus Christ our Lord most high,
    Who with the Holy Ghost and Thee
    Doth live and reign eternally!
                                John Mason Neale

57 *"Until the day dawn, and the Day Star arise in your hearts."* [HARMONY GROVE

LORD God of morning and of night,
We thank Thee for Thy gift of light;
As in the dawn the shadows fly,
We seem to find Thee now more nigh.

2 Yet whilst Thy will we would pursue,
Oft what we would we cannot do;
The sun may stand in zenith skies,
But on the soul thick midnight lies.

3 O Lord of lights! 'tis Thou alone
Canst make our darkened hearts Thine own:
Though this new day with joy we see,
Great Dawn of God! we cry for Thee!

4 Praise God, our Maker and our Friend!
Praise Him through time, till time shall end!
Till psalm and song His Name adore
Through Heaven's great day of Evermore!

Francis Turner Palgrave

58 *"Christ shall give thee light."* [LISBON

BEHOLD the morning sun
  Begins his glorious way;
His beams through all the nations run,
  And life and light convey.

2 But where the gospel comes
  It spreads diviner light;
It calls dead sinners from their tombs,
  And gives the blind their sight.

3 How perfect is Thy word!
  And all Thy judgments just!
For ever sure Thy promise, Lord,
  And men securely trust.

4 While with my heart and tongue
   I spread Thy praise abroad,
  Accept the worship and the song,
   My Saviour and my God.
                    Isaac Watts

59 *"Thou shalt guide me with Thy counsel,* [PARK STREET
     and afterward receive me to glory."

God of the morning, at whose voice
   The cheerful sun makes haste to rise,
  And like a giant doth rejoice
   To run his journey through the skies:

2 O, like the sun, may I fulfill
   The appointed duties of the day,
  With ready mind and active will,
   March on, and keep my heavenly way.

3 But I shall rove and lose the race,
   If God, my Sun, shall disappear,
  And leave me in the world's wide maze
   To follow every wandering star.

4 Give me Thy counsel for my guide,
   And then receive me to Thy bliss;
  All my desires and hopes beside
   Are faint and cold, compared with this.
                    Isaac Watts

                              [EVENING PRAYER
60 *"Thou, Lord, only, makest me to dwell in safety."*

The day is past and over:
   All thanks, O Lord, to Thee!
  I pray Thee that offenceless
   The hours of dark may be.
  O Jesus! keep me in Thy sight,
  And save me through the coming night!

2 The joys of day are over:
   I lift my heart to Thee,
And call on Thee, that sinless
   The hours of sin may be.
O Jesus! make their darkness light,
And save me through the coming night!

3 The toils of day are over:
   I raise the hymn to Thee,
And ask that free from peril
   The hours of fear may be.
O Jesus! keep me in Thy sight,
And guard me through the coming night!

4 Lighten mine eyes, O Saviour,
   Or sleep in death shall I;
And he, my wakeful tempter,
   Triumphantly shall cry:
'He could not make their darkness light,
Nor guard them through the hours of night.'

5 Be Thou my soul's preserver,
   O God, for Thou dost know
How many are the perils
   Through which I have to go:
O loving Jesus! hear my call,
And guard and save me from them all!
John Mason Neale

61 "*The Lord will bless His people with peace.*" [ZOELLNER

HAIL tranquil hour of closing day!
   Begone disturbing care!
And look, my soul, from earth away
   To Him who heareth prayer.

2 How sweet the tear of penitence,
   Before His throne of grace,
While, to the contrite spirit's sense,
   He shows His smiling face.

3 How sweet, through long-remembered years,
   His mercies to recall,
   And, pressed with wants and griefs and fears,
   To trust His love for all.

4 How sweet to look, in thoughtful hope,
   Beyond this fading sky,
   And hear Him call His children up
   To His fair home on high.

5 Calmly the day forsakes our heaven
   To dawn beyond the west;
   So let my soul, in life's last even,
   Retire to glorious rest.
                        Leonard Bacon

62   *"The darkness hideth not from Thee."*   [SEYMOUR

SOFTLY, now, the light of day
Fades upon my sight away;
Free from care, from labor free,
Lord! I would commune with Thee.

2 Thou, whose all-pervading eye
   Naught escapes, without, within,
   Pardon each infirmity,
   Open fault, and secret sin.

3 Soon, for me, the light of day
   Shall for ever pass away;
   Then, from sin and sorrow free,
   Take me, Lord! to dwell with Thee.

4 Thou who, sinless, yet hast known
   All of man's infirmity;
   Then, from Thine eternal throne,
   Jesus, look with pitying eye.
                  George Washington Doane

For Morning and Evening

63   *"Abide with us."*

ABIDE with me! fast falls the even-tide;
The darkness deepens; Lord, with me abide!
When other helpers fail, and comforts flee,
Help of the helpless, O abide with me!

2 Swift to its close ebbs out life's little day;
Earth's joys grow dim; its glories pass away;
Change and decay in all around I see;
O Thou, who changest not, abide with me!

3 Not a brief glance I beg, a passing word;
But, as Thou dwelt'st with Thy disciples, Lord,
Familiar, condescending, patient, free,
Come, not to sojourn, but abide, with me!

4 Come not in terrors, as the King of kings;
But kind and good, with healing in Thy wings;
Tears for all woes, a heart for every plea;
Come, Friend of sinners, and thus 'bide with me!

5 I need Thy presence every passing hour;
What but Thy grace can foil the tempter's power?
Who like Thyself my guide and stay can be?
Through cloud and sunshine, O abide with me!

Henry Francis Lyte

64   [TALLIS' EVENING HYMN
"Under His wings shalt thou trust."

ALL praise to Thee, my God, this night,
For all the blessings of the light;
Keep me, O keep me, King of kings,
Beneath Thine own almighty wings!

2 Forgive me, Lord, for Thy dear Son,
   The ill that I this day have done;
   That with the world, myself, and Thee,
   I, ere I sleep, at peace may be.

3 Teach me to live, that I may dread
   The grave as little as my bed!
   To die, that this vile body may
   Rise glorious at the awful day!

4 O may my soul on Thee repose;
   And may sweet sleep mine eyelids close;
   Sleep, that may me more vigorous make
   To serve my God when I awake!

5 When in the night I sleepless lie,
   My soul with heavenly thoughts supply!
   Let no ill dreams disturb my rest,
   No powers of darkness me molest!

6 Praise God, from whom all blessings flow;
   Praise Him, all creatures here below!
   Praise Him above, ye heavenly host;
   Praise Father, Son, and Holy Ghost!
                              Thomas Ken

65 "*The Lord redeemeth the soul of His servants.*" [WARE

Thus far the Lord has led me on;
   Thus far His power prolongs my days;
And every evening shall make known
   Some fresh memorial of His grace.

2 Much of my time has run to waste,
      And I, perhaps, am near my home;
   But He forgives my follies past,
      And gives me strength for days to come.

3 Faith in His name forbids my fear:
   O may Thy presence ne'er depart!
   And in the morning make me hear
   The love and kindness of Thy heart.

4 Thus, when the night of death shall come,
   My flesh shall rest beneath the ground,
   And wait Thy voice to rouse my tomb,
   With sweet salvation in the sound.
                              Isaac Watts

66   "*Thy sun shall no more go down.*"   [DEDICATION

   SUN of my soul, Thou Saviour dear,
   It is not night if Thou be near;
   O! may no earth-born cloud arise
   To hide Thee from Thy servant's eyes!

2 When the soft dews of kindly sleep
   My wearied eyelids gently steep,
   Be my last thought, how sweet to rest
   For ever on my Saviour's breast!

3 Abide with me from morn till eve,
   For without Thee I cannot live!
   Abide with me when night is nigh,
   For without Thee I dare not die!

4 If some poor wandering child of Thine
   Have spurned, to-day, the voice divine,
   Now, Lord, the gracious work begin;
   Let him no more lie down in sin!

5 Watch by the sick, enrich the poor
   With blessings from Thy boundless store!
   Be every mourner's sleep to-night
   Like infants' slumbers, pure and light!

6 Come near and bless us when we wake,
   Ere through the world our way we take;
   Till in the ocean of Thy love
   We lose ourselves in heaven above.
                                John Keble

67 *"The Lord shall preserve thy going out* [ST. GEORGE
       and thy coming in."

SHINE on our souls, Eternal God,
   With rays of beauty shine!
O let Thy favor crown our days,
   And all their round be Thine!

2 Did we not raise our hands to Thee,
   Our hands might toil in vain;
Small joy success itself could give,
   If Thou Thy love restrain.

3 With Thee let every week begin,
   With Thee each day be spent;
For Thee each fleeting hour improved,
   Since each by Thee is lent.

4 Thus cheer us through this desert road,
   Till all our labors cease,
And heaven refresh our weary souls
   With everlasting peace!
                        Philip Doddridge

God the Creator

68 *"Who can show forth all His praise?"* [ROCKINGHAM]

THEE we adore, Eternal God!
We praise Thy Name with one accord;
Thy saints, who here Thy goodness see,
Through all the world do worship Thee.

2 To Thee aloud all angels cry,
And ceaseless raise their songs on high,
Both cherubin and seraphin,
The heavens and all the powers therein.

3 The apostles join the glorious throng;
The prophets swell the immortal song;
The martyrs' noble army raise
Eternal anthems to Thy praise.

4 Thee, Holy, holy, holy King!
Thee, O Lord God of hosts, they sing;
Thus earth below, and heaven above,
Resound Thy glory and Thy love.
Thomas Cotterill

69 *"They rest not day nor night, saying, Holy, holy, holy, Lord God Almighty."* [NICÆA]

HOLY, holy, holy, Lord God Almighty!
 Early in the morning our song shall rise to Thee;
Holy, holy, holy! merciful and mighty!
 God in three persons, blessed Trinity.

2 Holy, holy, holy! All the saints adore Thee,
　　Casting down their golden crowns around
　　　　the glassy sea;
　　Cherubim and seraphim falling down before
　　　　Thee,
　　Which wert, and art, and evermore shalt be!

3 Holy, holy, holy! Though the darkness hide
　　　　Thee,
　　Though the eye of sinful man Thy glory
　　　　may not see,
　　Only Thou art holy, there is none beside Thee,
　　Perfect in power, in love, and purity!

4 Holy, holy, holy, Lord God Almighty!
　　All Thy works shall praise Thy name, in
　　　　earth, and sky, and sea;
　　Holy, holy, holy! merciful and mighty!
　　God in three persons, blessed Trinity!
　　　　　　　　　　　　Reginald Heber

70　　*"Glory to God in the highest."*　　[TE DEUM
　　To God be glory, peace on earth,
　　　　To all mankind good will;
　　We bless, we praise, we worship Thee,
　　　　And glorify Thee still;

2 And thanks for Thy great glory give,
　　　　That fills our souls with light,
　　O Lord God, Heavenly King, the God
　　　　And Father of all might!

3 And Thou, begotten Son of God,
　　　　Before all time begun;
　　O Jesus Christ, God, Lamb of God,
　　　　The Father's Only Son!

4 Have mercy, Thou that tak'st the sins
   Of all the world away;
  Have mercy, Saviour of mankind,
   And hear us when we pray!

5 O Thou, who sitt'st at God's right hand,
   Upon the Father's throne,
  Have mercy on us, Thou, O Christ,
   Who art the Holy One!

6 Thou Lord, who with the Holy Ghost,
   Whom earth and heaven adore,
  In glory of the Father art
   Most high for evermore!

71   [OLD HUNDRED
"I will praise Thee, O Lord, among the people."

BE Thou exalted, O my God!
   Above the heavens where angels dwell;
  Thy power on earth be known abroad,
   And land to land Thy wonders tell.

2 My heart is fixed: my song shall raise
   Immortal honors to Thy name;
  Awake, my tongue, to sound His praise,
   My tongue, the glory of my frame.

3 High o'er the earth Thy mercy reigns,
   And reaches to the utmost sky;
  Thy truth to endless years remains,
   When lower worlds dissolve and die.

4 Be Thou exalted, O my God!
   Above the heavens where angels dwell;
  Thy power on earth be known abroad,
   And land to land Thy wonders tell.
                               Isaac Watts

72

"Te Deum laudamus." [TRINITY

LORD God of Hosts, by all adored!
Thy name we praise with one accord;
The earth and heavens are full of Thee,
Thy light, Thy love, Thy majesty.

2 Loud hallelujahs to Thy name
Angels and seraphim proclaim;
Eternal praise to Thee is given
By all the powers and thrones in heaven.

3 The apostles join the glorious throng;
The prophets aid to swell the song;
The noble and triumphant host
Of martyrs make of Thee their boast.

4 The holy church in every place
Throughout the world exalts Thy praise;
Both heaven and earth do worship Thee,
Thou Father of eternity!

5 From day to day, O Lord, do we
Highly exalt and honor Thee!
Thy name we worship and adore,
World without end, for evermore.

73

"Praise Him for His mighty acts; praise [ASCENSION
Him according to His excellent greatness."

PRAISE the Lord, His glories show,
Saints within His courts below,
Angels round His throne above,
All that see and share His love.
Earth to heaven, and heaven to earth,
Tell His wonders, sing His worth;
Age to age, and shore to shore,
Praise Him, praise Him, evermore!

2 Praise the Lord, His mercies trace,
Praise His providence and grace,
All that He for man hath done,
All He sends us through His Son:
Strings and voices, hands and hearts,
In the concert bear your parts;
All that breathe, your Lord adore,
Praise Him, praise Him, evermore!
Henry Francis Lyte

74 *"Praise ye the Name of the Lord."* [ITALIAN HYMN

Come, Thou Almighty King,
Help us Thy Name to sing,
   Help us to praise:
Father all glorious,
O'er all victorious,
Come and reign over us,
   Ancient of days.

2 Jesus, our Lord, arise;
Scatter our enemies,
   And make them fall;
Let Thine almighty aid
Our sure defence be made;
Our souls on Thee be stayed;
   Lord, hear our call.

3 Come, Thou Incarnate Word,
Gird on Thy mighty sword,
   Our prayer attend:
Come, and Thy people bless,
And give Thy word success:
Spirit of holiness,
   On us descend.

4 Come, Holy Comforter,
   Thy sacred witness bear
      In this glad hour:
   Thou who Almighty art,
   Now rule in every heart,
   And ne'er from us depart,
      Spirit of power.

5 To the great One and Three
   Eternal praises be
      Hence, evermore:
   His sovereign majesty
   May we in glory see,
   And to eternity
      Love and adore.
                                Charles Wesley

75 *"Serve the Lord with gladness."* [OLD HUNDRED

ALL people that on earth do dwell,
   Sing to the Lord with cheerful voice:
Him serve with fear, His praise forth tell,
   Come ye before Him, and rejoice.

2 The Lord ye know is God indeed,
   Without our aid He did us make:
  We are His flock, He doth us feed,
   And for His sheep He doth us take.

3 O enter then His gates with praise,
   Approach with joy His courts unto;
  Praise, laud, and bless His name always,
   For it is seemly so to do.

4 For why? the Lord our God is good,
   His mercy is for ever sure;
  His truth at all times firmly stood,
   And shall from age to age endure.
                                William Kethe

76   *"I will praise Thy name, O Lord, for it is good."*   [TRINITY

O THOU whom neither time nor space
    Can circle in, unseen, unknown,
Nor faith in boldest flight can trace,
    Save through Thy Spirit and Thy Son!

2 And Thou that from Thy bright abode,
    To us in mortal weakness shown,
Didst graft the manhood into God,
    Eternal, Co-eternal Son!

3 And Thou, whose unction from on high
    By comfort, light, and love is known!
Who with the Parent Deity,
    Dread Spirit, art for ever one!

4 Great First and Last! Thy blessing give;
    And grant us faith, Thy gift alone,
To love and praise Thee while we live,
    And do whate'er Thou would'st have done!
                            Reginald Heber

77   *"Thou, O Lord, remainest for ever."*   [ALL SAINTS

GREAT God! how infinite art Thou,
    What worthless worms are we!
Let the whole race of creatures bow,
    And pay their praise to Thee.

2 Thy throne eternal ages stood,
    Ere seas or stars were made:
Thou art the Ever-living God,
    Were all the nations dead.

3 Eternity, with all its years,
    Stands present in Thy view;
To Thee there's nothing old appears—
    Great God! there's nothing new.

4 Our lives through various scenes are drawn,
    And vexed with trifling cares;
    While Thine eternal thought moves on
    Thine undisturbed affairs.

5 Great God! how infinite art Thou!
    What worthless worms are we!
    Let the whole race of creatures bow,
    And pay their praise to Thee. *Isaac Watts*

78   [ST. GEORGE'S CHAPEL
   "*The whole earth is full of His glory.*"

HOLY, holy, holy Lord,
God of Hosts! when heaven and earth,
    Out of darkness at Thy word,
    Issued into glorious birth,
        All Thy works before Thee stood,
        And Thine eye beheld them good,
        While they sang with sweet accord,
        Holy, holy, holy Lord!

2   Holy, holy, holy! Thee,
    One Jehovah evermore,
        Father, Son, and Spirit! we,
    Dust and ashes, would adore;
        Lightly by the world esteemed,
        From that world by Thee redeemed,
        Sing we here with glad accord,
        Holy, holy, holy Lord!

3   Holy, holy, holy! All
    Heaven's triumphant choirs shall sing,
        When the ransomed nations fall
    At the footstool of their King:
        Then shall saints and seraphim,
        Hearts and voices, swell one hymn,
        Round the throne with full accord,
        Holy, holy, holy Lord!
                    James Montgomery

God the Creator

79   *"Jubilate Deo."*   [OLD HUNDRED

BEFORE Jehovah's awful throne,
  Ye nations, bow with sacred joy;
Know that the Lord is God alone;
  He can create, and He destroy.

2 His sovereign power, without our aid,
    Made us of clay, and formed us men;
  And when like wandering sheep we strayed,
    He brought us to His fold again.

3 We'll crowd Thy gates with thankful songs,
    High as the heavens our voices raise;
  And earth, with her ten thousand tongues,
    Shall fill Thy courts with sounding praise.

4 Wide as the world is Thy command,
    Vast as eternity Thy love;
  Firm as a rock Thy truth must stand,
    When rolling years shall cease to move.
                                    Isaac Watts

80   *"Who hath called you out of darkness into*   [PALESTINE
         His marvelous light."

LORD of all being! throned afar,
Thy glory flames from sun and star;
Center and soul of every sphere,
Yet to each loving heart how near!

2 Sun of our life, Thy quickening ray
  Sheds on our path the glow of day;
  Star of our hope, Thy softened light
  Cheers the long watches of the night.

3 Our midnight is Thy smile withdrawn;
  Our noontide is Thy gracious dawn;
  Our rainbow arch Thy mercy's sign;
  All, save the clouds of sin, are Thine!

4 Lord of all life, below, above,
Whose light is truth, whose warmth is love,
Before Thy ever-blazing throne
We ask no luster of our own.

5 Grant us Thy truth, to make us free,
And kindling hearts that burn for Thee,
Till all Thy living altars claim
One holy light, one heavenly flame!
Oliver Wendell Holmes

81   *"His name alone is excellent."*   [HADDAM

The Lord Jehovah reigns,
    His throne is built on high,
The garments He assumes
    Are light and majesty.
His glories shine with beams so bright,
No mortal eye can bear the sight.

2 The thunders of His hand
    Keep this wide world in awe;
His wrath and justice stand
    To guard His holy law;
And where His love resolves to bless,
His truth confirms and seals the grace.

3 Through all His ancient works
    Surprising wisdom shines,
Confounds the powers of hell,
    And breaks their curst designs:
Strong is His arm, and shall fulfill
His great decrees, His sovereign will.

4 And can this mighty King
    Of glory condescend?
And will He write His name,
    My Father and my Friend?
I love His name, I love His word:
Join all my powers, and praise the Lord.
Isaac Watts

God the Creator

82   *"O Lord my God, Thou art very great."*   [HANOVER

O WORSHIP the King, all glorious above;
O gratefully sing His power and His love;
Our Shield and Defender, the Ancient of days,
Pavilioned in splendor, and girded with praise.

2 O tell of His might, O sing of His grace,
Whose robe is the light, whose canopy space;
His chariots of wrath deep thunder-clouds form,
And dark is His path on the wings of the storm.

3 Frail children of dust, and feeble as frail,
In Thee do we trust, nor find Thee to fail:
Thy mercies how tender! how firm to the end!
Our Maker, Defender, Redeemer, and Friend!

4 O measureless Might! ineffable Love!
While angels delight to hymn Thee above,
The humbler creation, though feeble their lays,
With true adoration shall lisp to Thy praise.
Sir Robert Grant

[HELP
83   *"Even from everlasting to everlasting, Thou art God."*

OUR God, our Help in ages past,
    Our Hope for years to come,
Our Shelter from the stormy blast,
    And our Eternal Home!

2 Under the shadow of Thy throne
    Thy saints have dwelt secure;
Sufficient is Thine arm alone,
    And our defence is sure.

3 Before the hills in order stood,
    Or earth received her frame,
From everlasting Thou art God,
    To endless years the same.

4 A thousand ages in Thy sight
   Are like an evening gone;
   Short as the watch that ends the night,
   Before the rising sun.

5 Our God, our Help in ages past,
   Our Hope for years to come,
   Be Thou our Guard while troubles last,
   And our Eternal Home!
                            Isaac Watts

[TE DEUM

84 "*It is a good thing to give thanks unto the Lord.*"

LIFT up to God the voice of praise,
   Whose breath our souls inspired;
   Loud and more loud the anthem raise,
   With grateful ardor fired.

2 Lift up to God the voice of praise,
   Whose goodness, passing thought,
   Loads every moment, as it flies,
   With benefits unsought.

3 Lift up to God the voice of praise,
   From whom salvation flows,
   Who sent His Son our souls to save
   From everlasting woes.

4 Lift up to God the voice of praise,
   For hope's transporting ray,
   Which lights through darkest shades of death
   To realms of endless day.
                            Ralph Wardlaw

God the Creator

85   *"My help cometh from the Lord."*   [DAVID

    UPWARD I lift mine eyes;
      From God is all my aid;
    The God that built the skies,
      And earth and nature made:
God is the tower | His grace is nigh
To which I fly; | In every hour.

  2 My feet shall never slide,
      Nor fall in fatal snares,
    Since God, my Guard and Guide,
      Defends me from my fears:
Those wakeful eyes | Shall Israel keep
That never sleep, | When dangers rise.

  3 No burning heats by day,
      Nor blasts of evening air,
    Shall take my health away,
      If God be with me there:
Thou art my Sun, | To guard my head
And Thou my Shade, | By night or noon.

  4 Hast Thou not given Thy word
      To save my soul from death?
    And I can trust my Lord
      To keep my mortal breath:
I'll go and come, | Till from on high
Nor fear to die, | Thou call me home.
                    Isaac Watts

86   *"Holiness, without which no man shall see*   [WATCH
      the Lord."

    HOLY and reverend is the name
      Of our Eternal King:
    Thrice holy Lord! the angels cry;
      Thrice holy! let us sing.

2 The deepest reverence of the mind,
　Pay, O my soul, to God;
　Lift with thy hands a holy heart
　　To His sublime abode.

3 With sacred awe pronounce His name
　Whom words nor thoughts can reach;
　A contrite heart shall please Him more
　　Than noblest forms of speech.

4 Thou holy God! preserve our souls
　From all pollution free;
　The pure in heart are Thy delight,
　　And they Thy face shall see.
　　　　　　　　　John Needham

87　"*The Lord hath been mindful of us.*" [St. Thomas

My Maker and my King!
　To Thee my all I owe;
Thy sovereign bounty is the spring
　Whence all my blessings flow.

2 The creature of Thy hand,
　On Thee alone I live;
　My God, Thy benefits demand
　More praise than life can give.

3 Lord, what can I impart,
　When all is Thine before?
　Thy love demands a thankful heart:
　The gift, alas, how poor!

4 Shall I withhold Thy due?
　And shall my passions rove?
　Lord, form this wretched heart anew,
　And fill it with Thy love.
　　　　　　　　　Anne Steele

God the Creator

88 *"He shall feed His flock like a shepherd."* [BATTELL

The Lord my shepherd is,
 I shall be well supplied;
Since He is mine, and I am His,
 What can I want beside?

2 He leads me to the place
 Where heavenly pasture grows,
Where living waters gently pass,
 And full salvation flows.

3 If e'er I go astray,
 He doth my soul reclaim,
And guides me in His own right way,
 For His most holy name.

4 While He affords His aid
 I cannot yield to fear;
Though I should walk through death's dark shade,
 My Shepherd's with me there.

5 In spite of all my foes,
 Thou dost my table spread;
My cup with blessings overflows,
 And joy exalts my head.

6 The bounties of Thy love
 Shall crown my following days;
Nor from Thy house will I remove,
 Nor cease to speak Thy praise.
                    Isaac Watts

89 *"Holy, holy, holy, is the Lord of hosts."* [DES ANGES

Holy, holy, holy Lord!
Be Thy glorious name adored;
Lord, Thy mercies never fail:
Hail, celestial goodness, hail!

2 Though unworthy of Thine ear,
Deign our humble songs to hear;
Purer praise we hope to bring,
When around Thy throne we sing.

3 While on earth ordained to stay,
Guide our footsteps in Thy way,
Till we come to dwell with Thee,
Till we all Thy glory see.

4 Lord, Thy mercies never fail;
Hail, celestial goodness, hail!
Holy, holy, holy Lord!
Be Thy glorious name adored.
Benjamin Williams

90 [TRUST
"*Thine is the kingdom, and the power, and the glory.*"

BLEST be Thou, O God of Israel,
    Thou our Father and our Lord;
Blest Thy Majesty for ever,
    Ever be Thy name adored.

2 Thine, O Lord, are power and greatness,
    Glory, victory, are Thine own;
All is Thine in earth and heaven;
    Over all Thy boundless throne.

3 Riches come of Thee, and honor;
    Power and might to Thee belong;
Thine it is to make us prosper,
    Only Thine to make us strong.

4 Lord our God, for these Thy bounties
    Hymns of gratitude we raise;
To Thy name, for ever glorious,
    Ever we address our praise.

God the Creator

91 *"He hath not dealt with us after our sins."* [WELLS

PRAISE, my soul, the King of heaven;
    To His feet thy tribute bring;
Ransomed, healed, restored, forgiven,
    Who like thee His praise should sing?
        Praise Him! Praise Him!
    Praise the everlasting King!

2 Praise Him for His grace and favor
    To our fathers in distress;
Praise Him, still the same for ever,
    Slow to chide, and swift to bless;
        Praise Him! Praise Him!
    Glorious in His faithfulness!

3 Father-like He tends and spares us;
    Well our feeble frame He knows;
In His hands He gently bears us,
    Rescues us from all our foes:
        Praise Him! Praise Him!
    Widely as His mercy flows!

4 Angels, help us to adore Him,
    Ye behold Him face to face;
Sun and moon, bow down before Him;
    Dwellers all in time and space,
        Praise Him! Praise Him!
    Praise with us the God of grace!
                Henry Francis Lyte

92 *"Praise Him in the firmament of His power."* [STUDENT

PRAISE the Lord! ye heavens, adore Him;
    Praise Him, angels in the hight;
Sun and moon, rejoice before Him;
    Praise Him, all ye stars of light!

2 Praise the Lord—for He hath spoken;
    Worlds His mighty voice obeyed;
    Laws which never shall be broken,
    For their guidance He hath made.

3 Praise the Lord—for He is glorious;
    Never shall His promise fail;
    God hath made His saints victorious,
    Sin and death shall not prevail.

4 Praise the God of our salvation,
    Hosts on high His power proclaim;
    Heaven and earth, and all creation,
    Laud and magnify His name!

93 *"Bless the Lord, O my soul."* [GERMANY

Bless, O my soul, the living God,
Call home thy thoughts that rove abroad,
Let all the powers within me join
In work and worship so divine.

2 Bless, O my soul, the God of grace;
    His favors claim thy highest praise;
    Why should the wonders He hath wrought
    Be lost in silence and forgot?

3 'Tis He, my soul, that sent His Son
    To die for crimes which thou hast done;
    He owns the ransom; and forgives
    The hourly follies of our lives.

4 Let the whole earth His power confess,
    Let the whole earth adore His grace;
    The Gentile with the Jew shall join
    In work and worship so divine.   *Isaac Watts*

94 [ALLEIN GOTT
"O that men would praise the Lord for His goodness."

SING praise to God who reigns above,
  The God of all creation,
The God of power, the God of love,
  The God of our salvation;
With healing balm my soul He fills,
And every faithless murmur stills:
  To God all praise and glory!

2 The angel-host, O King of kings,
    Thy praise for ever telling,
  In earth and sky all living things
    Beneath Thy shadow dwelling,
  Adore the wisdom which could span,
  And power which formed creation's plan:
    To God all praise and glory!

3 What God's almighty power hath made
    His gracious mercy keepeth:
  By morning glow or evening shade,
    His watchful eye ne'er sleepeth;
  Within the kingdom of His might,
  Lo, all is just and all is right:
    To God all praise and glory!

4 O ye who bear Christ's holy name,
    Give God all praise and glory!
  All ye who own His power, proclaim
    Aloud the wondrous story;
  Cast each false idol from His throne,
  The Lord is God, and He alone:
    To God all praise and glory!
                              Frances E. Cox

95 *"Faithful is He that calleth you."* [GERMANY

THOU, Lord, of all the parent art,
Of all things Thou alone the end:
On Thee still fix our wavering heart;
To Thee let all our actions tend.

2 Thou, Lord, art light; Thy native ray
No change nor shadow ever knows;
To our dark souls Thy light display,
The glory of Thy face disclose.

3 Thou, Lord, art love; the fountain Thou
Whence mercy unexhausted flows;
On barren hearts, O shed it now,
And make the desert bear the rose!

4 So shall our every power to Thee
In love and holy service rise;
And body, soul, and spirit be
Thy ever-living sacrifice.

96 *" Thou compassest my path."* [LANDSTUHl

JEHOVAH, God! Thy gracious power
On every hand we see;
O may the blessings of each hour
Lead all our thoughts to Thee!

2 If, on the wings of morn, we speed
To earth's remotest bound,
Thy hand will there our journey lead,
Thy love our path surround.

3 Thy power is in the ocean deeps,
And reaches to the skies;
Thine eye of mercy never sleeps,
Thy goodness never dies.

4 From morn till noon, till latest eve,
   Thy hand, O God, we see;
   And all the blessings we receive,
   Proceed alone from Thee.

5 In all the varying scenes of time,
   On Thee our hopes depend;
   Through every age, in every clime,
   Our Father and our Friend.
                                John Thomson

97 *"All things are naked and opened unto the*   [SILLIMAN
     eyes of Him with whom we have to do."

LORD, Thou hast searched and seen me through;
Thine eye commands with piercing view
My rising and my resting hours,
My heart and flesh with all their powers.

2 My thoughts, before they are my own,
   Are to my God distinctly known;
   He knows the words I mean to speak,
   Ere from my opening lips they break.

3 Within Thy circling power I stand;
   On every side I find Thy hand:
   Awake, asleep, at home, abroad,
   I am surrounded still with God.

4 Amazing knowledge, vast and great!
   What large extent! what lofty hight!
   My soul with all the powers I boast
   Is in the boundless prospect lost.

5 O may these thoughts possess my breast,
   Where'er I rove, where'er I rest!
   Nor let my weaker passions dare
   Consent to sin, for God is there.
                                Isaac Watts

98 *"Whither shall I flee from Thy presence?"* [DES ANGES

WHITHER shall a creature run,
    From Jehovah's Spirit fly?
How Jehovah's presence shun,
    Screened from His all-seeing eye?
Holy Ghost, before Thy face
    Where shall I myself conceal?
Thou art God in every place,
    God incomprehensible.

2 If to heaven I take my flight,
    With beatitude unknown
Filling all the realms of light,
    There Thou sittest on Thy throne!
If to hell I could retire,
    Gloomy pit of endless pains,
There is the consuming fire,
    There Almighty Vengeance reigns!

3 If the morning's wings I gain,
    Fly to earth's remotest bound,
Could I hid from Thee remain,
    In a world of waters drowned?
Leaving lands and seas behind,
    Could I the Omniscient leave?
There Thy quicker hand would find,
    There arrest, Thy fugitive.

4 Covered by the darkest shade,
    Should I hope to lurk unknown,
By a sudden light betrayed,
    By an uncreated Sun,
Naked at the noon of night
    Should I not to Thee appear?
Forced to acknowledge in Thy sight,
    God is light, and God is here!

Charles Wesley

99 *"The eyes of the Lord are in every place."* [LANDSTUHL

In all my vast concerns with Thee
  In vain my soul would try
To shun Thy presence, Lord, or flee
  The notice of Thine eye.

2 Thy all-surrounding sight surveys
  My rising and my rest,
My public walks, my private ways,
  And secrets of my breast.

3 My thoughts lie open to the Lord,
  Before they're formed within;
And ere my lips pronounce the word,
  He knows the sense I mean.

4 O wondrous knowledge, deep and high!
  Where can a creature hide?
Within Thy circling arms I lie,
  Beset on every side.

5 So let Thy grace surround me still,
  And like a bulwark prove,
To guard my soul from every ill,
  Secured by sovereign love.
      Isaac Watts

100 *"His mercy endureth for ever."* [WINCHESTER OLD

When all Thy mercies, O my God,
  My rising soul surveys,
Transported with the view, I'm lost
  In wonder, love, and praise.

2 Unnumbered comforts on my soul
  Thy tender care bestowed,
Before my infant heart conceived
  From whom those comforts flowed.

3 Ten thousand thousand precious gifts
   My daily thanks employ;
   Nor is the least a cheerful heart,
   That tastes those gifts with joy.

4 Through every period of my life,
   Thy goodness I'll pursue;
   And after death, in distant worlds,
   The glorious theme renew.

5 Through all eternity, to Thee
   A joyful song I'll raise:
   For, O! eternity's too short
   To utter all Thy praise!
                        Joseph Addison

                                    [ASCALON
101 *"The Lord reigneth, He is clothed with majesty."*

THE Lord Jehovah reigns,
   And royal state maintains,
His head with awful glories crowned;
   Arrayed in robes of light,
   Begirt with sovereign might,
And rays of majesty around.

2 Upheld by Thy commands,
   The world securely stands,
And skies and stars obey Thy word:
   Thy throne was fixed on high
   Before the starry sky:
Eternal is Thy kingdom, Lord.

3 Thy promises are true,
   Thy grace is ever new;
There fixed, Thy Church shall ne'er remove;
   Thy saints with holy fear
   Shall in Thy courts appear,
And sing Thine everlasting love. *Isaac Watts*

God the Creator

[Portuguese Hymn

102 *"He leadeth me in the paths of righteousness."*

The Lord is my Shepherd, no want shall I know,
   I feed in green pastures, safe-folded I rest;
He leadeth my soul where the still waters flow,
   Restores me when wandering, redeems when opprest.

2 Through the valley and shadow of death though I stray,
   Since Thou art my Guardian, no evil I fear;
Thy rod shall defend me, Thy staff be my stay;
   No harm can befall, with my Comforter near.

3 In the midst of affliction my table is spread;
   With blessings unmeasured my cup runneth o'er;
With perfume and oil Thou anointest my head;
   O! what shall I ask of Thy providence more?

4 Let goodness and mercy, my bountiful God!
   Still follow my steps till I meet Thee above;
I seek—by the path which my forefathers trod,
   Through the land of their sojourn—Thy kingdom of love.
                  James Montgomery

103 *"With Thee is the fountain of life."* [Cathedral

High in the heavens, Eternal God,
   Thy goodness in full glory shines;
Thy truth shall break through every cloud
   That veils and darkens Thy designs.

2 For ever firm Thy justice stands,
   As mountains their foundations keep;
Wise are the wonders of Thy hands;
   Thy judgments are a mighty deep.

3 My God! how excellent Thy grace,
    Whence all our hope and comfort springs!
  The sons of Adam, in distress,
    Fly to the shadow of Thy wings.

4 From the provisions of Thy house
    We shall be fed with sweet repast:
  There mercy like a river flows,
    And brings salvation to our taste.

5 Life, like a fountain rich and free,
    Springs from the presence of my Lord;
  And in Thy light our souls shall see
    The glories promised in Thy word.
                               Isaac Watts

104 *"The Lord hath His way in the whirlwind* [WONDER
        and in the storm."

THE Lord our God is full of might;
    The winds obey His will;
  He speaks, and in his heavenly hight
    The rolling sun stands still.

2 Rebel, ye waves, and o'er the land
    With threatening aspect roar:
  The Lord uplifts His awful hand,
    And chains you to the shore.

3 Howl, winds of night; your force combine;
    Without His high behest,
  Ye shall not in the mountain pine
    Disturb the sparrow's nest.

4 His voice sublime is heard afar,
    In distant peals it dies;
  He yokes the whirlwind to His car,
    And sweeps the howling skies.

5 Ye nations, bend, in reverence bend;
　　Ye monarchs, wait His nod;
　　And bid the choral song ascend
　　　To celebrate our God.
　　　　　　　　　Henry Kirke White

105　　　　　　　　　　　　[WARWICK
　　"Bow Thy heavens, O Lord, and come down."
THE Lord descended from above,
　　And bowed the heavens most high;
　　And underneath His feet He cast
　　　The darkness of the sky.

2 On cherubs and on cherubim
　　Full royally He rode,
　　And on the wings of mighty winds
　　　Came flying all abroad.

3 The Lord doth sit upon the floods,
　　Their fury to restrain;
　　And He, as sovereign Lord and King,
　　　For evermore shall reign.

4 The Lord will give His people strength
　　Whereby they shall increase;
　　And He will bless His chosen flock
　　　With everlasting peace.

5 Give glory to His holy name,
　　And honor Him alone;
　　Give worship to His majesty
　　　Upon His holy throne.
　　　　　　　　　Thomas Sternhold

106　　*"God is a refuge for us."*　　[ALL SAINTS
THE floods, O Lord, lift up their voice,
　　The mighty floods lift up their roar;
　　The floods in tumult loud rejoice,
　　　And climb in foam the sounding shore.

2 But mightier than the mighty sea,
   The Lord of glory reigns on high:
   Far o'er its waves we look to Thee,
   And see their fury break and die.

3 Thy word is true, Thy promise sure,
   That ancient promise, sealed in love;
   Here be Thy temple ever pure
   As Thy pure mansions shine above.
                              George Burgess

107 "*The heavens declare the glory of God.*" [CREATION
   THE spacious firmament on high,
   With all the blue ethereal sky,
   And spangled heavens, a shining frame,
   Their great Original proclaim.
   The unwearied sun from day to day,
   Does his Creator's power display,
   And publishes to every land
   The work of an Almighty hand.

2 Soon as the evening shades prevail,
   The moon takes up the wondrous tale,
   And nightly to the listening earth
   Repeats the story of her birth;
   Whilst all the stars that round her burn,
   And all the planets, in their turn,
   Confirm the tidings, as they roll,
   And spread the truth from pole to pole.

3 What though in solemn silence all
   Move round the dark terrestrial ball?
   What though nor real voice nor sound
   Amid their radiant orbs be found?
   In reason's ear they all rejoice,
   And utter forth a glorious voice,
   For ever singing, as they shine,
   'The Hand that made us is divine.'
                              Joseph Addison

108 "*O satisfy us early with Thy mercy.*" [ALLEIN GOTT

Lord, Thou hast been Thy people's rest,
   Through all their generations,
Their refuge when by danger prest,
   Their hope in tribulations;
Thou, ere the mountains sprang to birth,
Or ever Thou hadst formed the earth,
   Art God from everlasting!

2 The sons of men return to clay,
   When Thou the word hast spoken,
As with a torrent borne away,
   Gone like a dream when broken:
A thousand years are, in Thy sight,
But as a watch amid the night,
   Or yesterday departed.

3 Lo! Thou hast set before Thine eyes
   All our misdeeds and errors;
Our secret sins from darkness rise,
   At Thine awakening terrors:
Who shall abide the trying hour?
Who knows the thunder of Thy power?
   We flee unto Thy mercy.

4 Lord, teach us so to mark our days
   That we may prize them duly;
So guide our feet in wisdom's ways,
   That we may love Thee truly:
Return, O Lord! our griefs behold,
And with Thy goodness, as of old,
   O satisfy us early!

James Montgomery

Our Lord Jesus Christ

109 *"When they saw the star, they rejoiced with exceeding great joy."*

BRIGHTEST and best of the sons of the morning!
  Dawn on our darkness, and lend us thine aid!
Star of the east, the horizon adorning,
  Guide where our infant Redeemer is laid!

2 Cold on His cradle the dew-drops are shining,
  Low lies His head with the beasts of the stall,
Angels adore Him in slumber reclining—
  Maker, and Monarch, and Saviour of all.

3 Say, shall we yield Him, in costly devotion,
  Odors of Edom, and offerings divine?
Gems of the mountain, and pearls of the ocean,
  Myrrh from the forest, or gold from the mine?

4 Vainly we offer each ample oblation;
  Vainly with gifts would His favor secure;
Richer by far is the heart's adoration;
  Dearer to God are the prayers of the poor.

5 Brightest and best of the sons of the morning!
  Dawn on our darkness, and lend us thine aid!
Star of the east, the horizon adorning,
  Guide where our infant Redeemer is laid!

Reginald Heber

Our Lord Jesus Christ

110 *"We have seen His star in the east, and are come to worship Him."* [ANTHEM

ANGELS, from the realms of glory,
   Wing your flight o'er all the earth;
Ye who sang creation's story,
   Now proclaim Messiah's birth;
    Come and worship,
Worship Christ, the new-born King.

2 Shepherds, in the field abiding,
   Watching o'er your flocks by night,
God with man is now residing,
   Yonder shines the infant light;
    Come and worship,
Worship Christ, the new-born King.

3 Sages, leave your contemplations,
   Brighter visions beam afar;
Seek the great Desire of nations,
   Ye have seen His natal star;
    Come and worship,
Worship Christ, the new-born King.

4 Saints, before the altar bending,
   Watching long in hope and fear,
Suddenly the Lord, descending,
   In His temple shall appear;
    Come and worship,
Worship Christ, the new-born King.

5 Sinners, wrung with true repentance,
   Doomed for guilt to endless pains,
Justice now revokes the sentence,
   Mercy calls you,—break your chains!
    Come and worship,
Worship Christ, the new-born King.

James Montgomery

III *"I am the bright and morning Star."* [ROSEFIELD

As with gladness men of old
Did the guiding star behold;
As with joy they hailed its light,
Leading onward, beaming bright;
So, most gracious God, may we
Evermore be led by Thee.

2 As with joyful steps they sped
To that lowly manger-bed;
There to bend the knee before
Him whom heaven and earth adore;
So may we with willing feet
Ever seek Thy mercy-seat.

3 As they offered gifts most rare
At that manger rude and bare;
So may we with holy joy,
Pure, and free from sin's alloy,
All our costliest treasures bring,
Christ, to Thee, our Heavenly King.

4 Holy Jesus! every day
Keep us in the narrow way;
And, when earthly things are past,
Bring our ransomed souls at last
Where they need no star to guide,
Where no clouds Thy glory hide.

5 In the heavenly country bright
Need they no created light;
Thou its Light, its Joy, its Crown,
Thou its Sun, which goes not down;
There for ever may we sing
Hallelujah to our King.

William Chatterton Dix

112 *"Unto you is born this day . . a Saviour* [GOSPEL
which is Christ the Lord."

HARK, the herald angels sing,
'Glory to the new-born King!
Peace on earth, and mercy mild,
God and sinners reconciled!'
Joyful, all ye nations, rise,
Join the triumph of the skies;
Universal nature say,
'Christ the Lord is born to-day.'

2 Christ, by highest heaven adored,
Christ the Everlasting Lord!
Late in time behold Him come,
Offspring of a Virgin's womb!
Veiled in flesh the Godhead see,
Hail, the incarnate Deity!
Pleased as man with men to dwell,
Jesus, our Immanuel.

3 Hail, the heavenly Prince of peace!
Hail, the Sun of righteousness!
Light and life to all He brings,
Risen with healing in His wings.
Mild He lays His glory by,
Born that man no more may die,
Born to raise the sons of earth,
Born to give them second birth.

4 Come, Desire of nations, come!
Fix in us Thy humble home;
Rise, the woman's conquering Seed,
Bruise in us the serpent's head.
Now display Thy saving power,
Ruined nature now restore;
Now in mystic union join
Thine to ours, and ours to Thine.

Charles Wesley

113 *"Greater love hath no man than this."* [PETERSBURG

   All praise to Thee, eternal Lord,
   Clothed in the garb of flesh and blood;
   Choosing a manger for Thy throne,
   While worlds on worlds are Thine alone.

2 Once did the skies before Thee bow;
   A Virgin's arms contain Thee now;
   Angels who did in Thee rejoice
   Now listen for Thine infant voice.

3 A little child Thou art our guest,
   That weary ones in Thee may rest;
   Forlorn and lowly is thy birth,
   That we may rise from heaven to earth.

4 Thou comest in the darksome night,
   To make us children of the light,
   To make us, in the realms divine,
   Like Thine own angels round Thee shine.

5 All this for us Thy love hath done;
   By this to Thee our love is won;
   For this we tune our cheerful lays,
   And shout our thanks in ceaseless praise.
                             Martin Luther

114 *"We have peace with God through our Lord Jesus Christ."* [MELANCHTHON

   It came upon the midnight clear,—
      That glorious song of old,
   From angels bending near the earth
      To touch their harps of gold:
   'Peace on the earth, good-will to men,
      From heaven's all-gracious King!'
   The world in solemn stillness lay
      To hear the angels sing.

2 Still through the cloven skies they come,
   With peaceful wings unfurled;
  And still their heavenly music floats
   O'er all the weary world:
  Above its sad and lowly plains
   They bend on hovering wing,
  And ever o'er its Babel sounds
   The blessed angels sing.

3 Yet with the woes of sin and strife
   The world has suffered long;
  Beneath the angel-strain have rolled
   Two thousand years of wrong;
  And men, at war with men, hear not
   The love-song which they bring:
  Oh! hush the noise, ye men of strife,
   And hear the angels sing!

4 And ye, beneath life's crushing load
   Whose forms are bending low,
  Who toil along the climbing way
   With painful steps and slow;
  Look now! for glad and golden hours
   Come swiftly on the wing:
  O! rest beside the weary road,
   And hear the angels sing!

5 For lo! the days are hastening on,
   By prophet-bards foretold,
  When with the ever-circling years
   Comes round the age of gold;
  When peace shall over all the earth
   Its ancient splendors fling,
  And the whole world send back the song
   Which now the angels sing.
                    Edmund Hamilton Sears

Our Lord Jesus Christ

115 [LAUDA SION
"Behold I bring you good tidings of great joy."

HARK! what mean those holy voices,
    Sweetly sounding through the skies?
Lo! the angelic host rejoices;
    Loudest hallelujahs rise.

2 Listen to the wondrous story,
    Which they chant in hymns of joy:—
'Glory in the highest, glory!
    Glory be to God most high!

3 'Peace on earth, good-will from heaven,
    Reaching far as man is found;
Souls redeemed, and sins forgiven;—
    Loud our golden harps shall sound.

4 'Christ is born, the great Anointed;
    Heaven and earth His praises sing!
Glad receive whom God appointed,
    For your Prophet, Priest and King!

5 'Hasten, mortals, to adore Him;
    Learn His name, and taste His joy;
Till in heaven ye sing before Him,—
    Glory be to God most high!'
John Cawood

116 *"Mine eyes have seen Thy salvation."* [ALLELUIA

THE race that long in darkness walked
    Have seen a glorious light;
The people dwell in day, who dwelt
    In death's surrounding night.

2 To hail Thy rise, Thou better Sun,
    The gathering nations come;
They joy as when the reapers bear
    The harvest-treasures home.

3 For unto us a Child is born,
   To us a Son is given:
And on His shoulder ever rests
   All power in earth and heaven.

4 His name shall be the Prince of peace,
   The God by all adored,
The Wonderful, the Counsellor,
   The Everlasting Lord.

5 His power increasing still shall spread,
   His reign no end shall know,
Justice and judgment guard His throne,
   And peace abound below.
                    John Morrison

117   *"King of Kings, and Lord of Lords."* [CORONATION

ALL hail the power of Jesus' name!
   Let angels prostrate fall;
Bring forth the royal diadem,
   To crown Him Lord of all!

2 Crown Him, ye morning stars of light,
   Who fixed this floating ball;
Now hail the Strength of Israel's might,
   And crown Him Lord of all!

3 Ye chosen seed of Israel's race,
   Ye ransomed of the fall,
Hail Him who saves you by His grace,
   And crown Him Lord of all!

4 Sinners, whose love can ne'er forget
   The wormwood and the gall,
Go, spread your trophies at His feet,
   And crown Him Lord of all!

5 Let every tribe and every tongue
    That hear the Saviour's call,
  Now shout in universal song,
    And crown Him Lord of all!
                            Edward Perronet

118 *"The oil of joy for mourning, the garment* [CAMBRIDGE
      of praise for the spirit of heaviness."

  HARK, the glad sound, the Saviour comes,
    The Saviour promised long!
  Let every heart prepare a throne,
    And every voice a song.

2 On Him, the Spirit, largely poured,
    Exerts its sacred fire;
  Wisdom and might, and zeal and love,
    His holy breast inspire.

3 He comes, the prisoners to release,
    In Satan's bondage held;
  The gates of brass before Him burst,
    The iron fetters yield.

4 He comes, from thickest films of vice
    To clear the mental ray;
  And, on the eyes oppressed with night,
    To pour celestial day.

5 He comes, the broken heart to bind,
    The bleeding soul to cure;
  And, with the treasures of His grace,
    To enrich the humble poor.

6 Our glad hosannas, Prince of peace,
    Thy welcome shall proclaim;
  And heaven's eternal arches ring
    With Thy beloved name.
                            Philip Doddridge

119 "*God was manifest in the flesh.*" [SPANISH HYMN]

    Songs of thankfulness and praise,
    Jesus, Lord, to Thee we raise,
    Manifested by the Star
    To the sages from afar;
    Branch of royal David's stem
    In Thy birth at Bethlehem,
    Anthems be to Thee addrest,
    God in man made manifest.

2 Manifest at Jordan's stream,
    Prophet, Priest, and King supreme;
    And at Cana, wedding-guest,
    In Thy Godhead manifest;
    Manifest in power divine,
    Changing water into wine;
    Anthems be to Thee addrest,
    God in man made manifest.

3 Sun and moon shall darkened be,
    Stars shall fall, the heavens shall flee;
    Christ will then like lightning shine,
    All will see His glorious sign;
    All will then the trumpet hear;
    All will see the Judge appear,
    Who by all will be confest,
    God in man made manifest.

4 Grant us grace to see Thee, Lord,
    Mirrored in Thy holy word;
    May we imitate Thee now,
    And be pure, as pure art Thou;
    That we like to Thee may be
    At Thy great Epiphany;
    And may praise Thee, ever blest,
    God in man made manifest.
                      Christopher Wordsworth

Our Lord Jesus Christ

120   *"Behold, I bring you good tidings of great joy."*   [ANTIOCH

Joy to the world! the Lord is come;
   Let earth receive her King;
Let every heart prepare Him room,
   And heaven and nature sing.

2 Joy to the earth! the Saviour reigns;
   Let men their songs employ;
While fields and floods, rocks, hills, and plains
   Repeat the sounding joy.

3 No more let sins and sorrows grow,
   Nor thorns infest the ground;
He comes to make His blessings flow
   Far as the curse is found.

4 He rules the world with truth and grace,
   And makes the nations prove
The glories of His righteousness,
   And wonders of His love.
                    Isaac Watts

121   *"Hosanna to the Son of David."*   [JERUSALEM

ALL glory, laud, and honor,
   To Thee, Redeemer King!
To whom the lips of children
   Made sweet Hosannas ring!

2 Thou art the King of Israel;
   Thou David's Royal Son;
Who in the Lord's name comest,
   The King and Blessed One.

3 The company of angels
   Are praising Thee on high:
And mortal men and all things
   Created make reply.

4 The people of the Hebrews
    With palms before Thee went;
Our praise, and prayer, and anthems
    Before Thee we present.

5 To Thee before Thy Passion,
    They raised their hymns of praise:
To Thee amid Thy glory,
    Our melody we raise.

6 Thou didst accept their praises;
    Accept the prayers we bring,
Who in all good delightest,
    Thou good and gracious King!

John Mason Neale

122 "*His name is called the Word of God.*" [Elysium

O heavenly Word, Eternal Light,
Begotten of the Father's might,
Who, in these latter days, art born
For succor to a world forlorn;

2 Our hearts enlighten from above,
  And kindle with Thine own true love;
  That we, who hear Thy call to-day,
  May cast earth's vanities away.

3 And when as Judge Thou drawest nigh,
  The secrets of all hearts to try;
  When sinners meet their awful doom,
  And saints attain their heavenly home;

4 O let us not, for evil past,
  Be driven from Thy face at last;
  But with the blessed evermore
  Behold Thee, love Thee, and adore.

123 *"Ye are Christ's, and Christ is God's."* [SALZBURG

Hail, thou once despised Jesus!
　　Hail, thou Galilean King!
Thou didst suffer to release us,
　　Thou didst free salvation bring:
Hail, thou agonizing Saviour,
　　Bearer of our sin and shame;
By Thy merits we find favor;
　　Life is given through Thy name!

2 Paschal Lamb, by God appointed,
　　All our sins were on Thee laid;
By almighty love anointed
　　Thou hast full atonement made:
All Thy people are forgiven
　　Through the virtue of Thy blood;
Opened is the gate of heaven;
　　Peace is made 'twixt man and God.

3 Jesus, hail! enthroned in glory,
　　There for ever to abide;
All the heavenly host adore Thee,
　　Seated at Thy Father's side:
There for sinners Thou art pleading;
　　There Thou dost our place prepare;
Ever for us interceding
　　Till in glory we appear.

4 Worship, honor, power, and blessing,
　　Thou art worthy to receive;
Loudest praises, without ceasing,
　　Meet it is for us to give!
Help, ye bright angelic spirits,
　　Bring your sweetest, noblest lays;
Help to sing our Saviour's merits,
　　Help to chant Immanuel's praise!

John Bakewell

124   *"Christ is all, and in all."*   [TRIUMPH

    Join all the glorious names
        Of wisdom, love, and power,
    That ever mortals knew,
        That angels ever bore;
    All are too mean to speak His worth,
    Too mean to set my Saviour forth.

2 Great Prophet of my God,
        My tongue would bless Thy name;
    By Thee the joyful news
        Of our salvation came;
    The joyful news of sins forgiven,
    Of hell subdued, and peace with heaven.

3 Jesus, my great High-Priest,
        Offered His blood and died;
    My guilty conscience seeks
        No sacrifice beside;
    His powerful blood did once atone,
    And now it pleads before the throne.

4 My dear Almighty Lord,
        My Conqueror and my King,
    Thy scepter and Thy sword,
        Thy reigning grace, I sing:
    Thine is the power: behold I sit
    In willing bonds beneath Thy feet!
                    Isaac Watts

125   *"A light to lighten the Gentiles."*   [CHIMES

    Infinite excellence is thine,
      Thou glorious Prince of grace!
    Thine uncreated beauties shine
      With never-fading rays.

2 Sinners, from earth's remotest end,
  Come bending at Thy feet;
  To Thee their prayers and songs ascend,
  In Thee their wishes meet.

3 Millions of happy spirits live
  On Thine exhaustless store;
  From Thee they all their bliss receive,
  And still Thou givest more.

4 Thou art their triumph and their joy;
  They find their all in Thee;
  Thy glories will their tongues employ
  Through all eternity.
                              John Fawcett

126 "*My grace is sufficient for thee.*"   [REST

Fountain of grace, rich, full, and free,
What need I, that is not in Thee!
Full pardon, strength to meet the day,
And peace which none can take away!

2 Doth sickness fill my heart with fear?
  'Tis sweet to know that Thou art near;
  Am I with dread of justice tried?
  'Tis sweet to know that Christ hath died.

3 In life, Thy promises of aid
  Forbid my heart to be afraid;
  In death, peace gently veils the eyes;
  Christ rose, and I shall surely rise.

4 O all-sufficient Saviour, be
  This all-sufficiency to me;
  Nor pain, nor sin, nor death can harm
  The weakest, shielded by Thine arm.

127   *"Make His praise glorious."*   [ARIEL

O COULD I speak the matchless worth,
O could I sound the glories forth,
  Which in my Saviour shine!
I'd soar, and touch the heavenly strings,
And vie with Gabriel while he sings
  In notes almost divine.

2 I'd sing the precious blood He spilt,
My ransom from the dreadful guilt
  Of sin and wrath divine:
I'd sing His glorious righteousness,
In which all-perfect, heavenly dress
  My soul shall ever shine.

3 I'd sing the characters he bears,
And all the forms of love He wears,
  Exalted on His throne:
In loftiest songs of sweetest praise,
I would to everlasting days
  Make all His glories known.

4 Well, the delightful day will come,
When my dear Lord will bring me home,
  And I shall see His face:
Then, with my Saviour, Brother, Friend,
A blest eternity I'll spend,
  Triumphant in His grace.
                  Samuel Medley

128   *"A Name which is above every name."*   [CALVARY

JESUS! Name of wondrous love!
Name all other names above!
Unto which must every knee
Bow in deep humility.

2 Jesus! Name of priceless worth
To the fallen sons of earth,
For the promise that it gave—
'Jesus shall His people save.'

3 Jesus! Name of mercy mild,
Given to the Holy Child,
When the cup of human woe
First He tasted here below.

4 Jesus! only Name that's given
Under all the mighty heaven,
Whereby man to sin enslaved,
Bursts his fetters, and is saved.

5 Jesus! Name of wondrous love!
Human name of God above!
Pleading only this we flee,
Helpless, O our God, to Thee.
William Walsham How

[ANGEL'S SONG
129 *"Ye are dead, and your life is hid with Christ in God."*

Thou who didst leave Thy Father's breast,
  Eternal Word sublime,
And cam'st to aid a world distrest,
  In Thine appointed time!
Our hearts enlighten, Lord, we pray,
  And kindle with Thy love,
That, dead to earthly things, we may
  Live but to things above.

2 So, when before the Judgment-seat
  The sinner hears his doom,
And when a voice divinely sweet
  Shall call the righteous home;
Safe from the burning, fiery flood,
  Safe from the dread abyss,
May we behold the face of God
  In everlasting bliss!

Our Lord Jesus Christ

130 [CHIMES
"*To know the love of Christ, which passeth knowledge.*"

    JESUS! the very thought of Thee
      With sweetness fills the breast;
    But sweeter far Thy face to see,
      And in Thy presence rest.

2 Nor voice can sing, nor heart can frame,
      Nor can the memory find
    A sweeter sound than Thy blest name,
      O Saviour of mankind!

3 O Hope of every contrite heart!
      O Joy of all the meek!
    To those who fall, how kind Thou art!
      How good to those who seek!

4 But what to those who find? Ah, this
      Nor tongue nor pen can show:
    The love of Jesus, what it is,
      None but His loved ones know.

5 Jesus, our only Joy be Thou,
      As Thou our Prize wilt be;
    Jesus, be Thou our Glory now,
      And through eternity!
                      Edward Caswall.

131 [SALZBURG
"*I will never leave thee, nor forsake thee.*"

    ONE there is above all others,
      Well deserves the name of Friend;
    His is love beyond a brother's,
      Costly, free, and knows no end.
    Which of all our friends, to save us,
      Could or would have shed his blood?
    But our Jesus died to have us
      Reconciled in Him to God.

2 When He lived on earth abased,
 Friend of sinners was His name;
 Now above all glory raised,
 He rejoices in the same.
 O for grace our hearts to soften;
 Teach us, Lord, at length to love;
 We, alas, forget too often
 What a Friend we have above.
                    John Newton

132 *"The Way, the Truth, and the Life."*   [ST. ANNA
 HOLY Jesus, Saviour blest,
 When, by passion strong possessed,
 Through this world of sin we stray,
 Thou to guide us art the Way.

2 Holy Jesus, when, like night,
 Error dims our clouded sight,
 Through the mists of sin to shine,
 Thou dost rise, the Truth divine.

3 Holy Jesus, when our power
 Fails us in temptation's hour,
 All unequal for the strife,
 Thou to aid us art the Life.

4 Who would reach his heavenly home,
 Who would to the Father come,
 Who His glorious presence see,
 Jesus, he must come by Thee.

5 Image of the Father's face,
 Giver of the Spirit's grace,
 Thee we praise, Incarnate Son!
 Glory to the Three in One!
                Richard Mant

133 *"Thy people shall be willing in the day of Thy power."* [DARWELL

  GIRD on Thy conquering sword,
   Ascend Thy shining car,
  And march, Almighty Lord,
   To wage Thy holy war.
Before His wheels, | Ye valleys rise,
In glad surprise, | And sink ye hills.

2 Fair truth, and smiling love,
  And injured righteousness,
Under Thy banners move,
  And seek from Thee redress:
Thou in their cause | And far and wide
Shalt prosperous ride, | Dispense Thy laws.

3 Before Thine awful face,
  Millions of foes shall fall,
The captives of Thy grace,
  The grace that conquers all.
The world shall know, | What wondrous things
Great King of kings, | Thine arm can do.

4 Here to my willing soul,
  Bend Thy triumphant way;
Here every foe control,
  And all Thy power display.
My heart, Thy throne, | Bows low to Thee,
Blest Jesus, see | To Thee alone.
       Philip Doddridge

134 *"If we deny Him, He also will deny us."* [REST

JESUS! and shall it ever be,
A mortal man ashamed of Thee?
Ashamed of Thee whom angels praise,
Whose glories shine through endless days?

2 Ashamed of Jesus! sooner far
  Let evening blush to own a star;
  He sheds the beams of light divine
  O'er this benighted soul of mine.

3 Ashamed of Jesus! that dear Friend
  On whom my hopes of heaven depend!
  No; when I blush—be this my shame,
  That I no more revere His name.

4 Ashamed of Jesus! yes, I may,
  When I've no guilt to wash away;
  No tear to wipe, no good to crave,
  No fear to quell, no soul to save.

5 Till then, nor is my boasting vain,
  Till then I boast a Saviour slain!
  And O may this my glory be,
  That Christ is not ashamed of me!
  Joseph Grigg

135 *"Behold My Servant, whom I have chosen."* [EXAMPLE
  My dear Redeemer and my Lord,
  I read my duty in Thy word;
  But in Thy life the law appears,
  Drawn out in living characters.

2 Such was Thy truth, and such Thy zeal,
  Such deference to Thy Father's will,
  Such love, and meekness so divine,
  I would transcribe and make them mine.

3 Cold mountains, and the midnight air,
  Witnessed the fervor of Thy prayer;
  The desert Thy temptations knew,
  Thy conflict, and Thy victory too.

4 Be Thou my pattern; make me bear
  More of Thy gracious image here!
  Then God, the Judge, shall own my name,
  Among the followers of the Lamb. *Isaac Watts*

136 *"As we have borne the image of the earthly,* [HOSTIA
we shall also bear the image of the heavenly."

O MEAN may seem this house of clay,
   Yet 'twas the Lord's abode;
Our feet may mourn this thorny way,
   Yet here Emmanuel trod.

2 This fleshly robe the Lord did wear,
   This watch the Lord did keep,
These burdens sore the Lord did bear,
   These tears the Lord did weep.

3 O vale of tears no longer sad,
   Wherein the Lord did dwell!
O holy robe of flesh that clad
   Our own Emmanuel!

4 But not this fleshly robe alone
   Shall link us, Lord, to Thee;
Not only in the tear and groan
   Shall the dear kindred be.

5 We shall be reckoned for Thine own,
   Because Thy heaven we share,
Because we sing around Thy throne,
   And Thy bright raiment wear.

6 O mighty grace, our life to live,
   To make our earth divine!
O mighty grace, Thy heaven to give
   And lift our life to Thine!
              Thomas Hornblower Gill

137 *"Never man spake like this Man."* [ENTREATY

How sweetly flowed the gospel's sound
   From lips of gentleness and grace,
When listening thousands gathered round,
   And joy and reverence filled the place!

2 From heaven He came, of heaven He spoke,
   To heaven He led his followers' way;
   Dark clouds of gloomy night He broke,
   Unveiling an immortal day.

3 'Come, wanderers, to My Father's home;
   Come, all ye weary ones, and rest:'
   Yes, sacred Teacher, we will come,
   Obey Thee, love Thee, and be blest.

4 Decay, then, tenements of dust;
   Pillars of earthly pride, decay:
   A nobler mansion waits the just,
   And Jesus has prepared the way.
                          John Bowring

138 *"Truly this man was the Son of God."* [WILMINGTON

PRAISE to the Holiest in the hight,
   And in the depth be praise:
In all His words most wonderful,
   Most sure in all His ways!
O loving wisdom of our God!
   When all was sin and shame,
A second Adam to the fight
   And to the rescue came.

2 O wisest love! that flesh and blood,
     Which did in Adam fail,
   Should strive afresh against the foe,
     Should strive and should prevail;
   And that a higher gift than grace
     Should flesh and blood refine,
   God's Presence and His very Self,
     And Essence all-divine.

3 O generous love! that He who smote
   In man for man the foe,
The double agony in man
   For man should undergo;
And in the garden secretly,
   And on the cross on high,
Should teach His brethren and inspire
   To suffer and to die!   *John Henry Newman*

139   *"The unsearchable riches of Christ."*   [EXAMPLE

O LOVE, how deep! how broad! how high!
It fills the heart with ecstacy,
That God, the Son of God, should take
Our mortal form for mortals' sake.

2 He sent no angel to our race,
Of higher or of lower place,
But clothed Himself in human frame
And to redeem this lost world came.

3 For us He prayed, for us He taught,
For us his daily works He wrought,
By words, and signs, and actions, thus
Still seeking not Himself, but us.

4 For us to wicked men betrayed,
Scourged, mocked, in purple robe arrayed,
He bore the shameful cross and death,
For us at length gave up His breath.

5 For us He rose from death again,
For us He went on high to reign,
For us He sent His Spirit here
To guide, to strengthen, and to cheer.

6 To Him whose boundless love has won
Salvation for us through the Son,
To God the Father, glory be,
Both now and through eternity.
                John Mason Neale

140 *"And I, if I be lifted up from the earth,* [JOACHIM
will draw all men unto Me."

From the cross uplifted high
Where the Saviour deigns to die,
What melodious sounds I hear,
Bursting on my ravished ear!
'Love's redeeming work is done,
Come and welcome, sinner, come!

2 'Sprinkled now with blood the throne,
Why beneath thy burdens groan?
On My pierced body laid,
Justice owns the ransom paid;
Bow the knee, and kiss the Son,
Come and welcome, sinner, come!

3 'Spread for thee, the festal board
See with richest dainties stored;
To thy Father's bosom prest
Yet again a child confest,
Never from His house to roam;
Come and welcome, sinner, come!

4 'Soon the days of life shall end:
Lo I come, your Saviour, Friend!
Safe your spirit to convey
To the realms of endless day,
Up to My eternal home:
Come and welcome, sinner, come!'
Thomas Haweis

141 *"Who loved me, and gave Himself for me."* [PHRYGIA

O Sacred Head! once wounded,
  With grief and shame weighed down,
Once scornfully surrounded
  With thorns, Thy only crown;
O Sacred Head! what glory,
  What bliss, till now was Thine;
Yet, though despised and gory,
  I joy to call Thee mine.

2 What Thou, my Lord, hast suffered,
  Was all for sinners' gain:
Mine, mine, was the transgression,
  But Thine the deadly pain.
Lo! here I fall, my Saviour;
  'Tis I deserve Thy place;
Look on me with Thy favor,
  Vouchsafe to me Thy grace.

3 What language shall I borrow
  To thank Thee, dearest Friend,
For this, Thy dying sorrow,
  Thy pity without end!
O make me Thine for ever;
  And should I fainting be,
Lord, let me never, never,
  Outlive my love to Thee.

4 And when I am departing,
  O part not Thou from me!
When mortal pangs are darting,
  Come, Lord, and set me free!
And when my heart must languish
  Amid the final throe,
Release me from mine anguish
  By Thine own pain and woe!

5 Be near me when I'm dying,
  O show Thy cross to me;
And, for my succor flying,
  Come, Lord, and set me free!
These eyes new faith receiving
  From Jesus shall not move;
For he, who dies believing,
  Dies safely through Thy love.

Paul Gerhardt

142 *"God forbid that I should glory,* [UNSER HERRSCHER
save in the cross of our Lord Jesus Christ."

IN the cross of Christ I glory,
  Towering o'er the wrecks of time;
All the light of sacred story
  Gathers round its head sublime.

2 When the woes of life o'ertake me,
    Hopes deceive, and fears annoy,
  Never shall the cross forsake me;
    Lo, it glows with peace and joy.

3 When the sun of bliss is beaming
    Light and love upon my way,
  From the cross the radiance streaming
    Adds more luster to the day.

4 Bane and blessing, pain and pleasure,
    By the cross are sanctified;
  Peace is there, that knows no measure,
    Joys that through all time abide.

5 In the cross of Christ I glory,
    Towering o'er the wrecks of time;
  All the light of sacred story
    Gathers round its head sublime.
                              John Bowring

143 *"Jesus Christ, the same yesterday, and to-* [SAMSON
day, and for ever."

O CHRIST! our King, Creator, Lord!
Saviour of all who trust Thy word!
To them who seek Thee ever near,
Now to our praises bend Thine ear.

2 In Thy dear cross a grace is found—
It flows from every streaming wound—
Whose power our inbred sin controls,
Breaks the firm bond, and frees our souls!

3 Thou didst create the stars of night,
Yet Thou hast veiled in flesh Thy light;
Hast deigned a mortal form to wear,
A mortal's painful lot to bear.

4 When Thou didst hang upon the tree,
The quaking earth acknowledged Thee;
When Thou didst there yield up Thy breath,
The world grew dark as shades of death.

5 Now in the Father's glory high,
Great Conquerer, never more to die,
Us by Thy mighty power defend,
And reign through ages without end!

Ray Palmer

144 *"Thou wast slain, and hast redeemed us to God by Thy blood."* [UNSER HERRSCHER

HE who once in righteous vengeance
   Whelmed the world beneath the flood,
Once again in mercy cleansed it,
   With His own most precious blood;
Coming from His throne on high
On the bitter cross to die.

2 O the wisdom of the Eternal!
   O the depth of love divine!
O the sweetness of that mercy
   Which in Jesus Christ doth shine!
We were sinners doomed to die—
Jesus paid our penalty.

3 When before the Judge we tremble,
    Conscious of His broken laws,
  May His blood in that dread moment
    Cry aloud, and plead our cause;
  Bid our fears for ever cease,
  Be our pardon and our peace.

4 Prince and Author of salvation,
    Lord, of majesty supreme,
  Jesus, praise to Thee be given
    By the world Thou didst redeem;
  Glory to the Father be,
  And the Spirit, One with Thee!
                    Edward Caswall

145 [ANGEL'S SONG
"I am He that liveth and was dead."

  THE shade and gloom of life are fled,
    This Resurrection day;
  Henceforth in Christ are no more dead,
    The grave hath no more prey;
  In Christ we live, in Christ we sleep,
    In Christ we wake and rise,
  And the sad tears death makes us weep,
    He wipes from all our eyes.

2 Then wake, glad heart, awake! awake!
    And seek Thy risen Lord;
  Joy in His resurrection take,
    And comfort in His word;
  And let thy life, through all its ways,
    One long thanksgiving be;
  Its theme of joy, its song of praise,
    'Christ died and rose for me!'

146   "*O grave, where is thy victory?*"   [TRIUMPH

    YES, the Redeemer rose;
      The Saviour left the dead;
    And o'er our hellish foes
      High raised His conquering head.
In wild dismay, | Fell to the ground,
The guards around | And sunk away.

2 Lo! the angelic bands
     In full assembly meet,
  To wait His high commands,
     And worship at His feet:
Joyful they come, | From realms of day
And wing their way | To such a tomb.

3 Then back to heaven they fly,
     The joyful news to bear:
  Hark! as they soar on high,
     What music fills the air!
Their anthems say, | Hath left the dead;
'Jesus, who bled, | He rose to-day.'

4 Ye mortals, catch the sound,
     Redeemed by Him from hell;
  And send the echo round
     The globe on which you dwell;
Transported cry, | Hath left the dead,
'Jesus, who bled, | No more to die.'

5 All hail, triumphant Lord,
     Who sav'st us with Thy blood!
  Wide be Thy name adored,
     Thou rising, reigning God!
With Thee we rise, | And empires gain
With Thee we reign, | Beyond the skies.
                     Philip Doddridge

147 *"If we be dead with Him, we shall also live with Him."* [HASTINGS

How calm and beautiful the morn
    That gilds the sacred tomb,
Where Christ the crucified was borne
    And veiled in midnight gloom!
O weep no more the Saviour slain!
The Lord is risen, He lives again!

2 Ye mourning saints, dry every tear
    For your departed Lord;
Behold the place, He is not here,
    The tomb is all unbarred:
The gates of death were closed in vain,
The Lord is risen, He lives again.

3 How tranquil now the rising day!
    'Tis Jesus still appears,
A risen Lord, to chase away
    Your unbelieving fears:
O weep no more your comforts slain!
The Lord is risen, He lives again!

4 And when the shades of evening fall,
    When life's last hour draws nigh,
If Jesus shines upon the soul,
    How blissful then to die!
Since He has risen that once was slain,
Ye die in Christ to live again.
                  Thomas Hastings

148 *"Death is swallowed up in victory."* [CHAPEL

'THE Lord is risen indeed;'
    The grave hath lost its prey;
With Him shall rise the ransomed seed
    To reign in endless day.

2 'The Lord is risen indeed;'
    He lives, to die no more;
    He lives the sinner's cause to plead,
    Whose curse and shame He bore.

3 'The Lord is risen indeed;'
    Attending angels, hear;
    Up to the courts of heaven, with speed,
    The joyful tidings bear.

4 Then take your golden lyres,
    And strike each cheerful chord;
    Join all the bright celestial choirs,
    To sing our risen Lord.   *Thomas Kelly*

149   "*Worthy is the Lamb that was slain.*"   [HERMON
GLORY to God on high!
Let praises fill the sky!
    Praise ye His name!
Angels His name adore,
Who all our sorrows bore;
Saints cry for evermore,
    Worthy the Lamb!

2 All they around the throne
Cheerfully join in one,
    Praising His name:
We, who have felt His blood
Sealing our peace with God,
Spread His dear name abroad,
    Worthy the Lamb!

3 Though we must change our place,
Our souls shall never cease
    Praising His name;
To Him we'll tribute bring,
Hail Him our gracious King,
And without ceasing sing,
    Worthy the Lamb!   *James Allen*

150 "*And on His head were many crowns.*" [HOLSTEIN

CROWN Him with crowns of gold,
 All nations great and small,
Crown Him, ye martyred saints of old,
 The Lamb once slain for all;
The Lamb once slain for them
 Who bring their praises now,
As jewels for the diadem
 That girds His sacred brow.

2 Crown Him the Son of God
 Before the worlds began,
And ye who tread where He hath trod,
 Crown Him the Son of Man;
Who every grief hath known
 That wrings the human breast,
And takes and bears them for His own
 That all in Him may rest.

3 Crown Him the Lord of light,
 Who o'er a darkened world
In robes of glory infinite
 His fiery flag unfurled,
And bore it raised on high,
 In heaven,—in earth,—beneath,
To all the sign of victory
 O'er Satan, sin, and death.

4 Crown Him the Lord of life,
 Who triumphed o'er the grave,
And rose victorious in the strife
 For those He came to save;
His glories now we sing
 Who died, and rose on high,
Who died, eternal life to bring,
 And lives, that death may die.
     Godfrey Thring

151 *"We have not an High Priest, which cannot be touched with the feeling of our infirmities."* [ALLELUIA

Come, let us join our songs of praise
　To our ascended Priest;
He entered heaven, with all our names
　Engraven on His breast.

2 Below He washed our guilt away,
　By His atoning blood;
Now He appears before the throne,
　And pleads our cause with God.

3 Clothed with our nature still, He knows
　The weakness of our frame,
And how to shield us from the foes
　Whom He Himself o'ercame.

4 Nor time, nor distance, e'er shall quench
　The fervor of His love;
For us He died in kindness here,
　For us He lives above.

5 O may we ne'er forget His grace,
　Nor blush to bear his name;
Still may our hearts hold fast His faith,
　Our lips His praise proclaim.

152 *"He that glorieth, let him glory in the Lord."* [WILMINGTON

O Christ! our Hope, our heart's Desire,
　Redemption's only Spring,
Creator of the world art Thou,
　Its Saviour and its King!

2 How vast the mercy and the love
　Which laid our sins on Thee,
And led Thee to a cruel death,
　To set Thy people free!

3 But now the bonds of death are burst,
   The ransom hath been paid;
   And Thou art on Thy Father's throne,
   In glorious might arrayed.

4 O may Thy wondrous love prevail
   Our sinful souls to spare!
   O may we come before Thy throne,
   And find acceptance there!

5 O Christ, be Thou our present Joy,
   Our future great Reward;
   Our only glory may it be
   To glory in the Lord.
                                John Chandler

[ELYSIUM
153 *"All power is given unto Me, in heaven and in earth."*

O LORD most high, Eternal King,
By Thee redeemed Thy praise we sing:
The bonds of death are burst by Thee,
And grace has won the victory.

2 Ascending to the Father's throne,
   Thou claim'st the kingdom as Thine own;
   Thy days of mortal weakness o'er,
   All power is Thine for evermore.

3 To Thee the whole creation now
   Shall, in its threefold order, bow,
   Of things on earth, and things on high,
   And things that underneath us lie.

4 Be Thou our Joy, O mighty Lord,
   As Thou wilt be our great Reward;
   Let all our glory be in Thee
   Both now and through eternity.
                                John Mason Neale

154 *"As rivers of water in a dry place, as the shadow of a great rock in a weary land."* [DEDHAM

HE who on earth as man was known,
  And bore our sins and pains,
Now, seated on the eternal throne,
  The God of glory reigns.

2 His hands the wheels of nature guide
   With an unerring skill,
  And countless worlds, extended wide,
   Obey His sovereign will.

3 This land, through which His pilgrims go,
   Is desolate and dry;
  But streams of grace from Him o'erflow,
   Their thirst to satisfy.

4 When troubles, like a burning sun,
   Beat heavy on their head,
  To this Almighty Rock they run,
   And find a pleasing shade.

5 How glorious He! how happy they
   In such a glorious Friend!
  Whose love secures them all the way,
   And crowns them at the end.
                            John Newton

155   *"Worthy is the Lamb that was slain."* [SAMSON

COME, let us sing the song of songs,—
  The saints in heaven began the strain,—
 The homage which to Christ belongs:
  'Worthy the Lamb, for He was slain!'

2 Slain to redeem us by His blood,
   To cleanse from every sinful stain,
  And make us kings and priests to God:
   'Worthy the Lamb, for He was slain!'

3 To Him who suffered on the tree,
    Our souls at His soul's price to gain,
  Blessing, and praise, and glory be:
    'Worthy the Lamb, for He was slain!'

4 To Him enthroned by filial right,
    All power in heaven and earth pertain,
  Honor, and majesty, and might:
    'Worthy the Lamb, for He was slain!'

5 Come, Holy Spirit, from on high,
    Our faith, our hope, our love sustain,
  Living to sing, and dying cry,
    'Worthy the Lamb, for He was slain!'
                              James Montgomery

156 [HADLEY
  "We shall be like Him, for we shall see Him as He is."

  'WE would see Jesus!'—for the shadows lengthen
    Across this little landscape of our life;
  'We would see Jesus!' our weak faith to strengthen
    For the last weariness, the final strife.

2 'We would see Jesus!' the great Rock-foundation,
    Whereon our feet were set by sovereign grace;
  Nor life nor death, with all their agitation,
    Can thence remove us, if we see His face.

3 'We would see Jesus!' sense is all too blinding,
    And heaven appears too dim, too far away;
  We would see Thee, Thyself our hearts reminding
    What Thou hast suffered, our great debt to pay.

4 'We would see Jesus!' this is all we're needing:
   Strength, joy, and willingness come with
      the sight;
   'We would see Jesus!' dying, risen, pleading;
   Then, welcome day, and farewell mortal
      night!

[Duke St.
157   *"He ever liveth to make intercession for us."*
   He lives, the great Redeemer lives,—
   What joy the blest assurance gives:
   And now, before His Father, God,
   Pleads the full merit of His blood.

2 Hence then, ye black, despairing thoughts:
   Above our fears, above our faults,
   His powerful intercessions rise,
   And guilt recedes, and terror dies.

3 In every dark, distressful hour,
   When sin and Satan join their power,
   Let this dear hope repel the dart,
   That Jesus bears us on His heart.

4 Great Advocate, Almighty Friend!
   On Him our humble hopes depend;
   Our cause can never, never fail,
   For Jesus pleads, and must prevail.
                              Anne Steele

158   *"Perfect through sufferings."*   [Watch
   The Head that once was crowned with thorns
      Is crowned with glory now;
   A royal diadem adorns
      The mighty Victor's brow.

2 The highest place that heaven affords,
  Is His, is His by right,
The King of kings, and Lord of lords,
  And heaven's eternal Light.

3 The Joy of all who dwell above,
  The Joy of all below
To whom He manifests His love,
  And grants His name to know.

4 To them the cross, with all its shame,
  With all its grace, is given;
Their name, an everlasting name,
  Their joy, the joy of heaven.

5 They suffer with their Lord below,
  They reign with Him above;
Their profit and their joy to know
  The mystery of His love.

6 The cross He bore is life and health,
  Though shame and death to Him;
His people's hope, His people's wealth,
  Their everlasting theme.
                              Thomas Kelly

159 *"And I heard the voice of many angels* [WOODSTOCK
       round about the Throne."

BEHOLD the glories of the Lamb,
  Amid His Father's throne;
Prepare new honors for His name,
  And songs before unknown.

2 Let elders worship at His feet;
  The church adore around;
With vials full of odors sweet,
  And harps of sweeter sound.

3 Those are the prayers of all the saints,
  And these the hymns they raise:
Jesus is kind to our complaints,
  He loves to hear our praise.

4 Now to the Lamb, that once was slain,
  Be endless blessings paid;
Salvation, glory, joy, remain
  For ever on Thy head.

5 Thou hast redeemed our souls with blood,
  Hast set the prisoners free,
Hast made us kings and priests to God,
  And we shall reign with Thee!

6 The worlds of nature and of grace
  Are put beneath Thy power;
Then shorten these delaying days,
  And bring the promised hour.
            Isaac Watts

160 *"Sing ye to the Lord, for He hath* [DUKE ST.
       triumphed gloriously."

LIFT up, lift up your voices now!
The whole wide world rejoices now!
The Lord hath triumphed gloriously!
The Lord shall reign victoriously!

2 In vain with stone the cave they barred,
  In vain the watch kept ward and guard;
  Majestic from the spoiled tomb,
  In pomp of triumph, Christ is come!

3 He binds in chains the ancient foe,
  A countless host he frees from woe,
  And heaven's high portal open flies,
  For Christ hath risen and man shall rise.

4 And all He did, and all He bare,
　He gives us as our own to share;
　And hope and joy and peace begin,
　For Christ hath won and man may win.

5 O Victor, aid us in the fight,
　And lead through death to realms of light;
　We safely tread where Thou hast trod;
　In Thee we die, to rise to God.

6 Thy flock, from sin and death set free,
　Glad Hallelujah raise to Thee;
　And ever, with the heavenly host,
　Praise Father, Son, and Holy Ghost!
　　　　　　　　John Mason Neale

161 *"Now is Christ risen from the dead."* [FRANKFORT

Jesus Christ is risen to-day,
Our triumphant holy day,
Who did once upon the cross
Suffer to redeem our loss.

2 Hymns of praise then let us sing
　Unto Christ our Heavenly King,
　Who endured the cross and grave,
　Sinners to redeem and save.

3 But the pain which He endured,
　Our salvation has procured:
　Now above the sky He's King,
　Where the angels ever sing.

4 Sing we to our God above
　Praise eternal as His love;
　Praise Him, all ye heavenly host,
　Father, Son, and Holy Ghost.

The Holy Spirit

162   *"That Holy Spirit of promise."*   [PENTECOST

LET songs of praises fill the sky:
    Christ, our ascended Lord,
Sends down His spirit from on high,
    According to His word:
All hail the day of Pentecost,
The coming of the Holy Ghost!

2 The Spirit, by His heavenly breath,
    New life creates within;
He quickens sinners from the death
    Of trespasses and sin:
All hail the day of Pentecost,
The coming of the Holy Ghost!

3 The things of Christ the Spirit takes
    And shows them unto men;
The fallen soul His temple makes:
    God's image stamps again:
All hail the day of Pentecost,
The coming of the Holy Ghost!

4 Come, Holy Spirit, from above,
    With Thy celestial fire;
Come, and with flames of zeal and love
    Our hearts and tongues inspire!
Be this our day of Pentecost,
The coming of the Holy Ghost!

Thomas Cotterill

163 *"The Spirit also helpeth our infirmities."* [WARD

Come, Holy Ghost, who ever One
Art with the Father and the Son:
Come, Holy Ghost, our souls possess
With Thy full flood of holiness.

2 Let flesh, and heart, and lips, and mind,
Sound forth our witness to mankind;
And love light up our mortal frame,
Till others catch the living flame.

3 Thou ever-blessed Three in One,
O Father and Coequal Son,
O Holy Ghost the Comforter,
Thy grace on Thy redeemed confer.
John Henry Newman

164 *"The Comforter, which is the Holy Ghost."* [STATE ST.

Come, Holy Spirit, come,
Let Thy bright beams arise,
Dispel the darkness from our minds,
And open all our eyes.

2 Revive our drooping faith,
Our doubts and fears remove,
And kindle in our breasts the flame
Of never-dying love.

3 Convince us of our sin,
Then lead to Jesus' blood,
And to our wondering view reveal
The secret love of God.

4 'Tis Thine to cleanse the heart,
To sanctify the soul,
To pour fresh life in every part,
And new-create the whole.

5 Dwell therefore in our hearts,
    Our minds from bondage free;
  Then we shall know, and praise, and love
    The Father, Son, and Thee!
                                    Joseph Hart

165   *"Ask, and it shall be given you."*   [ST. JOHN
  O THOU that hearest prayer,
      Attend our humble cry;
  And let Thy servants share
      Thy blessing from on high:
  We plead the promise of Thy word;
  Grant us Thy Holy Spirit, Lord!

2 If earthly parents hear
      Their children when they cry;
  If they, with love sincere,
      Their children's wants supply;
  Much more wilt Thou Thy love display,
  And answer when Thy children pray.

3 Our Heavenly Father Thou;
      We, children of Thy grace;
  O let Thy Spirit now
      Descend, and fill the place;
  That all may feel the heavenly flame,
  And all unite to praise Thy name.

4 O send Thy Spirit down
      On all the nations, Lord,
  With great success to crown
      The preaching of Thy word;
  Till heathen lands may own Thy sway,
  And cast their idol-gods away.
                                    John Burton

The Holy Spirit

166 *"He shall baptize you with the Holy Ghost and with fire."* [PSALM

Jesus, Thine all-victorious love
  Shed in my heart abroad:
Then shall my feet no longer rove,
  Rooted and fixed in God.

2 O that in me the sacred fire
  Might now begin to glow;
Burn up the dross of base desire,
  And make the mountains flow.

3 O that it now from heaven might fall,
  And all my sins consume:
Come, Holy Ghost, for Thee I call;
  Spirit of burning, come.

4 Refining Fire, go through my heart;
  Illuminate my soul,
Scatter Thy life through every part,
  And sanctify the whole.

5 My steadfast soul, from falling free,
  Shall then no longer move;
While Christ is all the world to me,
  And all my heart is love.
        Charles Wesley

167 *"If we ask anything according to His will, He heareth us."* [PESARO

Lord, show Thy glory, as of old,
  The work of heavenly love display,
And let our longing eyes behold
  Another Pentecostal day:
Our fervent wishes deign to crown,
And send Thy quickening Spirit down.

2 Thou seest, Lord, how far we stray,
    Opprest with ills we cannot flee;
  How sin hath drawn our hearts away
    From peace, from happiness, and Thee:
  Thy gracious Spirit, Lord, bestow,
  And snatch us from the depth of woe.

3 Now let a brighter day begin
    Than ever yet was witnessed here:
  Bid the dark-gathering clouds of sin
    Before Thy presence disappear;
  Reign in each heart; in every place
  Set up the empire of Thy grace.
William Hiley Bathurst

168 "*The love of God is shed abroad in our hearts* [GLUCK
      by the Holy Ghost."

SPIRIT Divine, attend our prayers,
  And make this house Thy home;
Descend with all Thy gracious powers,
  O come, Great Spirit, come!

2 Come as the light: to us reveal
    Our emptiness and woe,
  And lead us in those paths of life
    Where all the righteous go.

3 Come as the fire, and purge our hearts
    Like sacrificial flame;
  Let our whole soul an offering be
    To our Redeemer's name.

4 Come as the dove, and spread Thy wings,
    The wings of peaceful love;
  And let Thy church on earth become
    Blest as the church above.

5 Spirit Divine, attend our prayers;
    Make a lost world Thy home;
  Descend with all Thy gracious powers,
    O come, Great Spirit, come!
                                Andrew Reed

169   *"The Spirit giveth life."*   [VALENTIA
  COME, Holy Spirit, Heavenly Dove,
    With all Thy quickening powers;
  Kindle a flame of sacred love
    In these cold hearts of ours.

2 Look how we grovel here below,
    Fond of these trifling toys:
  Our souls can neither fly, nor go,
    To reach eternal joys.

3 In vain we tune our formal songs,
    In vain we strive to rise;
  Hosannas languish on our tongues,
    And our devotion dies.

4 Dear Lord! and shall we ever live
    At this poor dying rate,
  Our love so faint, so cold to Thee,
    And Thine to us so great?

5 Come, Holy Spirit, Heavenly Dove,
    With all Thy quickening powers;
  Come, shed abroad a Saviour's love,
    And that shall kindle ours.
                                Isaac Watts

170   *"As many as are led by the Spirit of God,*   [WARD
         they are the sons of God."
  COME, O Creator Spirit blest,
  And in our souls take up Thy rest;
  Come, with Thy grace and heavenly aid,
  And fill the hearts which Thou hast made.

2 Great Paraclete, to Thee we cry:
  O highest gift of God most high,
  O Fount of life, O Fire of love,
  And sweet Anointing from above!

3 Thou in Thy sevenfold gifts art known;
  Thee, Finger of God's hand, we own:
  The promise of the Father Thou,
  Who dost the tongue with power endow.

4 Our senses kindle from above,
  And make our hearts o'erflow with love:
  With Thine unfailing strength refresh
  The weakness of our mortal flesh.

5 Drive far from us the foe we dread,
  And grant us Thy true peace instead:
  With Thee for Guardian, Thee for Guide,
  No evil can our steps betide.

6 O let Thy grace on us bestow
  The Father and the Son to know,
  And Thee, through endless time confest,
  Of Both the Eternal Spirit blest.
                    Edward Caswall

171   "*Ye are the temple of the living God.*"   [PESARO

  SPIRIT of God, that moved of old
    Upon the water's darkened face,
  Come, when our faithless hearts are cold,
    And stir them with an inward grace.

2 Thou that art power and peace combined,
    All highest strength, all purest love,
  The rushing of the mighty wind,
    The brooding of the gentle dove:

3 Come, give us still Thy powerful aid,
   And urge us on, and make us Thine;
   Nor leave the hearts that once were made
   Fit temples for Thy grace divine.
                        Cecil Frances Alexander

172   *"He will guide you into all truth."*   [GERMANY
   COME, Holy Spirit, Heavenly Dove,
   My sinful maladies remove;
   Be Thou my Light, be Thou my Guide,
   O'er every thought and step preside.

2 The light of truth to me display,
   That I may know and choose my way;
   Plant holy fear within mine heart,
   That I from God may ne'er depart.

3 Conduct me safe, conduct me far
   From every sin and hurtful snare;
   Lead me to God, my final rest,
   In His enjoyment to be blest.

4 Lead me to Christ, the Living Way,
   Nor let me from His pastures stray:
   Lead me to heaven, the seat of bliss,
   Where pleasure in perfection is.

5 Lead me to holiness, the road
   That I must take to dwell with God;
   Lead to Thy word, that rules must give,
   And sure directions how to live.

6 Lead me to means of grace, where I
   May own my wants, and seek supply:
   Lead to Thyself, the Spring from whence
   To fetch all quickening influence.
                        Simon Browne

The Holy Spirit

173   *"He shall teach you all things."*   [ELIJAH

Come, blessed Spirit! Source of light,
  Whose power and grace are unconfined,
Dispel the gloomy shades of night,
  The thicker darkness of the mind.

2 To mine illumined eyes display
   The glorious truths Thy word reveals;
 Cause me to run the heavenly way;
   The book unfold, and loose the seals.

3 Thine inward teachings make me know
   The mysteries of redeeming love,
 The emptiness of things below,
   And excellence of things above.

4 While through this dubious maze I stray,
   Spread, like the sun, Thy beams abroad,
 To show the dangers of the way,
   And guide my feeble steps to God.
                        Benjamin Beddome

[GLUCK
174 *"Righteousness, and peace, and joy in the Holy Ghost."*

Thou blessed Spirit, by whose aid
  Life's path is safely trod,
Its varied scenes and duties made
  True progress home to God:

2 Come to our hearts, Lord, and abide
   A welcome guest therein:
 Help to withstand assaults of pride,
   To fight and conquer sin.

3 The grace and peace of Christ reveal,
   His everlasting love;
 Disperse the doubts that would conceal
   Our hope of rest above.

4 Come with the joy Thy love imparts,
   Sweet sense of sin forgiven:
   With patience fill our restless hearts,
   And guide us home to heaven.

175   *"Receive ye the Holy Ghost."*   [HENDON
   GOD, the everlasting God,
   Makes with mortals His abode;
   Whom the heavens cannot contain,
   He vouchsafes to dwell in man.

2 Never will He thence depart,
   Inmate of a humble heart;
   Carrying on His work within,
   Striving till He cast out sin.

3 Come, divine and peaceful Guest,
   Enter our devoted breast:
   Holy Ghost, our hearts inspire,
   Kindle there the gospel fire.

4 Crown the agonizing strife,
   Principle and Lord of life:
   Life divine in us renew,
   Thou the Gift and Giver too!
                    Charles Wesley

176   *"Walk in the Spirit, and ye shall not fulfill*   [PESARO
      the lust of the flesh."
   ETERNAL Spirit! we confess,
   And sing the wonders of Thy grace:
   Thy power conveys our blessings down
   From God the Father and the Son.

2 Enlightened by Thine heavenly ray,
   Our shades and darkness turn to day;
   Thine inward teachings make us know
   Our danger, and our refuge too.

3 Thy power and glory work within,
   And break the chains of reigning sin;
   Do our imperious lusts subdue,
   And form our wretched hearts anew.

4 The troubled conscience knows Thy voice;
   Thy cheering words awake our joys;
   Thy words allay the stormy wind,
   And calm the surges of the mind.
                               Isaac Watts

177 "*The earnest of the Spirit in our hearts.*" [ST. MARTIN
   ENTHRONED on high, Almighty Lord,
      Thy Holy Ghost send down;
   Fulfill in us Thy faithful word,
      And all Thy mercies crown.

2 Spirit of life, and light, and love,
      Thy heavenly influence give;
   Quicken our souls, born from above,
      In Christ that we may live.

3 To our benighted minds reveal
      The glories of His grace,
   And bring us where no clouds conceal
      The brightness of His face.

4 His love within us shed abroad,
      Life's ever-springing well;
   Till God in us, and we in God,
      In love eternal dwell.
                           Thomas Haweis

The Holy Spirit

[WORMS

178 *"The fruit of the Spirit is love, joy, peace."*

GRACIOUS Spirit, Dove Divine!
Let Thy light within me shine;
All my guilty fears remove,
Fill me with Thy heavenly love.

2 Speak Thy pardoning grace to me,
Set the burdened sinner free;
Lead me to the Lamb of God,
Wash me in His precious blood.

3 Life and peace to me impart;
Seal salvation on my heart;
Breathe Thyself into my breast,
Earnest of immortal rest.

4 Let me never from Thee stray;
Keep me in the narrow way;
Fill my soul with joy divine,
Keep me, Lord, for ever Thine.
                                John Stocker

[ST. MARTIN

179 *"The Spirit is life because of righteousness."*

HE's come! let every knee be bent,
   All hearts new joys resume;
Let nations sing with one consent,
   The Comforter is come!

2 What greater gift, what greater love
   Can God on man bestow!
'Tis half the angels' heaven above,
   And all our heaven below.

3 Hail, blessed Spirit! not a soul
    But doth Thy goodness feel;
  Thou dost our darling sins control,
    And fix our wavering zeal.

4 As pilots by the compass steer,
    Till they their harbor find,
  So do Thy sacred breathings here
    Guide every wandering mind.

5 The flesh may strive our course to impeach,
    The world's rough billows roar,
  But by Thy help we're sure to reach
    The safe, eternal shore.

Redemption

180   *"We have seen His star, in the east."*   [HEBRON

WHEN marshaled on the nightly plain,
    The glittering host bestud the sky,
One star alone, of all the train,
    Can fix the sinner's wandering eye.

2 Hark! hark! to God the chorus breaks,
    From every host, from every gem;
But one alone the Saviour speaks,
    It is the Star of Bethlehem.

3 Once on the raging seas I rode,
    The storm was loud, the night was dark,
The ocean yawned, and rudely blowed
    The wind that tost my foundering bark.

4 Deep horror then my vitals froze;
    Death-struck, I ceased the tide to stem;
When suddenly a star arose,—
    It was the Star of Bethlehem.

5 It was my guide, my light, my all;
    It bade my dark forebodings cease;
And, through the storm and danger's thrall,
    It led me to he port of peace.

6 Now safely moored, my perils o'er,
    I'll sing, first in night's diadem,
For ever and for evermore,
    The Star—the Star of Bethlehem!
                  Henry Kirke White

Redemption

181 *"The wages of sin is death: but the gift of God is eternal life through Jesus Christ our Lord."* [GORTON

How heavy is the night
   That hangs upon our eyes,
Till Christ with His reviving light
   Over our souls arise!

2 Our guilty spirits dread
   To meet the wrath of heaven!
But, in His righteousness arrayed,
   We see our sins forgiven.

3 Unholy and impure
   Are all our thoughts and ways:
His hands infected nature cure
   With sanctifying grace.

4 The powers of hell agree
   To hold our souls in vain;
He sets the sons of bondage free,
   And breaks the cursed chain.

5 Lord, we adore Thy ways
   To bring us near to God,
Thy sovereign power, Thy healing grace,
   And Thine atoning blood.
                            Isaac Watts

182 *"Come unto Me, all ye that labor and are heavy laden, and I will give you rest."*

COME, ye disconsolate, where'er ye languish:
   Come to the mercy-seat, fervently kneel;
Here bring your wounded hearts, here tell
      your anguish;
Earth has no sorrow that heaven cannot heal.

Redemption

2 Joy of the desolate, Light of the straying,
   Hope of the penitent, fadeless and pure,
  Here speaks the Comforter, tenderly saying,
   Earth has no sorrow that heaven cannot cure.

3 Here see the bread of life; see waters flowing
   Forth from the throne of God, pure from above;
  Come to the feast of love; come, ever knowing
   Earth has no sorrow but heaven can remove.
                             Thomas Moore

183   *"He is the propitiation for our sins."*   [ASHFORD

  How shall a contrite spirit pray,
   A broken heart its griefs make known,
  A weary wanderer find the way
   To peace and rest?—Through Christ alone.

2 He died that we might die to sin;
   He rose that we to God might rise;
  By His own blood He entered in
   The holy place beyond the skies.

3 Father, in Him we claim our part;
   For Thy Son's sake accept us now;
  In Him well pleased Thou always art,
   Well pleased with us through Him be Thou.

4 O look on Thine anointed One;
   Thy gift in Him is all our plea;
  Our righteousness, what He hath done;
   Our prayer, His prayer for us to Thee.

5 So, while He intercedes above,
   In His dear name may we believe,
  And all the fullness of Thy love
   Into our inmost souls receive.
                             James Montgomery

184   *"Him that loved us, and washed us from*   [COWPER
our sins in His own blood."

  THERE is a fountain filled with blood
    Drawn from Immanuel's veins;
  And sinners, plunged beneath that flood,
    Lose all their guilty stains.

2 The dying thief rejoiced to see
    That fountain in his day;
  And there have I, as vile as he,
    Washed all my sins away.

3 Dear dying Lamb! Thy precious blood
    Shall never lose its power,
  Till all the ransomed church of God
    Be saved, to sin no more.

4 E'er since, by faith, I saw the stream
    Thy flowing wounds supply,
  Redeeming love has been my theme,
    And shall be till I die.

5 Then in a nobler, sweeter song
    I'll sing Thy power to save,
  When this poor lisping, stammering tongue
    Lies silent in the grave.

6 Lord, I believe Thou hast prepared,
    Unworthy though I be,
  For me a blood-bought free reward,
    A golden harp for me:

7 'Tis strung, and tuned for endless years,
    And formed by power divine,
  To sound in God the Father's ears
    No other name but Thine.
                    William Cowper

Redemption

185 *"The Lord is my light and my salvation."* [ZERAH

Salvation! O the joyful sound!
'Tis pleasure to our ears;
A sovereign balm for every wound,
A cordial for our fears.

2 Buried in sorrow and in sin,
At hell's dark door we lay;
But we arise, by grace divine,
To see a heavenly day.

3 Salvation! let the echo fly
The spacious earth around;
While all the armies of the sky
Conspire to raise the sound.
Isaac Watts

186 *"Who gave Himself a ransom for all."* [ASHFORD

Jesus, Thy blood and righteousness
My beauty are, my glorious dress;
'Mid flaming worlds, in these arrayed,
With joy shall I lift up my head.

2 Bold shall I stand in Thy great day,
For who aught to my charge shall lay?
Fully absolved through these I am,
From sin and fear, from guilt and shame.

3 Lord, I believe were sinners more
Than sands upon the ocean shore,
Thou hast for all a ransom paid,
For all a full atonement made.

4 When from the dust of death I rise
To claim my mansion in the skies,
E'en then, this shall be all my plea:
Jesus hath lived, hath died for me.
John Wesley

187   *"By grace ye are saved."*   [SEASONS

Grace! 'tis a charming sound!
  Harmonious to my ear!
Heaven with the echo shall resound,
  And all the earth shall hear.

2 Grace first contrived a way
  To save rebellious man;
And all the steps that grace display,
  Which drew the wondrous plan.

3 Grace taught my wandering feet
  To tread the heavenly road;
And new supplies each hour I meet,
  While pressing on to God.

4 Grace all the work shall crown,
  Through everlasting days;
It lays in heaven the topmost stone,
  And well deserves the praise.
Philip Doddridge

188   *"Justified freely by His grace."*   [LANE

Ah, how shall fallen man
  Be just before his God!
If He contend in righteousness,
  We sink beneath His rod.

2 If He our ways should mark
  With strict inquiring eyes,
Could we for one of thousand faults
  A just excuse devise?

3 All-seeing, powerful God!
  Who can with Thee contend?
Or who that tries the unequal strife,
  Shall prosper in the end?

4 The mountains, in Thy wrath,
   Their ancient seats forsake!
   The trembling earth deserts her place,
   Her rooted pillars shake!

5 Ah, how shall guilty man
   Contend with such a God!
   None, none can meet him, and escape,
   But through the Saviour's blood.

189 *"With His stripes we are healed."* [INVOCATION

We sing the praise of Him who died,
   Of Him who died upon the cross;
   The sinner's hope let men deride,
   For this we count the world but loss.

2 Inscribed upon the cross we see,
   In shining letters, God is love;
   He bears our sins upon the tree,
   He brings us mercy from above.

3 The cross! it takes our guilt away;
   It holds the fainting spirit up;
   It cheers with hope the gloomy day,
   And sweetens every bitter cup;

4 It makes the coward spirit brave,
   And nerves the feeble arm for fight;
   It takes its terror from the grave,
   And gilds the bed of death with light;

5 The balm of life, the cure of woe,
   The measure and the pledge of love,
   The sinner's refuge here below,
   The angels' theme in heaven above.
                              Thomas Kelly

190 *"God forbid that I should glory, save in the cross of our Lord Jesus Christ."* [INVOCATION]

When I survey the wondrous cross
  On which the Prince of glory died,
My richest gain I count but loss,
  And pour contempt on all my pride.

2 Forbid it, Lord, that I should boast,
  Save in the death of Christ, my God;
All the vain things that charm me most,
  I sacrifice them to His blood.

3 See from His head, His hands, His feet,
  Sorrow and love flow mingled down!
Did e'er such love and sorrow meet,
  Or thorns compose so rich a crown?

4 Were the whole realm of nature mine,
  That were a present far too small;
Love so amazing, so divine,
  Demands my soul, my life, my all.
Isaac Watts

191 *"Being justified by faith, we have peace with God through our Lord Jesus Christ."* [REGENT SQUARE]

Ye that in His courts are found,
Listening to the joyful sound,
Lost and helpless as ye are,
Sons of sorrow, sin, and care,
Glorify the King of kings;
Take the peace the gospel brings.

2 Turn to Christ your longing eyes,
View His bleeding sacrifice;
See in Him your sins forgiven,
Pardon, holiness, and heaven:
Glorify the King of kings,
Take the peace the gospel brings.
Rowland Hill

Redemption

192   *"He that believeth not is condemned already."*   [Volkslied

Not to condemn the sons of men,
    Did Christ, the Son of God appear;
No weapons in His hands are seen,
    No flaming sword, nor thunder there.

2 Such was the pity of our God,
    He loved the race of man so well,
He sent His Son to bear our load
    Of sins, and save our souls from hell.

3 Sinners, believe the Saviour's word;
    Trust in His mighty name, and live;
A thousand joys His lips afford,
    His hands a thousand blessings give.
                    Isaac Watts

193   *"The exceeding riches of His grace."*   [Hebron

Now to the Lord a noble song!
Awake, my soul; awake, my tongue;
Hosanna to the eternal name,
And all His boundless love proclaim.

2 See where it shines in Jesus' face,
The brightest image of His grace;
God, in the person of His Son,
Has all His mightiest works outdone.

3 Grace! 'tis a sweet, a charming theme;
My thoughts rejoice at Jesus' name!
Ye angels, dwell upon the sound!
Ye heavens, reflect it to the ground!

4 O may I live to reach the place
Where He unveils His lovely face!
Where all His beauties you behold,
And sing His name to harps of gold!
                      Isaac Watts

194 "*The light of the glorious gospel of Christ.*" [HELP

PLUNGED in a gulf of dark despair
We wretched sinners lay,
Without one cheerful beam of hope,
Or spark of glimmering day.

2 With pitying eyes the Prince of grace
Beheld our helpless grief:
He saw, and O! amazing love!
He ran to our relief.

3 Down from the shining seats above
With joyful haste He fled;
Entered the grave in mortal flesh,
And dwelt among the dead.

4 O! for this love, let rocks and hills
Their lasting silence break,
And all harmonious human tongues
The Saviour's praises speak!

5 Angels, assist our mighty joys;
Strike all your harps of gold!
But, when you raise your highest notes,
His love can ne'er be told.
Isaac Watts

195 "*Christ Jesus came into the world to save sinners, of whom I am chief.*" [SACRIFICE

AMAZING grace,—how sweet the sound,—
That saved a wretch like me!
I once was lost, but now am found;
Was blind, but now I see.

2 'Twas grace that taught my heart to fear,
And grace my fears relieved;
How precious did that grace appear,
The hour I first believed!

3 Through many dangers, toils, and snares,
    Have I already come;
  But grace has brought me safe thus far,
    And grace will lead me home.

4 Yes, when this flesh and heart shall fail,
    And mortal life shall cease,
  I shall possess, within the veil,
    A life of joy and peace.
                                John Newton

                                    [RETURN
196 *"Worship the Lord in the beauty of holiness."*

  FATHER of glory! to Thy name
    Immortal praise we give,
  Who dost an act of grace proclaim,
    And bid us, rebels, live.

2 Immortal honor to the Son,
    Who makes Thine anger cease;
  Our lives He ransomed with His own,
    And died to buy our peace.

3 To Thine Almighty Spirit be
    Immortal glory given,
  Whose influence brings us near to Thee,
    And trains us up for heaven.

4 Let men, with their united voice,
    Adore the Eternal God;
  And spread His honors, and their joys,
    Through nations far abroad.

5 Let faith, and love, and duty join
    One general song to raise;
  And saints in earth and heaven combine
    In harmony and praise.
                                Isaac Watts

197 *"Him that cometh unto Me, I will in   [LANCASHIRE
no wise cast out."*

'Come unto Me, ye weary,
  And I will give you rest.'
O blessed voice of Jesus,
  Which comes to hearts opprest!
It tells of benediction,
  Of pardon, grace, and peace;
Of joy that hath no ending,
  Of love which cannot cease.

2 'Come unto Me, ye wanderers,
  And I will give you light.'
O loving voice of Jesus,
  Which comes to cheer the night!
Our hearts were filled with sadness,
  And we had lost our way,
But morning brings us gladness,
  And songs the break of day.

3 'Come unto me, ye fainting,
  And I will give you life.'
O cheering voice of Jesus,
  Which comes to aid our strife!
The foe is stern and eager,
  The fight is fierce and long;
But Thou hast made us mighty,
  And stronger than the strong.

4 'And whosoever cometh,
  I will not cast him out.'
O welcome voice of Jesus,
  Which drives away our doubt!
Which calls us, very sinners,
  Unworthy though we be
Of love so free and boundless,
  To come, dear Lord, to Thee!

William Chatterton Dix

198 [GORTON
"We which have believed do enter into rest."
O CEASE, my wandering soul,
On restless wing to roam;
All the wide world, to either pole,
Has not for thee a home.

2 Behold the ark of God;
Behold the open door;
Hasten to gain that dear abode,
And rove, my soul, no more.

3 There safe thou shalt abide,
There sweet shall be thy rest,
And every longing satisfied,
With full salvation blest.
William Augustus Muhlenberg

199 *"Ye shall find rest unto your souls."* [INVITATION
COME! said Jesus' sacred voice,
Come and make My paths your choice;
I will guide you to your home:
Weary pilgrim, hither come.

2 Thou, who homeless, and forlorn,
Long hast borne the proud world's scorn,
Long hast roamed the barren waste,
Weary pilgrim, hither haste.

3 Ye, who tost on beds of pain
Seek for ease, but seek in vain;
Ye, by fiercer anguish torn,
In remorse for guilt who mourn:—

4 Hither come, for here is found
Balm that flows for every wound!
Peace that ever shall endure,
Rest eternal, sacred, sure.
Anna Lætitia Barbauld

200   [ADMITTANCE
"Behold, I stand at the door and knock."

   BEHOLD! a Stranger's at the door!
He gently knocks, has knocked before,
Has waited long, is waiting still;
You treat no other friend so ill.

2 But will He prove a Friend indeed?
He will! the very Friend you need!
The Man of Nazareth, 'tis He,
With garments dyed at Calvary.

3 O lovely attitude! He stands
With melting heart, and laden hands!
O matchless kindness! and He shows
This matchless kindness to His foes.

4 Rise, touched with gratitude divine;
Turn out His enemy and thine,
That soul-destroying monster, sin;
And let the Heavenly Stranger in.

5 Admit Him, ere His anger burn;
His feet, departed, ne'er return!
Admit Him; or the hour's at hand
When at His door denied you'll stand.

6 Yet know, nor of the terms complain,
If Jesus comes, He comes to reign;
To reign, and with no partial sway;
Thoughts must be slain, that disobey!

7 Sovereign of souls! Thou Prince of peace!
O may Thy gentle reign increase!
Throw wide the door, each willing mind!
And be His empire all mankind!
                              Joseph Grigg

Redemption

201 *"Lord, Thou knowest that I love Thee."* [INNOCENTS

    HARK, my soul! it is the Lord,
    'Tis Thy Saviour, hear His word;
    Jesus speaks, and speaks to thee:
    'Say, poor sinner, lov'st thou Me?

2 'I delivered thee when bound,
   And, when bleeding, healed thy wound;
   Sought thee wandering, set thee right,
   Turned thy darkness into light.

3 'Can a woman's tender care
   Cease toward the child she bare?
   Yes, she may forgetful be;
   Yet will I remember thee!

4 'Mine is an unchanging love,
   Higher than the lights above,
   Deeper than the depths beneath,
   Free and faithful, strong as death.

5 'Thou shalt see my glory soon,
   When the work of grace is done;
   Partner of my throne shalt be:
   Say, poor sinner, lov'st thou Me?'

6 Lord! it is my chief complaint,
   That my love is weak and faint;
   Yet I love Thee and adore!
   Oh! for grace to love Thee more!
                     William Cowper

202 *"The Spirit and the Bride say, Come."* [DEDICATION

    THE Spirit, in our hearts,
      Is whispering, 'Sinner, come;'
    The Bride, the Church of Christ, proclaims
      To all His children, 'Come!'

2 Let him that heareth say
    To all about him, 'Come!'
  Let him that thirsts for righteousness,
    To Christ, the Fountain, come!

3 Yes, whosoever will,
    O let him freely come,
  And freely drink the stream of life;
    'Tis Jesus bids him come.

4 Lo! Jesus, who invites,
    Declares, 'I quickly come:'
  Lord, even so! I wait Thine hour;
    Jesus, my Saviour, come!
                    Henry Ustick Onderdonk

203 *"His commandments are not grievous."* [FEDERAL ST.
  'COME hither, all ye weary souls,
    Ye heavy laden sinners, come;
  I'll give you rest from all your toils,
    And raise you to My heavenly home.

2 'They shall find rest that learn of Me;
    I'm of a meek and lowly mind;
  But passion rages like the sea,
    And pride is restless as the wind.

3 'Blest is the man whose shoulders take
    My yoke, and bear it with delight!
  My yoke is easy to his neck,
    My grace shall make the burden light.'

4 Jesus, we come at Thy command;
    With faith, and hope, and humble zeal,
  Resign our spirits to Thy hand,
    To mold and guide us at Thy will.
                            Isaac Watts

204 *"We have an Advocate with the Father,* [FEDERAL ST.
Jesus Christ the righteous."

WHEREWITH, O Lord, shall I draw near
   And bow myself before Thy face?
How in Thy purer eyes appear?
   What shall I bring to gain Thy grace?

2 Whoe'er to Thee themselves approve,
   Must take the path Thy word hath showed:
Justice pursue, and mercy love,
   And humbly walk by faith with God.

3 But though my life henceforth be Thine,
   Present for past can ne'er atone;
Though I to Thee the whole resign,
   I only give Thee back Thine own.

4 Guilty I stand before Thy face;
   On me I feel Thy wrath abide;
'Tis just the sentence should take place;
   'Tis just:—but, O, Thy Son hath died!

5 He ever lives for me to pray;
   He prays that I with Him may reign;
Amen to what my Lord doth say!
   Jesus, Thou canst not pray in vain!
                      Charles Wesley

205 *"By the works of the law shall no flesh* [SACRIFICE
be justified."

IN vain we seek for peace with God
   By methods of our own;
Nothing, O Saviour! but Thy blood
   Can bring us near the throne.

2 The threatenings of the broken law
   Impress the soul with dread:
If God His sword of vengeance draw,
   It strikes the spirit dead.

3 But Thine illustrious sacrifice
    Hath answered these demands;
And peace and pardon from the skies
    Are offered by Thy hands.

4 'Tis by Thy death we live, O Lord!
    'Tis on Thy cross we rest:
For ever be Thy love adored,
    Thy name for ever blest.
Isaac Watts

206   *"No man cometh unto the Father, but by Me."*   [LATOUR

THOU art the Way—to Thee alone
    From sin and death we flee;
And he who would the Father seek,
    Must seek him, Lord, by Thee.

2 Thou art the Truth—Thy word alone
    True wisdom can impart;
Thou only canst inform the mind,
    And purify the heart.

3 Thou art the Life—the rending tomb
    Proclaims Thy conquering arm,
And those who put their trust in Thee
    Nor death, nor hell shall harm.

4 Thou art the Way—the Truth—the Life;
    Grant us that Way to know,
That Truth to keep, that Life to win,
    Whose joys eternal flow.
George Washington Doane

207   *"God was in Christ, reconciling the world unto Himself."*   [FEDERAL ST.

THOU blest Creator of the world,
    Redeemer of our fallen race,
True God of God! in whom we see
    The brightness of the Father's face.

2 Thy love! the mighty love, which made
   The starry sky, and sea, and earth,
   Took pity on our lost estate,
   And brake the bondage of our birth.

3 For this Thy sacred side was pierced,
     Whence mystic blood and water flowed,
   To cleanse us from the stain of guilt,
   And reconcile the world to God.

4 O Jesus! in Thy heart divine
   That self-same love doth ever glow;
   For ever mercy to mankind
   Doth from that ceaseless fountain flow.

208   *"Look unto Me, and be ye saved."*   [DEDICATION

THE Lord on high proclaims
   His Godhead from His throne;—
'Mercy and Justice are the names,
   By which I will be known.'

2 'Ye dying souls, that sit
     In darkness and distress,
   Look from the borders of the pit
     To My recovering grace.'

3 Sinners shall hear the sound;
     Their thankful tongues shall own,
   'Our righteousness and strength is found
     In Thee, the Lord, alone.'

4 In Thee shall Israel trust,
     And see their guilt forgiven;
   God will pronounce the sinners just,
     And take the saints to heaven.
                              Isaac Watts

Redemption

[HAMBURG
209 *"Christ, the Power of God and the Wisdom of God."*

Nature with open volume stands,
　To spread her Maker's praise abroad,
And every labor of His hands
　Shows something worthy of a God.

2 But in the grace that rescued man,
　　His brightest form of glory shines;
Here on the cross, 'tis fairest drawn
　　In precious blood, and crimson lines.

3 Oh! the sweet wonders of that cross,
　　Where God the Saviour loved, and died!
Her noblest life my spirit draws
　　From His dear wounds, and bleeding side.

4 I would for ever speak His name,
　　In sounds to mortal ears unknown;
With angels join to praise the Lamb,
　　And worship at His Father's throne.
　　　　　　　　　　　　Isaac Watts

[VOLKSLIED
210 *"Be ye doers of the word, and not hearers only."*

Why will ye waste on trifling cares
That life which God's compassion spares,
While, in the various range of thought,
The one thing needful is forgot?

2 Shall God invite you from above?
Shall Jesus urge His dying love?
Shall troubled conscience give you pain?
And all these pleas unite in vain?

3 Not so your eyes will always view
Those objects which you now pursue;
Not so will heaven and hell appear,
When death's decisive hour is near.

4 Almighty God! Thy grace impart;
   Fix deep conviction on each heart;
   Nor let us waste on trifling cares
   That life which Thy compassion spares.
                              Philip Doddridge

211   *"He left not Himself without witness."*   [WARE

THE heavens declare Thy glory, Lord,
   In every star Thy wisdom shines;
But when our eyes behold Thy word,
   We read Thy name in fairer lines.

2 The rolling sun, the changing light,
   And nights and days Thy power confess;
But the blest volume Thou hast writ
   Reveals Thy justice and Thy grace.

3 Sun, moon, and stars convey Thy praise
   Round the whole earth, and never stand;
So, when Thy truth began its race,
   It touched and glanced on every land.

4 Nor shall Thy spreading gospel rest,
   Till through the world Thy truth has run;
Till Christ has all the nations blest
   That see the light or feel the sun.

5 Great Sun of righteousness, arise;
   Bless the dark world with heavenly light;
Thy gsopel makes the simple wise;
   Thy laws are pure, Thy judgments right.

6 Thy noblest wonders here we view,
   In souls renewed and sins forgiven:
Lord, cleanse my sins, my soul renew,
   And make Thy word my guide to heaven.
                              Isaac Watts

212 [ADVENT
"Where is the word of the Lord? Let it come now."

   O Saviour! is Thy promise fled?
     Nor longer might Thy grace endure
  To heal the sick, and raise the dead,
     And preach Thy gospel to the poor?

2 Come, Jesus, come! return again;
     With brighter beam Thy servants bless,
  Who long to feel Thy perfect reign,
     And share Thy kingdom's happiness!

3 Come, Jesus, come! and as of yore
     The prophet went to clear Thy way,
  A harbinger Thy feet before,
     A dawning to Thy brighter day;

4 So now may grace, with heavenly shower,
     Our stony hearts for truth prepare;
  Sow in our souls the seed of power,
     Then come, and reap Thy harvest there!

                            Reginald Heber

213   *"Let there be light."*   [LIGHT

  Thou, whose Almighty word
  Chaos and darkness heard,
     And took their flight;
  Hear us, we humbly pray;
  And, where the gospel's day
  Sheds not its glorious ray,
     Let there be light!

2 Thou who didst come to bring
  On Thy redeeming wing
     Healing and sight,
  Health to the sick in mind,
  Sight to the inly blind,
  O now to all mankind
     Let there be light!

3 Spirit of truth and love,
   Life-giving, holy Dove,
      Speed forth Thy flight!
   Move on the waters' face,
   Bearing the lamp of grace,
   And in earth's darkest place
      Let there be light!

4 Holy and blessed Three,
   Glorious Trinity,
      Wisdom, Love, Might!
   Boundless as ocean's tide
   Rolling in fullest pride,
   Through the earth, far and wide,
      Let there be light!
               John Marriott

214 [LANE
"*Let God arise, let His enemies be scattered.*"
O LORD our God, arise,
   The cause of truth maintain,
And wide o'er all the peopled world
   Extend her blessed reign.

2 Thou Prince of life, arise,
   Nor let Thy glory cease;
Far spread the conquests of Thy grace,
   And bless the earth with peace.

3 Thou Holy Ghost, arise,
   Expand Thy quickening wing,
And o'er a dark and ruined world
   Let light and order spring.

4 O all ye nations, rise,
   To God the Saviour sing;
From shore to shore, from earth to heaven,
   Let echoing anthems ring.
               Ralph Wardlaw

Redemption

215   *"Behold, I make all things new."*   [LATOUR

    SPIRIT of power and might, behold
      A world by sin destroyed:
    Creator-Spirit, as of old,
      Move on the formless void.

2 Give Thou the word:—that healing sound
      Shall quell the deadly strife,
    And earth again, like Eden crowned,
      Produce the tree of life.

3 If sang the morning stars for joy,
      When nature rose to view,
    What strains will angel-harps employ
      When Thou shalt all renew!

4 And if the sons of God rejoice
      To hear a Saviour's name,
    How will the ransomed raise their voice,
      To whom that Saviour came!

5 So every kindred, tongue, and tribe,
      Assembling round the throne,
    Thy new creation shall ascribe
      To sovereign love alone.
                  James Montgomery

[ABEND

216   *"I will pour out of My Spirit upon all flesh."*

    O SPIRIT of the living God!
      In all Thy plenitude of grace,
    Where'er the foot of man hath trod,
      Descend on our apostate race.

2 Give tongues of fire and hearts of love,
      To preach the reconciling word;
    Give power and unction from above,
      Whene'er the joyful sound is heard.

3 Be darkness, at Thy coming, light;
　　Confusion, order in Thy path;
　Souls without strength inspire with might,
　　Bid mercy triumph over wrath.

4 O Spirit of the Lord! prepare
　　All the round world her God to meet;
　Breathe Thou abroad like morning air,
　　Till hearts of stone begin to beat.

5 Baptize the nations; far and nigh
　　The triumphs of the cross record;
　The name of Jesus glorify,
　　Till every kindred call Him Lord.
　　　　　　　　　James Montgomery

[INNOCENTS
217　"*In His days shall the righteous flourish.*"

Hasten, Lord, the glorious time,
　　When, beneath Messiah's sway,
　Every nation, every clime,
　　Shall the gospel call obey.

2 Mightiest kings His power shall own,
　　Heathen tribes His name adore;
　Satan and his host, o'erthrown,
　　Bound in chains, shall hurt no more.

3 Then shall wars and tumults cease,
　　Then be banished grief and pain;
　Righteousness, and joy, and peace,
　　Undisturbed shall ever reign.

4 Bless we, then, our gracious Lord,
　　Ever praise His glorious name;
　All His mighty acts record,
　　All His wondrous love proclaim.
　　　　　　　　　Harriet Auber

218   *"Come over and help us."*   [MISSIONARY HYMN

FROM Greenland's icy mountains,
    From India's coral strand,
Where Afric's sunny fountains
    Roll down their golden sand,
From many an ancient river,
    From many a palmy plain,
They call us to deliver
    Their land from error's chain.

2 What though the spicy breezes
    Blow soft o'er Ceylon's isle;
Though every prospect pleases,
    And only man is vile;
In vain with lavish kindness
    The gifts of God are strown;
The heathen in his blindness
    Bows down to wood and stone.

3 Can we, whose souls are lighted
    With wisdom from on high,
Can we to men benighted
    The lamp of life deny?
Salvation! O salvation!
    The joyful sound proclaim,
Till each remotest nation
    Has learnt Messiah's Name.

4 Waft, waft, ye winds, His story,
    And you, ye waters, roll,
Till like a sea of glory
    It spreads from pole to pole;
Till o'er our ransomed nature
    The Lamb for sinners slain,
Redeemer, King, Creator,
    In bliss returns to reign.

                                            Reginald Heber

Redemption

219 *"He shall have dominion from sea to sea."* [HAMBURG

Great God, whose universal sway
The known and unknown worlds obey,
Now give the kingdom to Thy Son,
Extend His power, exalt His throne.

2 As rain on meadows newly mown,
So shall He send His influence down;
His grace on fainting souls distils
Like heavenly dew on thirsty hills.

3 The heathen lands, that lie beneath
The shades of overspreading death,
Revive at His first dawning light,
And deserts blossom at the sight.

4 The saints shall flourish in His days,
Drest in the robes of joy and praise;
Peace, like a river, from His throne
Shall flow to nations yet unknown.
Isaac Watts

220 *"Of His kingdom there shall be no end."* [BENEVENTO

Wake the song of jubilee,
Let it echo o'er the sea!
Now is come the promised hour;
Jesus reigns with glorious power!

2 All ye nations, join and sing,
Praise your Saviour, praise your King;
Let it sound from shore to shore,—
'Jesus reigns for evermore!'

3 Hark! the desert lands rejoice;
And the islands join their voice;
Joy! the whole creation sings,—
'Jesus is the King of kings!'
Leonard Bacon

Redemption

221   *"The morning cometh."*   [GOSPEL

WATCHMAN! tell us of the night,
  What its signs of promise are:
Traveler! o'er yon mountain hight,
  See that glory-beaming star!
Watchman! does its beauteous ray
  Aught of hope or joy foretell?
Traveler! yes; it brings the day,
  Promised day of Israel.

2 Watchman! tell us of the night;
  Higher yet that star ascends:
Traveler! blessedness and light,
  Peace and truth its course portends!
Watchman! will its beams alone
  Gild the spot that gave them birth?
Traveler! ages are its own,
  See, it bursts o'er all the earth!

3 Watchman! tell us of the night,
  For the morning seems to dawn:
Traveler! darkness takes its flight,
  Doubt and terror are withdrawn.—
Watchman! let thy wanderings cease;
  Hie thee to thy quiet home:
Traveler! lo! the Prince of peace,
  Lo! the Son of God is come!
John Bowring

222   *"All nations shall serve Him."*   [RELEASE

HAIL to the Lord's Anointed!
  Great David's greater Son!
Hail, in the time appointed,
  His reign on earth begun!
He comes to break oppression,
  To set the captive free;
To take away transgression,
  And rule in equity.

2 He comes, with succor speedy
    To those who suffer wrong;
  To help the poor and needy,
    And bid the weak be strong;
  To give them songs for sighing,
    Their darkness turn to light,
  Whose souls, condemned and dying,
    Were precious in His sight.

3 He shall come down like showers
    Upon the fruitful earth,
  And love and joy, like flowers,
    Spring in His path to birth:
  Before Him, on the mountains,
    Shall peace the herald go,
  And righteousness in fountains
    From hill to valley flow.

4 Kings shall fall down before Him,
    And gold and incense bring:
  All nations shall adore Him,
    His praise all people sing.
  For Him shall prayer unceasing
    And daily vows ascend;
  His kingdom still increasing,
    A kingdom without end.

5 O'er every foe victorious,
    He on His throne shall rest,
  From age to age more glorious,
    All-blessing and all-blest:
  The tide of time shall never
    His covenant remove;
  His name shall stand for ever;
    That name to us is—love.
                James Montgomery

223 "*Alleluia, for the Lord God Omnipotent reigneth.*" [BENEVENTO

HARK! the song of Jubilee;
Loud as mighty thunders roar,
Or the fullness of the sea,
When it breaks upon the shore:
Hallelujah! for the Lord
God Omnipotent shall reign;
Hallelujah! let the word
Echo round the earth and main.

2 Hallelujah! hark! the sound,
From the center to the skies,
Wakes above, beneath, around,
All creation's harmonies;
See Jehovah's banner furled,
Sheathed His sword: He speaks—'tis done,
And the kingdoms of this world
Are the kingdoms of His Son.

3 He shall reign from pole to pole
With illimitable sway;
He shall reign, when like a scroll
Yonder heavens have past away:
Then the end;—beneath His rod,
Man's last enemy shall fall;
Hallelujah! Christ in God,
God in Christ, is all in all.
James Montgomery

224 "*His Name shall endure for ever.*" [WARE

JESUS shall reign, where'er the sun
Does his successive journeys run;
His kingdom stretch from shore to shore,
Till moons shall wax and wane no more.

2 For Him shall endless prayer be made,
And praises throng to crown His head;
His name, like sweet perfume, shall rise
With every morning sacrifice.

3 People and realms of every tongue
Dwell on His love with sweetest song;
And infant voices shall proclaim
Their early blessings on His name.

4 Blessings abound where'er He reigns;
The prisoner leaps to lose his chains;
The weary find eternal rest,
And all the sons of want are blest.

5 Let every creature rise and bring
Peculiar honors to our King;
Angels descend with songs again,
And earth repeat the loud Amen!
Isaac Watts

[RETURN

225 *"Blessed is the people that know the joyful sound."*

BLEST are the souls that hear and know
  The gospel's joyful sound;
Peace shall attend the path they go,
  And light their steps surround.

2 Their joy shall bear their spirits up
  Through their Redeemer's name;
His righteousness exalts their hope,
  Nor Satan dares condemn.

3 The Lord, our glory and defence,
  Strength and salvation gives;
Israel, thy King for ever reigns,
  Thy God for ever lives.
Isaac Watts

The Church

226 *"Pray for the peace of Jerusalem; they shall prosper that love thee."* [HAYDN

I LOVE Thy kingdom, Lord,
  The house of Thine abode,
The church our blest Redeemer saved
  With His own precious blood.

2 I love Thy church, O God!
  Her walls before Thee stand,
Dear as the apple of Thine eye,
  And graven on Thy hand.

3 If e'er to bless Thy sons
  My voice or hands deny,
These hands let useful skill forsake,
  This voice in silence die.

4 If e'er my heart forget
  Her welfare or her wo,
Let every joy this heart forsake,
  And every grief o'erflow.

5 For her my tears shall fall,
  For her my prayers ascend;
To her my cares and toils be given,
  Till toils and cares shall end.

6 Beyond my highest joy
  I prize her heavenly ways,
Her sweet communion, solemn vows,
  Her hymns of love and praise.

7 Jesus, thou Friend Divine,
 Our Saviour and our King,
Thy hand from every snare and foe
 Shall great deliverance bring.

8 Sure as Thy truth shall last,
 To Zion shall be given
The brightest glories earth can yield,
 And brighter bliss of heaven.
   Timothy Dwight

227 *"He hath put a new song in my mouth."* [GRACE

Awake, and sing the song
 Of Moses and the Lamb,
Wake every heart and every tongue
 To praise the Saviour's name.

2 Sing of His dying love;
 Sing of His rising power;
Sing how He intercedes above
 For those whose sins He bore.

3 Sing, till we feel our hearts
 Ascending with our tongues;
Sing, till the love of sin departs,
 And grace inspires our songs.

4 Sing on your heavenly way,
 Ye ransomed sinners, sing;
Sing on, rejoicing every day
 In Christ, the Eternal King.

5 Soon shall ye hear Him say,
 Ye blessed children, come;
Soon will He call you hence away,
 And take His wanderers home.
   William Hammond

228 *"Beautiful for situation, the joy of the whole earth, is Mount Zion."* [St. Matthew

O where are kings and empires now,
  Of old that went and came!
But, Lord, Thy church is praying yet,
  A thousand years the same!
We mark her holy battlements,
  And her foundations strong;
And hear within her ceaseless voice,
  And her unending song.

2 For not like kingdoms of the world,
    The holy church of God!
  Though earthquake shocks be threatening her,
    And tempest is abroad;
  Unshaken as eternal hills,
    Unmovable she stands,
  A mountain that shall fill the earth,
    A house unbuilt by hands!

3 O ye that in these latter days
    The citadel defend,
  Perchance for you the Saviour said,
    'I'm with you to the end:'
  Stand therefore girt about, and hold
    Your burning lamps in hand,
  And standing listen for your Lord,
    And till He cometh—stand!
            Arthur Cleveland Coxe

[Phuvah

229 *"Behold, the tabernacle of God is with men."*

O Lord of life, and truth, and grace,
  Ere nature was begun!
Make welcome to our erring race
  Thy Spirit and Thy Son.

2 We hail the church, built high o'er all
   The heathen's rage and scoff;
   Thy providence its fenced wall,
   The Lamb the light thereof.

3 Thy Christ hath reached His heavenly seat
   Through sorrows and through scars;
   The golden lamps are at His feet,
   And in His hand the stars.

4 O may He walk among us here,
   With His rebuke and love,—
   A brightness o'er this lower sphere,
   A ray from worlds above!
                    Nathaniel Langdon Frothingham

230 [GREENVILLE
"*The city of the living God, the heavenly Jerusalem.*"

GLORIOUS things of thee are spoken,
   Zion, city of our God;
He, whose word cannot be broken,
   Formed thee for His own abode:
On the rock of ages founded—
   What can shake thy sure repose!
With salvation's walls surrounded,
   Thou may'st smile at all thy foes.

2 See, the streams of living waters,
   Springing from eternal love,
Well supply thy sons and daughters,
   And all fear of want remove:
Who can faint while such a river
   Ever will thy thirst assuage?
Grace, which like the Lord, the Giver,
   Never fails from age to age.
                              John Newton

The Church

231 *"Fear not, little flock; for it is your Father's good pleasure to give you the kingdom."* [PHUVAH

CHURCH of the Ever-living God,
  The Father's gracious choice,
Amid the voices of this earth
  How feeble is thy voice!

2 A little flock! so calls He thee
  Who bought thee with His blood;
A little flock, disowned of men,
  But owned and loved of God.

3 But the Chief Shepherd comes at length;
  Their feeble days are o'er,
No more a handful in the earth,
  A little flock no more.

4 No more a lily among thorns,
  Weary and faint and few;
But countless as the stars of heaven,
  Or as the early dew.

5 Then entering the eternal halls,
  In robes of victory,
That mighty multitude shall keep
  The joyous jubilee.

6 Unfading palms they bear aloft;
  Unfaltering songs they sing;
Unending festival they keep,
  In presence of the King.
              Horatius Bonar

232   *"That they all may be one."*   [STEPHENS

LET saints below in concert sing
  With those to glory gone:
For all the servants of our King
  In earth and heaven are one.

2 One family we dwell in Him,
   One church, above, beneath,
Though now divided by the stream,
   The narrow stream of death.

3 One army of the living God,
   To His command we bow;
Part of the host have crossed the flood,
   And part are crossing now.

4 Some to their everlasting home
   This solemn moment fly;
And we are to the margin come,
   And soon expect to die.

5 Lord Jesus, be our constant Guide:
   And, when the word is given,
Bid death's cold flood its waves divide,
   And land us safe in heaven.
                              Charles Wesley

233 "*Fellowcitizens with the saints, and of the household of God.*" [DUNDEE

Not to the terrors of the Lord,
   The tempest, fire, and smoke;
Not to the thunder of that word
   Which God on Sinai spoke :—

2 But we are come to Zion's hill,
   The city of our God;
Where milder words declare His will
   And spread His love abroad.

3 Behold the innumerable host
   Of angels clothed in light!
Behold the spirits of the just,
   Whose faith is turned to sight!

4 Behold the blest assembly there,
   Whose names are writ in heaven!
   And God, the Judge of all, declare
   Their vilest sins forgiven!

5 The saints on earth, and all the dead,
   But one communion make;
   All join in Christ, their living Head,
   And of His grace partake.

6 In such society as this
   My weary soul would rest;
   The man that dwells where Jesus is,
   Must be for ever blest.
                                Isaac Watts

234 "*The kingdom of God is come nigh unto you.*" [HAYDN

Come, kingdom of our God,
   Sweet reign of light and love,
Shed peace and hope and joy abroad,
   And wisdom from above.

2 Over our spirits first
   Extend Thy healing reign;
   Then raise and quench that sacred thirst
   That never pains again.

3 Come, kingdom of our God,
   And make the broad earth Thine;
   Stretch o'er her lands and isles the rod
   That flowers with grace divine.

4 Come, kingdom of our God,
   And raise the glorious throne
   In worlds by the undying trod
   When God shall bless His own.
                            Henry D. Johns

235 *"He is the Head of the body, the Church."* [Gotha

The Church's one foundation
  Is Jesus Christ her Lord;
She is His new creation
  By water and the word:
From heaven He came and sought her
  To be His holy bride;
With His own blood He bought her,
  And for her life He died.

2 Elect from every nation,
    Yet one o'er all the earth,
  Her charter of salvation
    One Lord, one faith, one birth,
  One holy name she blesses,
    Partakes one holy food,
  And to one hope she presses
    With every grace endued.

3 Mid toil and tribulation,
    And tumult of her war,
  She waits the consummation
    Of peace for evermore;
  Till with the vision glorious
    Her longing eyes are blest,
  And the great church victorious
    Shall be the church at rest.

4 Yet she on earth hath union
    With God, the Three in One,
  And mystic sweet communion
    With those whose rest is won;
  O happy ones and holy!
    Lord, give us grace that we,
  Like them, the meek and lowly,
    On high may dwell with Thee!
            Samuel John Stone

236 *"God is our Refuge and Strength."* [RUSSIAN HYMN]

God is the refuge of His saints,
  When storms of sharp distress invade:
Ere we can offer our complaints,
  Behold Him present with His aid.

2 Let mountains from their seats be hurled
   Down to the deep, and buried there;
Convulsions shake the solid world;—
  Our faith shall never yield to fear.

3 Loud may the troubled ocean roar,—
   In sacred peace our souls abide,
While every nation, every shore,
  Trembles, and dreads the swelling tide.

4 There is a stream whose gentle flow
   Supplies the city of our God;
Life, love, and joy, still gliding through,
  And watering our divine abode.

5 That sacred stream, Thine holy word,
   Our grief allays, our fear controls:
Sweet peace Thy promises afford,
  And give new strength to fainting souls.

6 Zion enjoys her Monarch's love,
   Secure against a threatening hour;
Nor can her firm foundations move,
  Built on His truth, and armed with power.
                                   Isaac Watts

237 [ROTHWELL
"Behold I create new heavens and a new earth."

O Lord, in perfect bliss above
Thou couldst not need created love;
And yet Thou didst Thy power display,
And earth's foundations firmly lay.

2 But even while the world came forth
   In all the beauty of its birth,
   In Thy deep thought Thou didst behold
   Another world of nobler mold.

3 For Thou didst will that Christ should frame
   A new creation by His name;
   Its seed, the living word of grace
   He scatters wide in every place;

4 Its home, when time shall be no more,
   In heaven with Thee for evermore;
   Accepted in Thy boundless love
   To share His throne and joy above.

5 O Father, bless, for they are Thine,
   O Son, direct in love divine,
   O Holy Ghost, with grace endue
   The old creation and the new!

Isaac Williams

238 *"Our fellowship is with the Father and with His Son Jesus Christ."* [PHUVAH

   Lord Jesus, are we one with Thee?
     O hight, O depth of love!
   Thou one with us on Calvary,
     We one with Thee above.

2 Such was Thy love, that for our sake
     Thou didst from heaven come down;
   Our mortal flesh and blood partake,
     In all our misery one.

3 Our sins, our guilt, in love divine,
     Confessed and borne by Thee;
   The sting, the curse, the wrath, were Thine
     To set Thy members free.

4 Ascended now, in glory bright,
    Still one with us Thou art;
  Nor life, nor death, nor depth, nor hight,
    Thy saints and Thee can part.

5 Ere long shall come that glorious day,
    When, seated on Thy throne,
  Thou shalt to wondering worlds display
    That we in Thee are one.
James George Deck

239 "*And they sung as it were a new song before the throne.*" [CHORAL

  SING we the song of those who stand
    Around the eternal throne,
  Of every kindred, clime, and land,
    A multitude unknown.

2 Life's poor distinctions vanish here;
    To-day the young, the old,
  Our Saviour and His flock, appear
    One Shepherd and one fold.

3 Toil, trial, suffering, still await
    On earth the pilgrim-throng,
  Yet learn we in our low estate
    The church triumphant's song.

4 'Worthy the Lamb for sinners slain,'
    Cry the redeemed above,
  'Blessing and honor to obtain,
    And everlasting love.'

5 'Worthy the Lamb!' on earth we sing,
    'Who died our souls to save;
  Henceforth, O Death! where is thy sting?
    Thy victory, O Grave?'

6 Then, hallelujah, power and praise
   To God in Christ be given;
   May all who now this anthem raise
   Renew the strain in heaven!
                    James Montgomery

240   *"Every one members one of another."*   [GRACE
   BLEST be the tie that binds
      Our hearts in Christian love;
   The fellowship of kindred minds
      Is like to that above.

2 Before our Father's throne,
      We pour our ardent prayers;
   Our fears, our hopes, our aims, are one,
      Our comforts and our cares.

3 We share our mutual woes,
      Our mutual burdens bear;
   And often for each other flows
      The sympathizing tear.

4 When we asunder part,
      It gives us inward pain;
   But we shall still be joined in heart,
      And hope to meet again.

5 This glorious hope revives
      Our courage by the way;
   While each in expectation lives,
      And longs to see the day.

6 From sorrow, toil, and pain,
      And sin, we shall be free;
   And perfect love and friendship reign
      Through all eternity.
                    John Fawcett

The Lord's Supper

241 *"Blessed are they that have not seen, and* [OAKSVILLE
yet have believed."

REMEMBER Me, the Saviour said,
  On that forsaken night,
When from His side the nearest fled,
  And death was close in sight.

2 Through all the following ages' track
    The world remembers yet;
  With love and worship gazes back,
    And never can forget.

3 O, blest are they, who have not seen,
    And yet believe Him still!
  They know Him, when His praise they mean,
    And when they do His will.

4 We hear His word along our way;
    We see His light above;—
  Remember, when we strive and pray,
    Remember, when we love.
              Nathaniel Langdon Frothingham

                              [FATHER HAYDN
242   *"It is the Spirit that beareth witness."*

COME, Thou Everlasting Spirit,
  Bring to every thankful mind
All the Saviour's dying merit,
  All His sufferings for mankind:

True Recorder of His passion,
  Now the living faith impart;
Now reveal His great salvation,
  Preach His gospel to our heart.

2 Come, Thou Witness of His dying;
    Come, Remembrancer Divine;
  Let us feel Thy power applying
    Christ to every soul, and mine;
  Let us groan Thine inward groaning,
    Look on Him we pierced, and grieve;
  All receive the grace atoning,
    All the sprinkled blood receive.
                    Charles Wesley

243 "*Ye are come unto Jesus, the Mediator of the new covenant.*" [INTROITUS

'THE promise of My Father's love
  Shall stand for ever good:'—
He said, and gave his soul to death,
  And sealed the grace with blood.

2 To this dear covenant of Thy word
    I set my worthless name;
  I seal the engagement to my Lord,
    And make my humble claim.

3 The light, and strength, and pardoning grace,
    And glory, shall be mine;
  My life and soul, my heart and flesh,
    And all my powers are Thine.

4 I call that legacy my own,
    Which Jesus did bequeath;
  'T was purchased with a dying groan,
    And ratified in death.

5 Sweet is the memory of His name,
   Who blest us in His will,
   And to His testament of love
   Made His own life the seal.
                              Isaac Watts

244 "*This cup is the new testament in My blood,* [SILLIMAN
        which is shed for you."

O JESUS, bruised and wounded more
   Than bursted grape, or bread of wheat,
The Life of life within our souls,
   The Cup of our salvation sweet!

2 We come to show Thy dying hour,
   Thy streaming vein, Thy broken flesh;
   And still the blood is warm to save,
   And still the fragrant wounds are fresh.

3 O Heart, that, with a double tide
   Of blood and water, maketh pure;
   O Flesh, once offered on the cross,
   The gift that makes our pardon sure:

4 Let never more our sinful souls
   The anguish of Thy cross renew;
   Nor forge again the cruel nails
   That pierced Thy victim body through.
                        Cecil Frances Alexander

245 "*My flesh is meat indeed, and My* [PLEYEL'S HYMN
        blood is drink indeed."

BREAD of heaven! on Thee we feed,
   For Thy flesh is meat indeed;
Ever may our souls be fed
   With this true and living Bread;
Day by day with strength supplied
   Through the life of Him who died.

2 Vine of heaven! Thy Blood supplies
This blest cup of sacrifice;
Lord! Thy wounds our healing give;
To Thy cross we look, and live.
Jesus, may we ever be
Rooted, grafted, built in Thee!
Josiah Conder

[LAUSANNE

246 *"We love Him, because He first loved us."*

O how could I forget Him
    Who ne'er forgetteth me?
Or tell the love that let Him
    Come down to set me free?
I lay in darkest sadness,
    Till He made all things new;
And still fresh love and gladness
    Flow from that heart so true.

2 For ever will I love Him
    Who saw my hopeless plight,
Who felt my sorrows move Him,
    And brought me life and light:
Whose arm shall be around me
    When my last hour is come,
And suffer none to wound me,
    Though dark the passage home.

3 He gives me pledges holy,
    His body and His blood;
He lifts the scorned and lowly,
    He makes my courage good;
For He will reign within me,
    And shed His graces there:
The heaven He died to win me
    Can I then fail to share?

4 In joy and sorrow ever
   Shine through me, Blessed Heart,
Who, bleeding for us, never
   Did shrink from sorest smart!
Whate'er I've loved or striven
   Or borne, I bring to Thee;
Now let Thy heart and heaven
   Stand open, Lord, to me!
Catherine Winkworth

247   [INTROITUS
"Lord, I believe; help Thou mine unbelief."

BEHOLD Thy servant drawing near
   Thine altar, Lord, to-day;
And though I come with doubt and fear,
   O! send me not away.

2 I would not dare to seek Thy throne
   With such a guilty soul,
But that Thy flesh and blood alone
   Can make a sinner whole.

3 In faith, in love, I would receive,
   With mingled joy and grief;
I would not question, but believe;
   Help Thou mine unbelief.

4 By each communion teach my feet
   To go from strength to strength;
Till I with all Thy faithful meet
   Around Thy throne at length.

248   [SILLIMAN
"He that cometh to Me shall never hunger."

JESUS, thou Joy of loving hearts!
   Thou Fount of Life! Thou Light of men!
From the best bliss that earth imparts,
   We turn unfilled to Thee again.

2 Thy truth unchanged hath ever stood;
   Thou savest those that on Thee call;
   To them that seek Thee, Thou art good,
   To them that find Thee, All in all!

3 We taste Thee, O Thou Living Bread,
   And long to feast upon Thee still!
   We drink of Thee, the Fountain Head,
   And thirst our souls from Thee to fill!

4 Our restless spirits yearn for Thee,
   Where'er our changeful lot is cast;
   Glad, when Thy gracious smile we see,
   Blest, when our faith can hold Thee fast.

5 O Jesus, ever with us stay!
   Make all our moments calm and bright!
   Chase the dark night of sin away,
   Shed o'er the world Thy holy light!
                                    Ray Palmer

[REDEMPTION

249   "*Ye do show the Lord's death till He come.*"

By Christ redeemed, in Christ restored,
We keep the memory adored,
And show the death of our dear Lord,
   Until He come.

2 His Body, broken in our stead,
   Is here in this memorial bread;
   And so our feeble love is fed,
      Until He come.

3 His fearful drops of agony,
   His life-blood shed for us we see:
   The wine shall tell the mystery,
      Until He come.

4 Until the trump of God be heard,
Until the ancient graves be stirred,
And with the great, commanding word,
The Lord shall come.

5 O blessed hope! with this elate,
Let not our hearts be desolate,
But strong in faith, in patience wait,
Until He come!

George Rawson

250 "*Abide in me, and I in you.*" [OAKSVILLE

If human kindness meets return
And owns the grateful tie;
If tender thoughts within us burn,
To feel a friend is nigh;—

2 O, shall not warmer accents tell
The gratitude we owe
To Him, who died, our fears to quell—
Who bore our guilt and wo!

3 While yet in anguish He surveyed
Those pangs He would not flee,
What love His latest words displayed,
'Meet and remember Me!'

4 Remember Thee, Thy death, Thy shame,
Our sinful hearts to share!
O memory! leave no other name
But His recorded there.

Gerald Thomas Noel

[MORNINGTON

251 "*Christ our Passover is sacrificed for us.*"

Not all the blood of beasts,
On Jewish altars slain,
Could give the guilty conscience peace,
Or wash away the stain.

2 But Christ, the Heavenly Lamb,
　　Takes all our sins away;
　　A sacrifice of nobler name
　　And richer blood than they.

3 My faith would lay her hand
　　On that dear head of Thine,
　　While like a penitent I stand,
　　And there confess my sin.

4 My soul looks back to see
　　The burdens Thou didst bear,
　　When hanging on the cursed tree,
　　And hopes her guilt was there.

5 Believing, we rejoice
　　To see the curse remove;
　　We bless the Lamb with cheerful voice,
　　And sing His bleeding love.
　　　　　　　　　　　Isaac Watts

252　　"*I am the Vine, ye are the branches.*"　　[LEBANON

LORD, when before Thy throne we meet,
　　Thy goodness to adore,
From Heaven, the eternal mercy-seat,
　　On us Thy blessing pour,
And make our inmost souls to be
An habitation meet for Thee!

2 The Body for our ransom given,
　　The Blood in mercy shed:
With this immortal food from Heaven,
　　Lord! let our souls be fed!
And, as we round Thy table kneel,
Help us Thy quickening grace to feel!

3 Be Thou, O Holy Spirit, nigh!
   Accept the humble prayer,
The contrite soul's repentant sigh,
   The sinner's heartfelt tear!
And let our adoration rise,
As fragrant incense, to the skies!
Tressilian George Nicholas

253 [ROSEFIELD
"*If ye love Me, keep My commandments.*"

MANY centuries have fled
Since our Saviour broke the bread,
And this sacred feast ordained,
Ever by His church retained:
Those His body who discern,
Thus shall meet till His return.

2 Through the churches' long eclipse,
When, from priest or pastor's lips,
Truth divine was never heard,—
Mid the famine of the word,
Still these symbols witness gave
To His love who died to save.

3 All who bear the Saviour's name,
Here their common faith proclaim;
Though diverse in tongue or rite,
Here, one body we unite;
Breaking thus one mystic bread,
Members of one common head.

4 Come, the blessed emblems share,
Which the Saviour's death declare;
Come, on truth immortal feed;
For His flesh is meat indeed:
Saviour! witness with the sign,
That our ransomed souls are Thine.
Josiah Conder

254 *"Except ye eat the flesh of the Son of man,* [LAUSANNE
and drink His blood, ye have no life in you."

O BREAD to pilgrims given,
   O food that angels eat,
O manna sent from heaven,
   For heaven-born natures meet:
Give us, for Thee, long pining,
   To eat till richly filled;
Till, earth's delights resigning,
   Our every wish is stilled!

2 O water, life-bestowing,
   From out the Saviour's heart,
A fountain purely flowing,
   A fount of love Thou art!
O let us, freely tasting,
   Our burning thirst assuage!
Thy sweetness, never wasting,
   Avails from age to age.

3 Jesus, this feast receiving,
   We Thee unseen adore;
Thy faithful word believing
   We take, and doubt no more:
Give us, Thou true and loving,
   On earth to live in Thee;
Then, death the veil removing,
   Thy glorious face to see.
                      Ray Palmer

255   *"This do in remembrance of Me."*   [INTROITUS

ACCORDING to Thy gracious word,
   In meek humility,
This will I do, my dying Lord!
   I will remember Thee!

The Lord's Supper

2 Thy body, broken for my sake,
   My bread from heaven shall be;
Thy testamental cup I take,
   And thus remember Thee!

3 Gethsemane can I forget?
   Or there Thy conflict see,
Thine agony and bloody sweat,
   And not remember Thee?

4 When to the cross I turn mine eye,
   And rest on Calvary,
O Lamb of God, my Sacrifice!
   I must remember Thee:—

5 Remember Thee, and all Thy pains
   And all Thy love to me;
Yea, while a breath, a pulse remains,
   Will I remember Thee.

6 And when these failing lips grow dumb,
   And mind and memory flee,
When Thou shalt in Thy kingdom come,
   Then, Lord, remember me!

James Montgomery

Repentance

[WALDSTEIN

256 *"Rest in the Lord, and wait patiently for Him."*

Does the gospel word proclaim
   Rest for those that weary be?
Then, my soul, assert thy claim;
   Sure, that promise speaks to thee.
Marks of grace I cannot show,
   All polluted is my best;
Yet I weary am, I know,
   And the weary long for rest.

2 Burdened with a load of sin,
   Harassed with tormenting doubt,
Hourly conflicts from within,
   Hourly crosses from without:
All my little strength is gone,
   Sink I must without supply;
Sure, upon the earth is none
   Can more weary be than I.

3 In the ark the weary dove
   Found a welcome resting-place;
Thus my spirit longs to prove
   Rest in Christ, the Ark of grace;
Tempest-tost I long have been,
   And the flood increases fast;
Open, Lord, and draw me in,
   Till the storm be overpast!

John Newton

Repentance

257 *"Return unto Me, and I will return unto you, saith the Lord of hosts."* [AUGUSTA

O Thou, whose tender mercy hears
   Contrition's humble sigh,
Whose hand indulgent wipes the tears
   From sorrow's weeping eye;

2 See, low before Thy throne of grace,
   A wretched wanderer mourn;
Hast Thou not bid me seek Thy face?
   Hast Thou not said, Return?

3 Absent from Thee, my Guide, my Light,
   Without one cheering ray,
Through dangers, fears, and gloomy night,
   How desolate my way!

4 O shine on this benighted heart,
   With beams of mercy shine!
And let Thy healing voice impart
   A taste of joys divine!
                           Anne Steele.

258 *"Seek ye the Lord while He may be found."* [LITOLF

Come, trembling sinner, in whose breast
   A thousand thoughts revolve,
Come, with your guilt and fear opprest,
   And make this last resolve:—

2 'I'll go to Jesus, though my sin
   Like mountains round me close;
I know His courts, I'll enter in,
   Whatever may oppose.

3 'Prostrate I'll lie before His throne,
   And there my guilt confess;
I'll tell Him I'm a wretch undone,
   Without His sovereign grace.

4 'I'll to the gracious King approach,
   Whose scepter pardon gives;
  Perhaps He may command my touch,
   And then the suppliant lives.

5 'Perhaps He will admit my plea,
   Perhaps will hear my prayer;
  But, if I perish, I will pray,
   And perish only there.

6 'I can but perish, if I go—
   I am resolved to try;
  For, if I stay away, I know
   I must for ever die.'   *Edmund Jones*

259 "*With His stripes we are healed.*" [STABAT MATER

  I saw One hanging on a tree,
   In agony and blood,
  Who fixed His languid eyes on me,
   As near His cross I stood.

2 Sure, never till my latest breath
   Can I forget that look;
  It seemed to charge me with His death,
   Though not a word He spoke.

3 Alas, I knew not what I did,
   But all my tears were vain;
  Where could my trembling soul be hid,
   For I the Lord had slain!

4 A second look He gave, that said,
   'I freely all forgive;
  This blood is for thy ransom paid;
   I die, that thou may'st live.'

5 Thus while His death my sin displays
   In all its blackest hue,
  Such is the mystery of grace,
   It seals my pardon too!   *John Newton*

Repentance

260 *"Hide Thy face from my sins, and blot out all mine iniquities."* [PORTSMOUTH

BLOT out our sins of old,
 When erst we went astray,
 When, Father, from Thy fold
  We wandered far away;
O King of heaven, | Ere yet we die,
To Thee we cry, | To be forgiven.

2 In this our hour of need,
 In hope we fly to Thee;
 Sow in our hearts the seed
  Of bright eternity;
O Lord, we pray, | Our strength renew
As morning dew, | From day to day.

3 Blot out our sins gone by,
 Blot out our sins to-day,
 And others ere we die;
  And give us, while we pray,
Undying faith | The victory
In Christ, to see | O'er sin and death.
     Godfrey Thring

261 [BETHLEHEM
"God be merciful to me a sinner."

THE abyss of many a former sin
Encloses me, and bars me in:
Like billows my transgressions roll;
Be Thou the Pilot of my soul,
And to salvation's harbor bring,
Thou Saviour and Thou glorious King!

2 My Father's heritage abused,
Wasted by lust, by sin misused;
To shame and want and misery brought,
The slave to many a fruitless thought,
I cry to Thee who lovest men,
O pity and receive again!

3 With that blest thief my prayer I make,
  Remember for Thy mercy's sake!
  With that poor publican I cry,
  Be merciful, O God most high!
  With that lost prodigal I fain
  Back to my home would turn again!

4 Mourn, mourn, my soul, with earnest care,
  And raise to Christ the contrite prayer;—
  O Thou, who freely wast made poor,
  My sorrows and my sins to cure,
  Me, poor of all good works, embrace,
  Enriching with Thy boundless grace!
                              John Mason Neale

262 *"Restore unto me the joy of Thy salvation."* [LITOLF

A SINNER, Lord, behold I stand,
  In thought, and word, and deed;
But Jesus sits at Thy right hand,
  For such to intercede.

2 To heaven can reach the softest word,
    A child's repenting prayer;
  And tears are seen, and sighs are heard,
    And thoughts regarded there.

3 And Thou canst change this evil heart,
    Canst give a holy mind,
  And wilt that heavenly grace impart
    Which those who seek shall find.

4 Then let me all my sins confess,
    Pardon and help implore,
  That I may love my follies less,
    And love my Saviour more.

263 *"Thou Son of David have mercy on me."* [DUNDEE

Jesus, if still Thou art to-day
   As yesterday the same,
Present to heal, in me display
   The virtue of Thy name.

2 If still Thou goest about to do
   Thy needy creatures good,
On me, that I Thy praise may show,
   Be all Thy wonders showed.

3 Thou seest me deaf to Thy commands;
   Open, O Lord, mine ear;
Bid me stretch out my withered hands,
   And lift them up in prayer.

4 Silent (alas! Thou know'st how long!)
   My voice I cannot raise;
But, O! when Thou shalt loose my tongue,
   The dumb shall sing Thy praise.

5 Lame, at the pool I still am found:
   Give, and my strength employ;
Light as a hart I then shall bound,
   The lame shall leap for joy.

6 Blind from my birth to guilt and Thee,
   And dark I am within:
The love of God I cannot see,
   The sinfulness of sin.

7 But Thou, they say, art passing by;
   O let me find Thee near;
Jesus, in mercy hear my cry,
   Thou Son of David, hear!

Repentance

8 Behold me waiting in the way,
  For Thee, the heavenly Light;
  Command me to be brought, and say,
  'Sinner, receive thy sight!'
                    Charles Wesley

264 *"Let us therefore come boldly unto the throne of grace, that we may obtain mercy."* [LAST HOPE

Hast thou sinned? Sin no more;
  Pardon ask, and pardon win;
  Mercy sits at mercy's door,
  Boldly knock and enter in.

2 Boldly to the throne of grace,
  Weeping for the bitter past,
  Go, though shame would hide its face,
  Go, and find a rest at last.

3 Christ, who died the lost to save,
  Never turned His face from pain;
  They who meekly pardon crave,
  Never cry to Him in vain.

4 Christ Himself is calling, 'Come,'
  Christ, who lived and died for thee,
  'Hasten, helpless sinner, home,
  Lay your weary load on Me.'

5 Stand not still to count the cost,
  Hasten while 'tis yet to-day;
  Time, too precious to be lost,
  Brooks not doubt;—away, away!

6 Yes, in this thy sorest need,
  Knock in faith at mercy's door;
  Go, and there for pardon plead,
  Go, for grace to sin no more.
                    Godfrey Thring

Repentance

265   *"Ho, every one that thirsteth."*   [OSGOOD

Come, ye sinners, poor and wretched,
    Weak and wounded, sick and sore;
Jesus ready stands to save you,
    Full of pity, joined with power:
        He is able,
    He is willing; doubt no more.

2 Ho, ye needy, come and welcome;
    God's free bounty glorify;
True belief, and true repentance,
    Every grace that brings us nigh,
        Without money,
    Come to Jesus Christ and buy.

3 Let not conscience make you linger,
    Nor of fitness fondly dream;
All the fitness He requireth
    Is to feel your need of Him:
        This He gives you;
    'Tis the Spirit's rising beam.

4 Come, ye weary, heavy laden,
    Lost and ruined by the fall!
If you tarry till you're better,
    You will never come at all:
        Not the righteous,
    Sinners, Jesus came to call.
                      Joseph Hart

266   *"Lord, what wilt thou have me to do?"*   [ARIEL

Lord, thou hast won—at length I yield,
My heart, by mighty grace compelled,
    Surrenders all to Thee;
Against Thy terrors long I strove,
But who can stand against Thy love?—
    Love conquers even me.

2 If Thou hadst bid Thy thunders roll,
   And lightnings flash to blast my soul,
     I still had stubborn been:
   But mercy has my heart subdued,
   A bleeding Saviour I have viewed,
     And now, I hate my sin.

3 Now, Lord, I would be Thine alone;
   Come, take possession of Thine own,
     For Thou hast set me free;
   Released from Satan's hard command,
   See all my powers in waiting stand,
     To be employed by Thee.
                   John Newton

267   "*Thou art my Rock.*"   [MATILDA

O JESUS, Saviour of the lost,
   My Rock and Hiding-place,
By storms of sin and sorrow tost,
   I seek Thy sheltering grace.

2 Guilty, forgive me, Lord! I cry;
   Pursued by foes I come;
   A sinner, save me or I die;
   An outcast, take me home.

3 Once safe in Thine almighty arms,
   Let storms come on amain;
There danger never, never harms;
   There death itself is gain.

4 And when I stand before Thy throne,
   And all Thy glory see,
Still be my righteousness alone
   To hide myself in Thee.
               Edward Henry Bickersteth

Repentance

268 *"If the righteous scarcely be saved, where*   [OLMUTZ
          shall the ungodly and the sinner appear?"

AND wilt Thou pardon, Lord,
   A sinner such as I,
Although Thy book his crimes record
   Of such a crimson dye?

2 So deep are they engraved,
      So terrible their fear,—
   The righteous scarcely shall be saved,
      And where shall I appear?

3 My soul, make all things known
      To Him who all things sees:
   That so the Lamb may yet atone
      For thine iniquities.

4 O Thou Physician blest,
      Make clean my guilty soul!
   And me, by many a sin opprest
      Restore, and keep me whole!

5 I know not how to praise
      Thy mercy and Thy love:
   But deign Thy servant to upraise,
      And I shall learn above!
                           John Mason Neale

269 *"God shall bring every work into judgment."*   [LITANY

ALMIGHTY God, Thy piercing eye
   Strikes through the shades of night;
And our most secret actions lie
   All open to Thy sight.

2 There's not a sin that we commit,
      Nor wicked word we say,
   But in Thy dreadful book 'tis writ
      Against the judgment-day.

3 And must the crimes that I have done
    Be read and published there,
  Be all exposed before the sun,
    While men and angels hear?

4 Lord! at Thy foot ashamed I lie,
    Upward I dare not look;
  Pardon my sins before I die,
    And blot them from Thy book.

5 Remember all the dying pains
    That my Redeemer felt,
  And let His blood wash out my stains,
    And answer for my guilt.
                        Isaac Watts

270 [MATILDA
"*With my whole heart have I sought Thee.*"

  My God, accept my heart this day,
    And make it always Thine,
  That I from Thee no more may stray,
    No more from Thee decline.

2 Before the cross of Him who died,
    Behold, I prostrate fall;
  Let every sin be crucified,
    Let Christ be all in all.

3 Anoint me with Thy heavenly grace,
    Adopt me for Thine own,
  That I may see Thy glorious face
    And worship at Thy throne!

4 Let every thought and work, and word,
    To Thee be ever given;
  Then life shall be Thy service, Lord,
    And death the gate of heaven!
                        Matthew Bridges

Repentance

271 [MONASTERY
"The sacrifices of God are a broken spirit."

O Thou, that hear'st when sinners cry,
Though all my crimes before Thee lie,
Behold them not with angry look,
But blot their memory from Thy book.

2 Create my nature pure within,
And form my soul averse to sin;
Let Thy good Spirit ne'er depart,
Nor hide Thy presence from my heart.

3 I cannot live without Thy light,
Cast out and banished from Thy sight;
Thine holy joys, my God, restore,
And guard me that I fall no more.

4 A broken heart, my God, my King,
Is all the sacrifice I bring;
The God of grace will ne'er despise
A broken heart for sacrifice.

5 O may Thy love inspire my tongue!
Salvation shall be all my song;
And all my powers shall join to bless
The Lord, my Strength and Righteousness.
Isaac Watts

272 *"My soul waiteth upon God."* [CRAMER

O that my load of sin were gone!
　O that I could at last submit
At Jesus' feet to lay it down,
　To lay my soul at Jesus' feet!

2 Rest for my soul I long to find;
　Saviour of all, if mine Thou art,
Give me Thy meek and lowly mind,
　And stamp Thine image on my heart.

3 Break off the yoke of inbred sin,
　　And fully set my spirit free;
　I cannot rest till pure within,
　　Till I am wholly lost in Thee.

4 Fain would I learn of Thee, my God;
　　Thy light and easy burden prove,
　The cross all stained with hallowed blood,
　　The labor of Thy dying love.

5 I would, but Thou must give me power;
　　My heart from every sin release;
　Bring near, bring near the joyful hour,
　　And fill me with Thy perfect peace.
　　　　　　　　　　　Charles Wesley

273　　　　"*God is love.*"　　　[LAST HOPE

Depth of mercy! can there be
Mercy still reserved for me?
Can my God His wrath forbear,—
Me, the chief of sinners, spare?

2 I have long withstood His grace;
　Long provoked Him to His face;
　Would not hearken to His calls;
　Grieved Him by a thousand falls.

3 Lord, incline me to repent;
　Let me now my fall lament;
　Deeply my revolt deplore;
　Weep, believe, and sin no more.

4 There for me the Saviour stands,
　Shows His wounds, and spreads His hands:
　God is love! I know, I feel;
　Jesus weeps, but loves me still.
　　　　　　　　　　Charles Wesley

Repentance

274   *"Create in me a clean heart, O God."*   [CRAMER

Show pity, Lord; O Lord, forgive;
Let a repenting rebel live;
Are not Thy mercies large and free?
May not a sinner trust in Thee?

2 My crimes are great, but don't surpass
The power and glory of Thy grace:
Great God, Thy nature hath no bound;
So let Thy pardoning love be found.

3 O, wash my soul from every sin,
And make my guilty conscience clean;
Here on my heart the burden lies,
And past offences pain mine eyes.

4 My lips with shame my sins confess
Against Thy law, against Thy grace;
Lord, should Thy judgment grow severe,
I am condemned, but Thou art clear.

5 Yet save a trembling sinner, Lord,
Whose hope, still hovering round Thy word,
Would light on some sweet promise there,
Some sure support against despair.
Isaac Watts

275   *"This is the love of God, that we keep His commandments."*   [STABAT MATER

Lord, as to Thy dear cross we flee
And plead to be forgiven,
So let Thy life our pattern be,
And form our souls for heaven.

2 Help us, through good report and ill,
Our daily cross to bear,
Like Thee to do our Father's will,
Our brethren's griefs to share.

Repentance

3 Let grace our selfishness expel,
   Our earthliness refine,
And kindness in our bosoms dwell,
   As free and true as Thine.

4 Should friends misjudge, or foes defame,
   Or brethren faithless prove,
Then, like Thine own, be all our aim
   To conquer them by love.

5 Kept peaceful in the midst of strife,
   Forgiving and forgiven,
O may we lead the pilgrim's life,
   And follow Thee to heaven!
            John Hampden Gurney

276   [MONASTERY
"And I, if I be lifted up, will draw all men unto Me."

Lord Jesus, when we stand afar
   And gaze upon Thy holy cross,
In love of Thee and scorn of self,
   O! may we count the world as loss.

2 When we behold Thy bleeding wounds,
   And the rough way that Thou hast trod,
Make us to hate the load of sin
   That lay so heavy on our God.

3 O holy Lord! uplifted high
   With outstretched arms, in mortal woe,
Embracing in Thy wondrous love
   The sinful world that lies below!

4 Give us an everliving faith
   To gaze beyond the things we see;
And in the mystery of Thy death
   Draw us and all men unto Thee!
            William Walsham How

Repentance

277   *"Rise: He calleth thee."*   [DUKE ST.

God calling yet! shall I not hear?
Earth's pleasures shall I still hold dear?
Shall life's swift passing years all fly
And still my soul in slumber lie?

2 God calling yet! shall I not rise?
Can I His loving voice despise
And basely His kind care repay?
He calls me still: can I delay?

3 God calling yet! and shall He knock,
And I my heart the closer lock?
He still is waiting to receive,
And shall I dare His Spirit grieve?

4 God calling yet! and shall I give
No heed, but still in bondage live?
I wait, but He does not forsake;
He calls me still: my heart, awake!

5 God calling yet! I cannot stay;
My heart I yield without delay:
Vain world, farewell, from thee I part;
The voice of God hath reached my heart.
                                        Gerhard Tersteegen

278   *"Whatsoever thy hand findeth to do, do it*   [WELLS
                        with thy might."

Life is the time to serve the Lord,
The time to insure the great reward;
And while the lamp holds out to burn
The vilest sinner may return.

2 Life is the hour that God hath given,
To escape from hell, and fly to heaven;
The day of grace, and mortals may
Secure the blessings of the day.

3 Then what my thoughts design to do,
My hands, with all your might pursue,
Since no device, nor work, is found,
Nor faith, nor hope, beneath the ground.

4 There are no acts of pardon past
In the cold grave to which we haste;
But darkness, death, and long despair
Reign in eternal silence there.
Isaac Watts

279 "*To-day, if ye will hear His voice, harden not your hearts.*" [GORTON

O WHERE shall rest be found,
  Rest for the weary soul?
'T were vain the ocean depths to sound,
  Or pierce to either pole.

2 The world can never give
  The bliss for which we sigh:
'T is not the whole of life to live,
  Nor all of death to die.

3 Beyond this vale of tears,
  There is a life above,
Unmeasured by the flight of years;
  And all that life is love.

4 There is a death whose pang
  Outlasts the fleeting breath:
O what eternal horrors hang
  Around the second death!

5 Lord God of truth and grace,
  Teach us that death to shun,
Lest we be banished from Thy face,
  And evermore undone.
James Montgomery

Repentance

280   *"A broken and a contrite heart, O God,*   [EVENTIDE
   Thou wilt not despise."

Lord, I am come! Thy promise is my plea,
Without Thy word I dare not venture nigh!
But Thou hast called the burdened soul to
  Thee;
A weary, burdened soul, O Lord, am I!

2 Bowed down beneath a heavy load of sin,
By Satan's fierce temptations sorely prest,
Beset without, and full of fears within,
Trembling and faint I come to Thee for rest.

3 Be Thou my Refuge, Lord, my Hiding-place;
I know no force can tear me from Thy side;
Unmoved I then may all accusers face
And answer every charge with—'Jesus died!'

281   [MORNINGTON
 "While we were yet sinners, Christ died for us."

  Did Christ o'er sinners weep,
   And shall our cheeks be dry?
  Let floods of penitential grief
   Burst forth from every eye.

2 The Son of God in tears
   Angels with wonder see!
  Be thou astonished, O my soul,
   He shed those tears for thee.

3 He wept that we might weep:
   Each sin demands a tear;
  In heaven alone no sin is found,
   And there's no weeping there.
        Benjamin Beddome.

Christian Joy and Hope

282   *"Mine eyes have seen Thy salvation."*   [GILEAD

    LIFT up your heads, ye mighty gates!
Behold, the King of glory waits;
The King of kings is drawing near,
The Saviour of the world is here.

2 The Lord is just, a Helper tried;
Mercy is ever at His side;
His kingly crown is holiness;
His scepter, pity in distress.

3 O blest the land, the city blest,
Where Christ the Ruler is confest!
O happy hearts and happy homes
To whom this King of triumph comes!

4 Fling wide the portals of your heart;
Make it a temple set apart
From earthly use for heaven's employ,
Adorned with prayer and love and joy.

5 Redeemer, come! I open wide
My heart to Thee; here, Lord, abide:
Let me Thine inner presence feel,
Thy grace and love in me reveal.

6 So come, my Sovereign, enter in;
Let new and nobler life begin;
Thy Holy Spirit guide us on
Until the glorious crown is won!

George Weissel

Christian Joy and Hope

283   [NUN DANKET ALLE GOTT
"This God is our God for ever and ever."

   Now thank we all our God,
     With heart and hand and voices,
 Who wondrous things hath done,
     In whom His world rejoices;
 Who from our mother's arms
     Hath blest us on our way
 With countless gifts of love,
     And still is ours to-day.

2 O may this bounteous God
     Through all our life be near us,
 With ever joyful hearts
     And blessed peace to cheer us;
 And keep us in His grace,
     And guide us when perplext,
 And free us from all ills
     In this world and the next.

3 All praise and thanks to God
     The Father now be given,
 The Son, and Him who reigns
     With Them in highest heaven!
 The One Eternal God
     Whom heaven and earth adore;
 For thus it was, is now,
     And shall be evermore!
                         Martin Rinkart

284 *"And I heard the voice of many* [UNSER HERRSCHER
     angels round about the throne."

HARK! ten thousand harps and voices
   Sound the note of praise above;
Jesus reigns, and heaven rejoices;
   Jesus reigns, the God of love:
See, He sits on yonder throne;
Jesus rules the world alone.

2 King of glory, reign for ever!
  Thine an everlasting crown:
Nothing from Thy love shall sever
  Those whom Thou hast made Thine own;
Happy objects of Thy grace,
Destined to behold Thy face.

3 Saviour, hasten Thine appearing;
  Bring, O bring the glorious day,
When, the awful summons hearing,
  Heaven and earth shall pass away:
Then, with golden harps, we'll sing,—
'Glory, glory to our King.'
Thomas Kelly

285 *"Thou art worthy, O Lord, to receive glory and honor and power."* [HEBRON]

WHAT equal honors shall we bring,
  To Thee, O Lord our God, the Lamb,
When all the notes that angels sing
  Are far inferior to Thy name?

2 Worthy is He that once was slain,
  The Prince of Peace that groaned and died,
Worthy to rise, and live, and reign
  At His Almighty Father's side.

3 Honor immortal must be paid
  Instead of scandal and of scorn;
While glory shines around His head,
  And a bright crown without a thorn.

4 Blessings for ever on the Lamb,
  Who bore the curse for wretched men;
Let angels sound His sacred name,
  And every creature say, Amen.
Isaac Watts

286
"O praise the Lord, all ye nations." [OLD HUNDRED]

From all that dwell below the skies
Let the Creator's praise arise;
Let the Redeemer's name be sung
Through every land by every tongue.

2 Eternal are Thy mercies, Lord;
Eternal truth attends Thy word;
Thy praise shall sound from shore to shore
Till suns shall rise and set no more.
Isaac Watts

287
[ACH GOTT UND HERR
"Thy loving-kindness is better than life."

O God, Thou art my God alone;
Early to Thee my soul shall cry;
A pilgrim in a land unknown,
A thirsty land whose springs are dry.

2 Yet, through this rough and thorny maze,
I follow hard on Thee, my God:
Thine hand unseen upholds my ways;
I safely tread where Thou hast trod.

3 Thee, in the watches of the night,
When I remember on my bed,
Thy presence makes the darkness light,
Thy guardian wings are round my head.

4 Better than life itself Thy love,
Dearer than all beside to me;
For whom have I in heaven above,
Or what on earth compared with Thee?

5 Praise with my heart, my mind, my voice,
For all Thy mercy I will give;
My soul shall still in God rejoice;
My tongue shall bless Thee while I live.
James Montgomery

288 [ORTONVILLE
"Unto you which believe He is precious."

How sweet the name of Jesus sounds
In a believer's ear!
It soothes his sorrows, heals his wounds,
And drives away his fear.

2 It makes the wounded spirit whole,
And calms the troubled breast;
'Tis manna to the hungry soul,
And to the weary, rest.

3 Dear name! the rock on which I build,
My shield and hiding-place,
My never-failing treasury, filled
With boundless stores of grace!

4 By Thee my prayers acceptance gain,
Although with sin defiled;
Satan accuses me in vain,
And I am owned a child.

5 Jesus! my Shepherd, Guardian, Friend,
My Prophet, Priest, and King;
My Lord, my Life, my Way, my End,
Accept the praise I bring!

6 Weak is the effort of my heart,
And cold my warmest thought;
But when I see Thee as Thou art,
I'll praise Thee as I ought.

7 Till then, I would Thy love proclaim,
With every fleeting breath;
And may the music of Thy name
Refresh my soul in death.

John Newton

Christian Joy and Hope

289 [ASHFORD
"The Lord hath dealt bountifully with thee."

REDEEMED from guilt, redeemed from fears,
My soul enlarged, and dried my tears,
What can I do, O Lord Divine,
What, to repay such gifts as Thine?

2 What can I do, so poor, so weak,
But from Thy hands new blessings seek,
A heart to feel Thy mercies more,
A soul to know Thee and adore?

3 O teach me at Thy feet to fall,
And yield Thee up myself, my all!
Before Thy saints my debts to own,
And live and die to Thee alone!

4 Thy Spirit, Lord, at large impart,
Expand and raise and fill my heart!
So may I hope my life shall be
Some faint return, O Lord, to Thee.
Henry Francis Lyte

290 *"The Spirit of God dwelleth in you."* [RETREAT

COME, ever-blessed Spirit, come,
And make Thy servants' hearts Thy home:
May each a living temple be,
Hallowed for ever, Lord, to Thee!

2 Enrich that temple's holy shrine
With sevenfold gifts of grace divine:
With wisdom, light, and knowledge bless,
Strength, counsel, fear, and godliness.

3 O Trinity in Unity,
One only God, and Persons Three!
In whom, through whom, by whom, we live,
To Thee we praise and glory give.

4 O grant us so to use Thy grace,
That we may see Thy glorious face,
And ever with the heavenly host
Praise Father, Son, and Holy Ghost!
Christopher Wordsworth

291 *"The Lord is my Shepherd."* [INTROITUS

My Shepherd will supply my need,
Jehovah is His name;
In pastures fresh He makes me feed,
Beside the living stream.

2 He brings my wandering spirit back,
When I forsake His ways;
And leads me, for His mercy's sake,
In paths of truth and grace.

3 When I walk through the shades of death,
Thy presence is my stay;
A word of Thy supporting breath
Drives all my fears away.

4 Thy hand, in spite of all my foes,
Doth still my table spread;
My cup with blessings overflows,
Thine oil anoints my head.

5 The sure provisions of my God
Attend me all my days;
O may Thy house be mine abode,
And all my work be praise!

6 There would I find a settled rest,
While others go and come;
No more a stranger, or a guest,
But like a child at home.
Isaac Watts

Christian Joy and Hope

292   *"I shall not want."*   [Waldhorn

My Shepherd is the living Lord,
  I therefore nothing need;
In pastures fair, near pleasant streams,
  He setteth me to feed.

2 He shall convert and glad my soul,
  And bring my mind in frame
To walk in paths of righteousness,
  For His most holy name.

3 Yea, though I walk the vale of death,
  Yet will I fear no ill:
Thy rod and staff do comfort me,
  And Thou art with me still.

4 And in the presence of my foes,
  My table Thou shalt spread;
Thou wilt fill full my cup, and Thou
  Anointed hast my head.

5 Through all my life Thy favor is
  So frankly shown to me,
That in Thy house for evermore
  My dwelling-place shall be.
                    Thomas Sternhold

293   *"The Desire of all nations shall come."*   [Elliot

Lift up your heads, eternal gates!
  Unfold to entertain
The King of glory: see, He comes
  With His celestial train.

2 Who is the King of glory? Who!
  The Lord for strength renowned;
In battle mighty; o'er His foes
  Eternal Victor crowned.

3 Lift up your heads, ye gates; unfold
  In state to entertain
The King of glory; see, He comes
With all His shining train.

4 Who is the King of glory? Who!
  The Lord of hosts renowned:
Of glory He alone is King
Who is with glory crowned.
            Tate and Brady

294 "*The angel of the Lord encampeth round   [COMFORT
     about them that fear Him.*"

Through all the changing scenes of life,
  In trouble, and in joy,
The praises of my God shall still
  My heart and tongue employ.

2 O magnify the Lord with me,
  With me exalt His name;
When in distress to Him I called,
  He to my rescue came.

3 The hosts of God encamp around
  The dwellings of the just;
Deliverance He affords to all,
  Who on His succor trust.

4 O make but trial of His love;
  Experience will decide
How blest are they, and only they,
  Who in His truth confide.

5 Fear Him, ye saints, and you will then
  Have nothing else to fear;
Make you His service your delight,
  Your wants shall be His care.
            Tate and Brady

295 "*The High and Lofty One that inhabiteth* [PHUVAH
eternity, whose name is Holy."

My God, how wonderful Thou art,
　Thy majesty how bright,
How beautiful Thy mercy-seat
　In depths of burning light!

2 How dread are Thine eternal years,
　　O Everlasting Lord!
　By prostrate spirits day and night
　　Incessantly adored!

3 How beautiful, how beautiful
　　The sight of Thee must be,
　Thine endless wisdom, boundless power,
　　And awful purity!

4 O how I fear Thee, living God,
　　With deepest, tenderest fears,
　And worship Thee with trembling hope
　　And penitential tears.

5 Yet I may love Thee too, O Lord!
　　Almighty as Thou art;
　For Thou hast stooped to ask of me
　　The love of this poor heart.

6 O then this worse than worthless heart
　　In pity deign to take,
　And make it love Thee for Thyself
　　And for Thy glory's sake!
　　　　　　Frederick William Faber

296 "*Praise waiteth for Thee, O God, in Zion.*" [ELLIOT

Thy praise alone, O Lord, doth reign
　In Zion Thine own hill;
Their vows to Thee they there maintain
　And promises fulfill.

2 For that Thou dost their prayers still hear,
　　And dost thereto agree,
　The people all, both far and near,
　　With trust shall come to Thee.

3 Our wicked life so far exceeds
　　That we shall fall therein;
　But, Lord, forgive our great misdeeds,
　　And purge us from our sin.

4 The man is blest whom Thou dost choose
　　Within Thy courts to dwell;
　Thy house and temple he shall use
　　With pleasures that excel.
　　　　　　　Sternhold and Hopkins

297 *"Unto Thee, O Lord, do I lift up my soul."* [GILEAD

Up to the Lord, that reigns on high,
　　And views the nations from afar,
　Let everlasting praises fly,
　　And tell how large His bounties are.

2 God, that must stoop to view the skies,
　　And bow to see what angels do,
　Down to our earth He casts His eyes,
　　And bends His footsteps downward too.

3 He overrules all mortal things,
　　And manages our mean affairs;
　On humble souls the King of kings
　　Bestows His counsels and His cares.

4 O, could our thankful hearts devise
　　A tribute equal to Thy grace,
　To the third heaven our songs should rise,
　　And teach the golden harps Thy praise.
　　　　　　　Isaac Watts

298 *"How shall we escape, if we neglect so great salvation?"* [BEETHOVEN

TREMBLING before Thine awful throne
O Lord! in dust my sins I own:
Justice and mercy for my life
Contend! O smile and heal the strife!

2 The Saviour smiles! upon my soul
New tides of hope tumultuous roll—
His voice proclaims my pardon found,
Seraphic transport wings the sound.

3 Earth has a joy unknown in heaven,
The new-born peace of sin forgiven!
Tears of such pure and sweet delight,
Ye angels! never dimmed your sight.

4 Ye saw of old on chaos rise
The beauteous pillars of the skies;
Ye know where morn exulting springs,
And evening folds her drooping wings.

5 Bright heralds of the eternal Will,
Abroad His errands ye fulfill;
Or, throned in floods of beamy day,
Symphonious in His presence play.

6 But I amid your choirs shall shine,
And all your knowledge will be mine:
Ye on your harps must lean to hear
A secret chord that mine will bear.
                              Augustus Lucas Hillhouse

299   *"Glory to God in the highest."*   [CALVARY

SONGS of praise the angels sang,
Heaven with hallelujahs rang,
When Jehovah's work begun,
When He spake and it was done.

2 Songs of praise awoke the morn,
   When the Prince of peace was born;
   Songs of praise arose when He
   Captive led captivity.

3 Heaven and earth must pass away,—
   Songs of praise shall crown that day:
   God will make new heavens and earth,—
   Songs of praise shall hail their birth.

4 And shall man alone be dumb,
   Till that glorious kingdom come?
   No! the church delights to raise
   Psalms, and hymns, and songs of praise.

5 Saints below, with heart and voice,
   Still in songs of praise rejoice;
   Learning here, by faith and love,
   Songs of praise to sing above.

6 Borne upon their latest breath,
   Songs of praise shall conquer death;
   Then, amid eternal joy,
   Songs of praise their powers employ.

   James Montgomery

300 *"Holy, holy, holy, Lord God Almighty."*   [TRUST

ROUND the Lord in glory seated
   Cherubim and seraphim
Filled His temple, and repeated
   Each to each the alternate hymn.

2 'Lord, Thy glory fills the heaven,
   Earth is with its fulness stored;
Unto Thee be glory given,
   Holy, holy, holy Lord!'

3 Heaven is still with glory ringing,
    Earth takes up the angels' cry,
  'Holy, holy, holy,' singing,
    'Lord of hosts, the Lord most High!'

4 With His seraph train before Him,
    With His holy church below,
  Thus conspire we to adore Him,
    Bid we thus our anthem flow:

5 'Lord, Thy glory fills the heaven,
    Earth is with its fulness stored;
  Unto Thee be glory given,
    Holy, holy, holy Lord!'
                        Richard Mant

301   *"These all died in faith."*   [CONTENTMENT

For all Thy saints, O Lord,
  Who strove in Thee to live,
Who followed Thee, obeyed, adored,
  Our grateful hymn receive.

2 For all Thy saints, O Lord,
    Accept our thankful cry,
  Who counted Thee their great reward,
    And strove in Thee to die.

3 They all in life and death,
    With Thee, their Lord, in view,
  Learned from Thy Holy Spirit's breath
    To suffer and to do.

4 For this Thy name we bless,
    And humbly pray that we
  May follow them in holiness,
    And live and die in Thee.
                        Richard Mant

302 [TEMA
"Just and true are Thy ways, Thou King of saints."

FROM all Thy saints in warfare,
    For all Thy saints at rest,
To Thee, O blessed Jesus,
    All praises be addrest.
Thou, Lord, didst win the battle
    That they might conquerors be;
Their crowns of living glory
    Are lit with rays from Thee.

2 For grace which did in mercy
    For all their sins atone;
For love which hath ingathered
    The blessed, one by one;
We praise Thy name, O Saviour,
    And pray that we with them
May shine as precious jewels
    In Thy bright diadem.

3 Apostles, prophets, martyrs,
    And all the later throng,
Who wear the spotless raiment,
    Who raise the ceaseless song;
For these, past on before us,
    Saviour, we Thee adore,
And walking in their footsteps
    Would serve Thee more and more.

4 Then praise we God the Father,
    And praise we God the Son,
And God the Holy Spirit,
    Eternal Three in One;
Till all the ransomed nation
    Fall down before the throne,
And honor, power, and glory
    Ascribe to God alone.

303 "*God be merciful unto us, and bless us, and* [CALVARY
cause His face to shine upon us."

GOD of mercy, God of grace!
Show the brightness of Thy face:
Shine upon us, Saviour! shine;
Fill Thy church with light divine;
And Thy saving health extend
Unto earth's remotest end.

2 Let the people praise Thee, Lord!
Be by all that live adored;
Let the nations shout and sing,
Glory to their Saviour King;
At Thy feet their tribute pay,
And Thy holy will obey.

3 Let the people praise Thee, Lord!
Earth shall then her fruits afford;
God to man His blessing give;
Man to God devoted live;
All below, and all above,
One in joy and light and love.
Henry Francis Lyte

304 "*O Lord of hosts, blessed is the man that* [SELDON
trusteth in Thee."

O GOD of hosts, the mighty Lord,
  How lovely is the place
Where Thou, enthroned in glory, showst
  The brightness of Thy face!

2 My longing soul faints with desire
  To view Thy blest abode:
My panting heart and flesh cry out
  For Thee, the living God.

3 Thrice happy they whose choice has Thee
   Their sure protection made;
   Who long to tread the sacred ways
   That to Thy dwelling lead.

4 For God, who is our Sun and Shield,
   Will grace and glory give;
   And no good thing will He withhold
   From them that justly live.

5 Thou God, whom heavenly hosts obey,
   How highly blest is he
   Whose hope and trust, securely placed,
   Are still reposed on Thee!
                              Tate and Brady

305 *"What shall I render unto the Lord for all* [ELLIOT
       his benefits?"

For mercies, countless as the sands,
   Which daily I receive
From Jesus my Redeemer's hands,
   My soul, what canst thou give?

2 Alas! from such a heart as mine,
   What I can bring Him forth?
   My best is stained and dyed with sin,
   My all is nothing worth.

3 The best return for one like me,
   So wretched and so poor,
   Is from His gifts to draw a plea,
   And ask Him still for more.

4 I cannot serve Him as I ought,
   No works have I to boast;
   Yet would I glory in the thought
   That I should owe Him most.
                              John Newton

306   *"Praise the Lord, O my soul."*   [WINCHESTER

Awake, my soul! in joyful lays,
And sing thy great Redeemer's praise;
He justly claims a song from me;
His loving-kindness, O how free!

2 He saw me ruined in the fall,
Yet loved me notwithstanding all;
He saved me from my lost estate;
His loving-kindness, O how great!

3 Through mighty hosts of cruel foes
Where earth and hell my way oppose,
He safely leads my soul along;
His loving-kindness, O how strong!

4 When trouble, like a gloomy cloud,
Has gathered thick and thundered loud,
He near my soul has always stood;
His loving-kindness, O how good!

5 When I shall pass death's gloomy vale,
And life and mortal powers must fail,
O may my last expiring breath
His loving-kindness sing in death!
                                        Samuel Medley

307   *"Looking unto Jesus."*   [ORTONVILLE

Majestic sweetness sits enthroned
   Upon the Saviour's brow;
His head with radiant glories crowned,
   His lips with grace o'erflow.

2 No mortal can with Him compare
   Among the sons of men;
Fairer is He than all the fair
   That fill the heavenly train.

3 He saw me plunged in deep distress,
    He flew to my relief;
  For me He bore the shameful cross,
    And carried all my grief.

4 To Him I owe my life, and breath,
    And all the joys I have:
  He makes me triumph over death,
    He saves me from the grave.

5 To heaven, the place of His abode,
    He brings my weary feet;
  Shows me the glories of my God,
    And makes my joy complete.

6 Since from His bounty I receive
    Such proofs of love divine,
  Had I a thousand hearts to give,
    Lord, they should all be Thine!
                              Samuel Stennett

308 *"The Lord is merciful and gracious."* [STATE ST.

  O BLESS the Lord, my soul!
    Let all within me join,
  And aid my tongue to bless His name,
    Whose favors are divine.

2 O bless the Lord, my soul!
    Nor let His mercies lie
  Forgotten in unthankfulness,
    And without praises die.

3 'Tis He forgives thy sins;
    'Tis He relieves thy pain;
  'Tis He that heals thy sicknesses,
    And makes thee young again.

4 He crowns thy life with love,
    When ransomed from the grave;
  He that redeemed my soul from hell
    Hath sovereign power to save.

5 He fills the poor with good,
    He gives the sufferers rest:
  The Lord hath judgments for the proud,
    And justice for the opprest.

6 His wondrous works and ways
    He made by Moses known;
  But sent the world His truth and grace
    By His beloved Son.
                  Isaac Watts

309   *"Who crowneth thee with loving-kindness."* [OLMUTZ

My soul, repeat His praise
    Whose mercies are so great;
  Whose anger is so slow to rise,
    So ready to abate.

2 God will not always chide;
    And, when His strokes are felt,
  His strokes are fewer than our crimes,
    And lighter than our guilt.

3 High as the heavens are raised
    Above the ground we tread,
  So far the riches of His grace
    Our highest thoughts exceed.

4 His power subdues our sins,
    And His forgiving love,
  Far as the east is from the west,
    Doth all our guilt remove.

5 Our days are as the grass,
    Or like the morning flower:
  If one sharp blast sweep o'er the field,
    It withers in an hour.

6 But Thy compassions, Lord,
    To endless years endure;
  And children's children ever find
    Thy words of promise sure.
                            Isaac Watts

310 *"Unite my heart to fear Thy Name."* [ABBE VOGLER

  O FOR a heart to praise my God,
    A heart from sin set free!
  A heart that always feels Thy blood,
    So freely spilt for me!

2 A heart resigned, submissive, meek,
    My dear Redeemer's throne;
  Where only Christ is heard to speak,
    Where Jesus reigns alone.

3 A humble, lowly, contrite heart,
    Believing, true, and clean;
  Which neither life nor death can part
    From Him that dwells within.

4 A heart in every thought renewed,
    And full of love divine;
  Perfect, and right, and pure, and good,
    A copy, Lord, of Thine.

5 Thy nature, gracious Lord, impart;
    Come quickly from above;
  Write Thy new name upon my heart,
    Thy new, best name of love.
                          Charles Wesley

311
"Into Thine hand I commit my spirit." [GRACE

Father of mercies, God of love,
  My Father and my God:
I'll sing the honors of Thy name
  And spread Thy praise abroad.

2 In every period of my life
  Thy kindest thoughts appear;
Thy mercies gild each transient scene,
  And crown each circling year.

3 In all these mercies may my soul
  A Father's bounty see,
Nor let the gifts Thy grace bestows
  Estrange my heart from Thee.

4 Teach me in times of deep distress
  To own Thy hand, O God,
And in submissive silence learn
  The lessons of Thy rod.

5 In every varying mortal state,
  Each bright, each dreary scene,
Give me a meek and humble mind,
  Still equal and serene.

6 Then shall I close mine eyes in death,
  Without one anxious fear;
For death itself, my God, is life,
  If Thou art with me there.
                    Ottiwell Heginbotham

312
"God is King of all the earth; sing ye praises [GILEAD
  with understanding."

The Lord is King! lift up thy voice,
O earth, and, all ye heavens, rejoice!
From world to world the joy shall ring,
The Lord Omnipotent is King.

2 The Lord is King! who then shall dare
   Resist His will, distrust His care,
   Or murmur at His wise decrees,
   Or doubt His royal promises?

3 The Lord is King! Child of the dust,
   The Judge of all the earth is just:
   Holy and true are all His ways:
   Let every creature speak His praise.

4 He reigns! ye saints, exalt your strains;
   Your God is King, your Father reigns:
   And He is at the Father's side,
   The Man of Love, the crucified.

5 Come, make your wants, your burdens known,
   He will present them at the throne;
   And angel bands are waiting there
   His messages of love to bear.

6 O when His wisdom can mistake,
   His might decay, His love forsake,
   Then may His children cease to sing,—
   The Lord Omnipotent is King.   *Josiah Conder*

313 *"The Lord is my light and my salvation."* [MIDNIGHT
   My God! the Spring of all my joys,
      The life of my delights,
   The glory of my brightest days,
      And comfort of my nights!

2 In darkest shades if He appear,
      My dawning is begun!
   He is my soul's sweet morning star,
      And He my rising sun.

3 The opening heavens around me shine
      With beams of sacred bliss,
   While Jesus shows His heart is mine,
      And whispers I am His.

4 My soul would leave this heavy clay
   At that transporting word,
Run up with joy the shining way,
   To embrace my dearest Lord.

5 Fearless of hell and ghastly death,
   I'd break through every foe;
The wings of love, and arms of faith,
   Should bear me conqueror through.
Isaac Watts

314 *"Rejoice in the Lord alway, and again* [SABBATH EVE
      I say, rejoice."

ALWAY in the Lord rejoice,
Lift, my soul, thy heart and voice,
Lift them holy, high, and pure,
For His mercies aye endure.

2 Up to heaven where He doth live,
Through the world which He doth give,
Raise thy heart and lift thy voice,
'And again I say, rejoice.'

3 Gently all thy trials take;
They are thine for Jesus' sake,
Meekly 'mid thy mercies move;
They are thine through Jesus' love.

4 All thou hast and all thou art
Own as His with thankful heart,
Use as His with heedful care,
For His coming to prepare.

5 Live in faith and live in prayer,
In His presence everywhere;
Live as angels, though on earth,
Children of the second birth.
John Samuel Bewley Monsell

315 *"Worthy is the Lamb that was slain."* [CAMBRIDGE

 COME, let us join our cheerful songs
  With angels round the throne;
 Ten thousand thousand are their tongues,
  But all their joys are one.

2 'Worthy the Lamb that died,' they cry,
  'To be exalted thus:'
 'Worthy the Lamb,' our lips reply,
  'For He was slain for us.'

3 Jesus is worthy to receive
  Honor and power divine;
 And blessings, more than we can give,
  Be, Lord, for ever Thine.

4 Let all that dwell above the sky,
  And air, and earth, and seas,
 Conspire to lift Thy glories high,
  And speak Thine endless praise.

5 The whole creation join in one,
  To bless the sacred name
 Of Him that sits upon the throne,
  And to adore the Lamb.
       Isaac Watts

316 [CAMBRIDGE
"My spirit hath rejoiced in God my Saviour."

 O FOR a thousand tongues to sing
  My dear Redeemer's praise,
 The glories of my God and King,
  The triumphs of His grace!

2 My gracious Master and my God,
  Assist me to proclaim,
 To spread through all the earth abroad,
  The honors of Thy name.

3 Jesus, the name that charms our fears,
    That bids our sorrows cease;
  'Tis music in the sinner's ears;
    'Tis life, and health, and peace!

4 He breaks the power of canceled sin;
    He sets the prisoner free;
  His blood can make the foulest clean;
    His blood availed for me.

5 He speaks, and, listening to His voice,
    New life the dead receive:
  The mournful, broken hearts rejoice:
    The humble poor believe.

6 Look unto Him, ye nations! own
    Your God, ye fallen race!
  Look, and be saved through faith alone,
    Be justified by grace!   *Charles Wesley*

317   *"Delight thyself in the Lord."*   [COMFORT

O LORD, I would delight in Thee,
  And on Thy care depend;
To Thee in every trouble flee,
  My best, my only Friend.

2 When all created streams are dried,
    Thy fulness is the same;
  May I with this be satisfied,
    And glory in Thy name!

3 No good in creatures can be found,
    But may be found in Thee;
  I must have all things, and abound,
    While God is God to me.

4 O that I had a stronger faith,
    To look within the veil;
  To credit what my Saviour saith,
    Whose word can never fail!

5 O Lord, I cast my care on Thee;
   I triumph and adore:
Henceforth my great concern shall be
   To love and please Thee more.
John Ryland

318 *"We have known and believed the love that God hath to us."* [AUTUMN

LOVE Divine, all love excelling,
   Joy of heaven, to earth come down!
Fix in us Thy humble dwelling,
   All Thy faithful mercies crown;
Jesus! Thou art all compassion,
   Pure, unbounded love Thou art;
Visit us with Thy salvation,
   Enter every trembling heart.

2 Breathe, O breathe thy loving Spirit,
   Into every troubled breast!
Let us all in Thee inherit,
   Let us find Thy promised rest;
Come, almighty to deliver,
   Let us all Thy life receive!
Speedily return, and never,
   Never more Thy temples leave.

3 Finish then Thy new creation,
   Pure and spotless let us be:
Let us see our whole salvation
   Perfectly secured by Thee!
Changed from glory into glory,
   Till in heaven we take our place;
Till we cast our crowns before Thee,
   Lost in wonder, love, and praise.
Charles Wesley

319 "*The unsearchable riches of Christ.*" [Heavenly Love

O Love divine, how sweet Thou art!
When shall I find my willing heart
   All taken up by Thee!
I thirst, and faint, and die to prove
The greatness of redeeming love,
   The love of Christ to me!

2 Stronger His love than death or hell;
Its riches are unsearchable:
   The first born sons of light
Desire in vain its depth to see;
They cannot reach the mystery,
   The length, and breadth, and hight.

3 God only knows the love of God:
O that it now were shed abroad
   In this poor stony heart!
For love I sigh, for love I pine;
This only portion, Lord, be mine,
   Be mine this better part!

4 O that I could for ever sit
With Mary at the Master's feet!
   Be this my happy choice:
My only care, delight, and bliss,
My joy, my heaven on earth, be this,
   To hear the Bridegroom's voice!

5 Thy only love do I require,
Nothing in earth beneath desire,
   Nothing in heaven above:
Let earth, and heaven, and all things go;
Give me Thy only love to know,
   Give me Thy only love!
                      Charles Wesley

Christian Joy and Hope

320 *"Behold what manner of love the Father hath bestowed upon us."* [MARTYN

BLESSED fountain, full of grace,
  Grace for sinners, grace for me,
To this source alone I trace
  What I am, and hope to be:
What I am, as one redeemed,
  Saved and rescued by the Lord;
Hating what I once esteemed,
  Loving what I once abhorred;

2 What I hope to be, ere long,
  When I take my place above,
When I join the heavenly throng,
  When I see the God of love;
Then I hope like Him to be,
  Who redeemed His saints from sin,
Whom I now obscurely see,
  Through a cloud that stands between.

3 When I see Him as He is,
  No corruption can remain:
Such their portion who are His,
  Such the happy state they gain.
Blessed fountain, full of grace,
  Grace for sinners, grace for me,
To this source alone I trace
  What I am, and hope to be.
Thomas Kelly

321 *"I have loved thee with an everlasting love."* [CAREY

O DRAW me, Father, after Thee!
  So shall I run, and never tire;
With gracious words still comfort me,
  Be Thou my hope, my sole desire;
Free me from every weight; nor fear
Nor sin can come, if Thou art here.

2 From all eternity, with love
   Unchangeable Thou hast me viewed;
Ere knew this beating heart to move,
   Thy tender mercies me pursued;
Ever with me may they abide,
And close me in on every side!

3 In suffering, be Thy love my peace;
   In weakness, be Thy love my power;
And when the storms of life shall cease,
   My God! in that transcendent hour,
In death, as life, be Thou my Guide,
And bear me through death's whelming tide.
John Wesley

322   *"With the Lord there is mercy."*   [TRUST

GOD is love; His mercy brightens
   All the path in which we rove;
Bliss He wakes, and woe He lightens:
   God is wisdom, God is love.

2 Chance and change are busy ever;
   Man decays, and ages move,
But His mercy waneth never:
   God is wisdom, God is love.

3 E'en the hour that darkest seemeth
   Will His changeless goodness prove;
From the mist His brightness streameth:
   God is wisdom, God is love.

4 He with earthly cares entwineth
   Hope and comfort from above;
Everywhere His glory shineth:
   God is wisdom, God is love.
John Bowring

323 *"My soul thirsteth for God."* [COVENTRY

As pants the hart for cooling streams,
  When heated in the chase,
So longs my soul, O God, for Thee
  And Thy refreshing grace.

2 For Thee, my God, the living God,
  My thirsty soul doth pine;
O when shall I behold Thy face,
  Thou Majesty Divine!

3 Why restless, why cast down, my soul?
  Trust God, who will employ
His aid for thee, and change these sighs
  To thankful hymns of joy.

4 Why restless, why cast down, my soul?
  Hope still, and thou shalt sing
The praise of Him, who is thy God,
  Thy health's eternal spring.
          Tate and Brady

324 *"We love Him, because He first loved us."* [PHUVAH

My God, I love Thee: not because
  I hope for heaven thereby,
Nor yet because who love Thee not
  Must die eternally.

2 Thou, O my Jesus, Thou didst me
  Upon the cross embrace:
For me didst bear the nails, and spear,
  And manifold disgrace.

3 And griefs and torments numberless,
  And sweat of agony,
Yea, death itself,—and all for me,
  Who was Thine enemy.

4 Then why, O blessed Jesus Christ,
    Should I not love Thee well?
  Not for the sake of winning heaven,
    Nor of escaping hell;

5 Not with the hope of gaining aught,
    Not seeking a reward,—
  But as Thyself hast loved me,
    O ever-loving Lord!

6 So would I love Thee, dearest Lord,
    And in Thy praise will sing;
  Solely because Thou art my God,
    And my Eternal King.
                    Edward Caswall

325 *"This is the love of God, that we keep His* [BELMONT
       commandments."

  O THOU, in whom our love doth find
    Its rest and perfect end,
  O Jesus, Saviour of mankind,
    And their Eternal Friend!

2 Stay with us, Lord, and with Thy light
    Illume the soul's abyss;
  Scatter the darkness of our night,
    And fill the world with bliss.

3 May every soul Thy love return,
    And strive to do Thy will;
  And, keeping Thy commandments, learn
    To love Thee better still!

4 Grant us, while here on earth we stay,
    Thy love to feel and know;
  And when from hence we pass away,
    To us Thy glory show.

326 *"We have known and believed the love that God hath to us."* [BELMONT

Thou Grace Divine, encircling all,
   A shoreless, soundless sea,
Wherein at last our souls must fall,
   O Love of God, most free!

2 When over dizzy hights we go,
   A soft hand blinds our eyes,
And we are guided safe and slow;
   O Love of God, most wise!

3 And though we turn us from Thy face,
   And wander wide and long,
Thou hold'st us still in kind embrace;
   O Love of God, most strong!

4 But not alone Thy care we claim,
   Our wayward steps to win;
We know Thee by a dearer name,
   O Love of God within!

5 And filled and quickened by Thy breath,
   Our souls are strong and free,
To rise o'er sin and fear and death,
   O Love of God, to Thee!
                              Eliza Scudder

327   *"Thou knowest that I love Thee."*   [POLAND

Do not I love Thee, O my Lord?
   Behold my heart and see;
And turn the dearest idol out
   That dares to rival Thee.

2 Is not Thy name melodious still
   To mine attentive ear?
Doth not each pulse with pleasure bound,
   My Saviour's voice to hear?

3 Hast Thou a lamb in all Thy flock
    I would disdain to feed?
Hast Thou a foe, before whose face
    I fear Thy cause to plead?

4 Would not my heart pour forth its blood
    In honor of Thy name,
And challenge the cold hand of death
    To damp the immortal flame?

5 Thou knowest that I love Thee, Lord;
    But O! I long to soar
Far from the sphere of mortal joys,
    And learn to love Thee more.
Philip Doddridge

328   *"Now are we the sons of God."*   [THACHER

BEHOLD what wondrous grace
    The Father hath bestowed
On sinners of a mortal race,
    To call them sons of God!

2 'Tis no surprising thing
    That we should be unknown;
The Jewish world knew not their King,
    God's Everlasting Son.

3 Nor doth it yet appear
    How great we must be made;
But when we see our Saviour here,
    We shall be like our Head.

4 A hope so much divine
    May trials well endure,
May purge our souls from sense and sin,
    As Christ the Lord is pure.

5 If in my Father's love
 I share a filial part,
 Send down Thy Spirit, like a dove,
 To rest upon my heart.

6 We would no longer lie
 Like slaves beneath the throne;
 Our faith shall Abba, Father, cry,
 And Thou the kindred own. *Isaac Watts*

[HAYDN
329 *"Waiting for the coming of our Lord Jesus Christ."*

Thou art gone up on high
 To mansions in the skies,
And round Thy throne unceasingly
 The songs of praise arise:
But we are lingering here
 With sin and care opprest;
Lord, send Thy promised Comforter,
 And lead us to Thy rest!

2 Thou art gone up on high:
 But Thou didst first come down
Through earth's most bitter agony
 To pass unto Thy crown:
And girt with griefs and fears
 Our onward course must be;
But only let that path of tears
 Lead us at last to Thee!

3 Thou art gone up on high:
 But Thou shalt come again
With all the bright ones of the sky
 Attendant in Thy train.
O by Thy saving power
 So make us live and die,
That we may stand, in that dread hour,
 At Thy right hand on high! *Emma Toke*

330 [ACH GOTT UND HERR
"I go to prepare a place for you."

O CHRIST, who hast prepared a place
For us around Thy throne of grace,
We pray Thee, lift our hearts above
And draw them with the cords of love!

2 Source of all good, Thou, Gracious Lord,
Art our exceeding great reward;
How transient is our present pain,
How boundless our eternal gain!

3 With open face and joyful heart,
We then shall see Thee as Thou art:
Our love shall never cease to glow,
Our praise shall never cease to flow.

4 Thy never-failing grace to prove,
A surety of Thine endless love,
Send down Thy Holy Ghost to be
The raiser of our souls to Thee.

5 O future Judge, Eternal Lord,
Thy name be hallowed and adored!
To God the Father, King of heaven,
And Holy Ghost, like praise be given.
John Chandler

331 [ST. MATTHIAS
"I will come again and receive you unto Myself."

THE golden gates are lifted up,
  The doors are opened wide,
The King of glory is gone in
  Unto His Father's side.

2 Thou art gone up before us, Lord,
  To make for us a place,
That we may be where now Thou art,
  And look upon God's face.

3 And ever on Thine earthly path
  A gleam of glory lies;
  A light still breaks behind the cloud
  That veiled Thee from our eyes.

4 Lift up our hearts, lift up our minds,
  Let Thy dear grace be given,
  That while we tarry here below,
  Our treasure be in heaven!

5 That where Thou art, at God's right hand,
  Our hope, our love, may be;
  Dwell Thou in us, that we may dwell
  For evermore in Thee.

332 *"Having a desire to depart and to be with Christ, which is far better."* [SARDIS

Let me be with Thee where Thou art,
  My Saviour, my eternal Rest!
Then only will this longing heart
  Be fully and for ever blest!

2 Let me be with Thee where Thou art,
  Thy unveiled glory to behold;
Then only will this wandering heart
  Cease to be treacherous, faithless, cold!

Let me be with Thee where Thou art,
  Where spotless saints Thy name adore;
Then only will this sinful heart
  Be evil and defiled no more!

Let me be with Thee where Thou art,
  Where none can die, where none remove;
There neither death nor life will part
  Me from Thy presence and Thy love!
           Charlotte Elliott

333 *"Strangers and pilgrims on the earth."* [AMSTERDAM

    RISE, my soul, and stretch thy wings,
        Thy better portion trace;
    Rise from transitory things
        Toward heaven, thy native place.
    Sun and moon and stars decay;
        Time shall soon this earth remove;
    Rise, my soul, and haste away
        To seats prepared above.

2 Rivers to the ocean run,
        Nor stay in all their course;
    Fire ascending seeks the sun;
        Both speed them to their source:
    So a soul derived from God
        Pants to view His glorious face,
    Upward tends to His abode,
        To rest in His embrace.

3 Cease, ye pilgrims, cease to mourn,
        Press onward to the prize;
    Soon our Saviour will return
        Triumphant in the skies:
    Yet a season, and you know
        Happy entrance will be given,
    All our sorrows left below,
        And earth exchanged for heaven.
                    Robert Seagrave

334 *"Every man that hath this hope in Him,* [MIDNIGHT
      purifieth himself, even as He is pure."

    O THOU who by a star didst guide
        The wise men on their way,
    Until it came and stood beside
        The place where Jesus lay;

2 Although by stars Thou dost not lead
   Thy servants now below,
   Thy Holy Spirit, when they need,
   Will show them how to go.

3 As yet we know Thee but in part;
   But still we trust Thy word,
   That blessed are the pure in heart,
   For they shall see the Lord.

4 O Saviour! give us, then, Thy grace,
   To make us pure in heart;
   That we may see Thee face to face
   Hereafter as Thou art.
                    John Mason Neale

335   "*Hope thou in God.*"   [GETHSEMANE
   IN true and patient hope,
     My soul, on God attend;
   And calmly confident look up,
     Till He salvation send.

2 I shall His goodness see,
     While on His name I call;
   He will defend and strengthen me,
     And I shall never fall.

3 Jesus, to Thee I fly,
     My refuge and my tower;
   Upon Thy faithful love rely,
     And find Thy saving power.

4 Trust in the Lord alone,
     Who aids us from above;
   In every strait surround His throne,
     And hang upon His love.
                    Charles Wesley

336 "*Your life is hid with Christ in God.*" [ABBE VOGLER

O HAPPY soul, that lives on high,
 While men lie groveling here!
His hopes are fixed above the sky,
 And faith forbids his fear.

2 His conscience knows no secret stings;
 While peace and joy combine
To form a life whose holy springs
 Are hidden and divine.

3 He waits in secret on his God,
 His God in secret sees;
Let earth be all in arms abroad,
 He dwells in heavenly peace.

4 His pleasures rise from things unseen,
 Beyond this world and time,
Where neither eyes nor ears have been,
 Nor thoughts of sinners climb.

5 He wants no pomp, nor royal throne,
 To raise his figure here;
Content and pleased to live unknown,
 Till Christ, his Life, appear.

6 He looks to heaven's eternal hill,
 To meet that glorious day;
And patient waits his Saviour's will,
 To fetch his soul away.
       Isaac Watts

337 "*Thou, Lord, wilt bless the righteous.*" [BEETHOVEN

BLEST are the humble souls that see
Their emptiness and poverty;
Treasures of grace to them are given,
And crowns of joy laid up in heaven.

2 Blest are the men of broken heart,
   Who mourn for sin with inward smart;
   The blood of Christ divinely flows,
   A healing balm for all their woes.

3 Blest are the meek, who stand afar
   From rage and passion, noise and war;
   God will secure their happy state,
   And plead their cause against the great.

4 Blest are the souls that thirst for grace,
   Hunger and long for righteousness;
   They shall be well supplied, and fed
   With living streams and living bread.

5 Blest are the merciful, who prove
   By acts their sympathy and love;
   From Christ, the Lord, shall they obtain
   Like sympathy and love again.

6 Blest are the pure, whose hearts are clean
   From the defiling power of sin;
   With endless pleasure they shall see
   A God of spotless purity.

7 Blest are the men of peaceful life,
   Who quench the coals of growing strife;
   They shall be called the heirs of bliss,
   The sons of God, the God of peace.

8 Blest are the sufferers, who partake
   Of pain and shame for Jesus' sake!
   Their souls shall triumph in the Lord,
   Glory and joy are their reward.

Isaac Watts

338 "*Because I live, ye shall live also.*" [ASHFORD

WHEN sins and fears prevailing rise,
  And fainting hope almost expires,
To Thee, O Lord, I lift mine eyes,
  To Thee I breathe my soul's desires.

2 Art Thou not mine, my living Lord?
  And can my hope, my comfort die—
Fixed on Thine everlasting word,
  That word which built the earth and sky?

3 If my immortal Saviour lives,
  Then my immortal life is sure;
His word a firm foundation gives;
  Here let me build, and rest secure.

4 Here let my faith unshaken dwell;
  For ever sure the promise stands:
Not all the powers of earth or hell
  Can e'er dissolve the sacred bands.

5 Here, O my soul, thy trust repose!
  If Jesus is for ever mine,
Not death itself—that last of foes—
  Shall break a union so divine.
                    Anne Steele

339 "*On Thee do I wait all the day.*" [GRIFFITH

To God, in whom I trust,
  I lift my heart and voice;
O let me not be put to shame,
  Nor let my foes rejoice.

2 To me Thy truth impart,
  And lead me in Thy way:
For Thou art He that brings me help;
  On Thee I wait all day.

3 Thy mercies and Thy love,
    O Lord, recall to mind;
   And graciously continue still,
    As Thou wert ever, kind.

4 Let all my youthful crimes
    Be blotted out by Thee;
   And for Thy wondrous goodness' sake
    In mercy think on me.

5 His mercy and His truth
    The righteous Lord displays,
   In bringing wandering sinners home,
    And teaching them His ways.
                            Tate and Brady

340 *"I will never leave thee nor forsake thee."* [DALTON

O HELP us, Lord! each hour of need,
  Thy heavenly succor give;
 Help us in thought, and word, and deed,
  Each hour on earth we live!

2 O help us when our spirits bleed
   With contrite anguish sore;
  And when our hearts are cold and dead,
   O help us, Lord, the more!

3 O help us through the prayer of faith,
   More firmly to believe;
  For still, the more the servant hath,
   The more shall he receive.

4 O help us, Jesus, from on high!
   We know no help but Thee:
  O help us so to live and die,
   As Thine in heaven to be.
                    Henry Hart Milman

341   *"Grace and truth came by Jesus Christ."*   [TRUST

Come, Thou Fount of every blessing,
  Tune my heart to sing Thy grace;
Streams of mercy never ceasing,
  Call for songs of loudest praise.

2 Teach me some melodious sonnet,
  Sung by flaming tongues above;
Praise the mount, I'm fixed upon it,
  Mount of God's unchanging love.

3 Jesus sought me, when a stranger,
  Wandering from the fold of God;
He, to rescue me from danger,
  Interposed His precious blood.

4 O! to grace how great a debtor,
  Daily I'm constrained to be:
Let that grace now, like a fetter,
  Bind my wandering heart to Thee!

5 Prone to wander, Lord, I feel it,
  Prone to leave the God I love:
Here's my heart, O take and seal it,
  Seal it from Thy courts above!
                      Robert Robinson

342   *"Blessed are the pure in heart."*   [ST. ANN'S

Blessed are they whose hearts are pure,
  From guile their spirits free:
To them shall God reveal Himself,
  They shall His glory see.

2 Their simple souls upon His word
  In fullest light of love
Place all their trust, and ask no more
  Than guidance from above.

3 Who in meek faith unmixed with doubt
  The engrafted word receive,
  Whom the first sign of heavenly power
  Persuades, and they believe:

4 They, as they walk the painful world,
  See hidden glories rise:
  Our God the sunshine of His love
  Unfolds before their eyes.

5 For them far greater things than these
  Doth Christ the Lord prepare:
  Whose bliss no heart of man can reach,
  No human voice declare.
              Josiah Conder

343   *"They shall see God."*   [THACHER

BLEST are the pure in heart,
  For they shall see our God:
The secret of the Lord is theirs,
  Their soul is Christ's abode.

2 The Lord, who left the heavens
    Our life and peace to bring,
  To dwell in lowliness with men,
    Their Pattern and their King:

3 Still to the lowly soul
    He doth Himself impart,
  And for His dwelling and His throne
    Chooseth the pure in heart.

4 Lord, we Thy presence seek;
    May ours this blessing be;
  Give us a pure and lowly heart,
    A temple meet for Thee!
              John Keble

Christian Joy and Hope

344   *"In the Lord Jehovah is everlasting strength."*   [TOPLADY]

ROCK of ages! cleft for me,
Let me hide myself in Thee!
Let the water and the blood,
From Thy riven side which flowed,
Be of sin the double cure,
Cleanse me from its guilt and power.

2 Not the labors of my hands
Can fulfil Thy laws' demands;
Could my zeal no respite know,
Could my tears for ever flow,
All for sin could not atone;
Thou must save, and Thou alone.

3 Nothing in my hand I bring;
Simply to Thy cross I cling;
Naked, come to Thee for dress;
Helpless, look to Thee for grace;
Foul, I to the Fountain fly;
Wash me, Saviour, or I die!

4 While I draw this fleeting breath,
When my eyelids close in death,
When I soar to worlds unknown,
See Thee on Thy judgment-throne;
Rock of ages, cleft for me,
Let me hide myself in Thee!

Augustus Montague Toplady

345   *"Thou shalt hide them in the secret of Thy presence."*   [MANCHESTER]

THERE is a safe and secret place
  Beneath the wings divine,
Reserved for all the heirs of grace;
  O be that refuge mine!

2 The least and feeblest there may bide,
    Uninjured and unawed;
  While thousands fall on every side,
    He rests secure in God.

3 He feeds in pastures large and fair
    Of love and truth divine:
  O child of God, O glory's heir,
    How rich a lot is thine!

4 A hand Almighty to defend,
    An ear for every call,
  An honored life, a peaceful end,
    And heaven to crown it all!
                Henry Francis Lyte

346 *"I have made a covenant with My chosen."* [COVENTRY

  UNITE, my roving thoughts, unite
    In silence soft and sweet:
  And thou, my soul, sit gently down
    At thy great Sovereign's feet.

2 Jehovah's awful voice is heard,
    Yet gladly I attend;
  For lo! the Everlasting God
    Proclaims Himself my friend.

3 Harmonious accents to my soul
    The sounds of peace convey;
  The tempest at His word subsides,
    And winds and seas obey.

4 By all its joys, I charge my heart,
    To grieve His love no more;
  But charmed by melody divine,
    To give its follies o'er.
                Philip Doddridge

Christian Joy and Hope

347   "*I flee unto Thee to hide me.*"   [ROBBINS

FAR from the world, O Lord, I flee,
  From strife and tumult far;
From scenes where Satan wages still
  His most successful war.

2 The calm retreat, the silent shade,
  With prayer and praise agree,
And seem by Thy sweet bounty made
  For those who follow Thee.

3 There, if Thy Spirit touch the soul,
  And grace her mean abode,
O with what peace, and joy, and love,
  Does she commune with God!

4 Author and Guardian of my life;
  Sweet Source of light divine;
And, all harmonious names in one,
  My Saviour! Thou art mine!

5 What thanks I owe Thee, and what love,—
  A boundless, endless store,—
Shall echo through the realms above
  When time shall be no more!
                William Cowper

348   "*Who loved me and gave Himself for me.*"   [CASSEL

THOU art my hiding-place, O Lord!
  In Thee I put my trust,
Encouraged by Thy holy word,—
  A feeble child of dust.
I have no argument beside,
  I urge no other plea;
And 'tis enough the Saviour died,
  The Saviour died for me!

2 When storms of fierce temptation beat
   And furious foes assail,
My refuge is the mercy-seat,
   My hope within the veil.
From strife of tongues and bitter words,
   My spirit flies to Thee;
Joy to my heart the thought affords,
   My Saviour died for me!

3 And when Thine awful voice commands
   This body to decay,
And life, in its last lingering sands,
   Is ebbing fast away;—
Then, though it be in accents weak,
   My voice shall call on Thee,
And ask for strength in death to speak,
   'My Saviour died for me!'
Thomas Raffles

349 *"I will fear no evil, for Thou art with me."* [TEMA

In heavenly love abiding,
   No change my heart shall fear;
And safe is such confiding,
   For nothing changes here.
The storm may roar without me,
   My heart may low be laid,
But God is round about me,
   And can I be dismayed?

2 Wherever He may guide me,
   No want shall turn me back;
My Shepherd is beside me,
   And nothing can I lack.
His wisdom ever waketh,
   His sight is never dim,
He knows the way He taketh,
   And I will walk with Him.

3 Green pastures are before me,
    Which yet I have not seen;
  Bright skies will soon be o'er me,
    Where darkest clouds have been.
  My hope I cannot measure,
    My path to life is free,
  My Saviour has my treasure,
    And He will walk with me.
                    Anna Lætitia Waring

350   "*The Lord is Thy Keeper.*"   [LEE
  How are Thy servants blest, O Lord,
    How sure is their defence!
  Eternal Wisdom is their guide,
    Their help, Omnipotence.

2 In foreign realms and lands remote,
    Supported by Thy care,
  Through burning climes they pass unhurt,
    And breathe in tainted air.

3 When by the dreadful tempest borne
    High on the broken wave,
  They know Thou art not slow to hear,
    Nor impotent to save.

4 The storm is laid, the winds retire,
    Obedient to Thy will;
  The sea, that roars at Thy command,
    At Thy command is still.

5 In midst of dangers, fears, and deaths,
    Thy goodness we'll adore;
  And praise Thee for Thy mercies past,
    And humbly hope for more.

6 Our life, while Thou preserv'st that life,
  Thy sacrifice shall be;
And death, when death shall be our lot,
  Shall join our souls to Thee.
                    Joseph Addison

351 *"Because he hath set his love upon Me, there-* [AUTUMN
        fore will I deliver him."

CALL Jehovah thy salvation,
  Rest beneath the Almighty's shade;
In His secret habitation
  Dwell, nor ever be dismayed:
There no tumult can alarm thee,
  Thou shalt dread no hidden snare;
Guile nor violence can harm thee,
  In eternal safeguard there.

2 From the sword at noon-day wasting,
  From the noisome pestilence,
In the depth of midnight blasting,
  God shall be thy sure defence:
Fear not thou the deadly quiver,
  When a thousand feel the blow;
Mercy shall thy soul deliver,
  Though ten thousand be laid low.

3 Since, with pure and firm affection,
  Thou on God hast set thy love,
With the wings of His protection,
  He will shield thee from above:
Thou shalt call on Him in trouble,
  He will hearken, He will save,
Here, for grief reward thee double,
  Crown with life beyond the grave.
                    James Montgomery

Christian Joy and Hope

352   *"His mercy endureth for ever."*   [BRATTLE ST.

WHILE Thee I seek, protecting Power,
  Be my vain wishes stilled;
And may this consecrated hour
  With better hopes be filled.
Thy love the powers of thought bestowed!
  To Thee my thoughts would soar;
Thy mercy o'er my life has flowed;
  That mercy I adore.

2 In each event of life, how clear
  Thy ruling hand I see!
Each blessing to my soul more dear,
  Because conferred by Thee.
In every joy that crowns my days,
  In every pain I bear,
My heart shall find delight in praise,
  Or seek relief in prayer.

3 When gladness wings my favored hour,
  Thy love my thoughts shall fill;
Resigned, when storms of sorrow lower,
  My soul shall meet Thy will.
My lifted eye, without a tear,
  The gathering storm shall see;
My steadfast heart shall know no fear;
  That heart shall rest on Thee.
              Helen Maria Williams

353   *"Above all, taking the shield of faith."*   [ST. JOHANNES

FAITH is the polar star
  That guides the Christian's way,
Directs his wanderings from afar
  To realms of endless day:
It points the course, where'er he roam,
And safely leads the pilgrim home.

2 Faith is the rainbow's form
  Hung on the brow of heaven,
  The glory of the passing storm,
  The pledge of mercy given;
  It is the bright, triumphal arch,
  Through which the saints to glory march.

3 The faith that works by love,
  And purifies the heart,
  A foretaste of the joys above
  To mortals can impart:
  It bears us through this earthly strife,
  And triumphs in immortal life.

[TAMWORTH

354 *"He hath remembered His covenant for ever."*

GUIDE me, O Thou great Jehovah,
  Pilgrim through this barren land;
I am weak, but Thou art mighty,
  Hold me with Thy powerful hand;
    Bread of heaven,
  Feed me till I want no more.

2 Open now the crystal fountain,
    Whence the healing waters flow;
  Let the fiery cloudy pillar
    Lead me all my journey through:
      Strong Deliverer,
    Be Thou still my strength and shield.

3 When I tread the verge of Jordan,
    Bid the swelling stream divide;
  Death of death, and hell's destruction,
    Land me safe on Canaan's side:
      Songs of praises
    I will ever give to Thee.

William Williams

355 *"The just shall live by faith."* [PRAYER

FAITH adds new charms to earthly bliss,
  And saves us from its snares;
Its aid in every duty brings,
  And softens all our cares.

2 It heals the deadly thirst of sin;
  It lights the sacred fire
Of love to God and heavenly things,
  And feeds the pure desire.

3 The wounded conscience knows its power,
  The healing balm to give;
That balm the saddest heart can cheer,
  And make the dying live.

4 It shows the precious promise, sealed
  With the Redeemer's blood;
And helps our feeble hope to rest
  Upon a faithful God.

5 Wide it unveils celestial worlds,
  Where deathless pleasures reign;
And bids us seek our portion there,
  Nor bids us seek in vain.
                                Daniel Turner

[PRAYER
356 *"God having provided some better thing for us."*

FAITH is the dawning of the day
  Where darkness was before,
The rising of a solar ray
  To set in night no more.

2 Faith gives a hand that holds the heart
  Within the mystic veil,
Fast by that Friend who will not part
  From those who will not fail.

3 Faith takes her balances of gold
  And weighs with skill sublime
  Eternal happiness untold,
  Against the dream of time.

4 O Lord, increase this grace in me,
  That with each fleeting breath
  I more and more may know of Thee,
  And hail the hand of death.

5 So faith shall in fruition end,
  And grace in glory cease,
  Where praise her powers can never spend
  Nor aught disturb their peace.
            Matthew Bridges

[BRADFORD

357 *"If thou canst believe, all things are possible."*

  LORD, I believe; Thy power I own,
  Thy word I would obey;
  I wander comfortless and lone,
  When from Thy truth I stray.

2 Lord, I believe; but gloomy fears
  Sometimes bedim my sight;
  I look to Thee with prayers and tears,
  And cry for strength and light.

3 Lord, I believe; but oft, I know,
  My faith is cold and weak:
  My weakness strengthen, and bestow
  The confidence I seek!

4 Yes! I believe; and only Thou
  Can give my soul relief:
  Lord! to Thy truth my spirit bow;
  Help Thou mine unbelief!
            John Reynell Wreford

358 *"Who is he that overcometh the world, but he that believeth that Jesus is the Son of God?"* [SELDON

O GIFT of gifts! O grace of faith!
My God, how can it be
That Thou who hast discerning love
Dost give that gift to me!

2 How many hearts Thou mightst have had
More innocent than mine!
How many souls more worthy far
Of that sweet touch of Thine!

3 Ah Grace! into unlikeliest hearts
It is Thy boast to come,
The glory of Thy light to find
In darkest spots a home.

4 How can they live, how will they die,
How bear the cross of grief,
Who have not got the light of faith,
The courage of belief?

5 The crowd of cares, the weightiest cross,
Seem trifles less than light;
Earth looks so little and so low,
When faith shines full and bright.

6 O happy, happy that I am!
If Thou canst be, O Faith,
The treasure that thou art in life,
What wilt Thou be in death!

7 Thy choice, O God of goodness, then,
I lovingly adore;
O give me grace to keep Thy grace,
And grace to merit more.

Frederick William Faber

359 *"We walk by faith, not by sight."* [ADMITTANCE

As when the weary traveler gains
  The hight of some o'erlooking hill,
His heart revives, if, 'cross the plains,
  He eyes his home though distant still;—

2 So when the Christian pilgrim views,
  By faith, his mansion in the skies;
The sight his fainting strength renews,
  And wings his speed to reach the prize.

3 'Tis there, he says, I am to dwell
  With Jesus in the realms of day:
Then I shall bid my cares farewell,
  And He will wipe my tears away.
                              John Newton

360 *"Blessed are they who have not seen, and* [ST. ANN'S
         yet have believed."

O Thou who didst, with love untold,
  Thy doubting servant chide,
And bade the eye of sense behold
  Thy wounded hands and side:

2 Grant us, like him, with heartfelt awe,
  To own Thee God and Lord,
And from his hour of doubt to draw
  Faith in the incarnate Word.

3 And grant that we may never dare
  Thy loving heart to grieve,
But at the last their blessing share
  Who see not, yet believe:

4 That when our life of faith is done,
  In realms of clearer light
We Thee may view, Incarnate Son,
  With full and endless sight.
                              Emma Toke

Christian Joy and Hope

361   [BRADFORD
"*We which have believed do enter into rest.*"

    LORD, I believe a rest remains,
      To all Thy people known;
    A rest where pure enjoyment reigns,
      And Thou art loved alone.

2 A rest·where all our souls' desire
      Is fixed on things above;
    Where fear and sin and grief expire,
      Cast out by perfect love.

3 O that I now the rest might know,
      Believe and enter in!
    Now, Saviour! now the power bestow,
      And let me cease from sin.

4 Remove the hardness of my heart,
      The unbelief remove;
    To me the rest of faith impart,
      The Sabbath of Thy love.
                    Charles Wesley

362   "*Behold the Lamb of God!*"   [OLIVET

    MY faith looks up to Thee,
    Thou Lamb of Calvary,
      Saviour divine:
    Now hear me while I pray;
    Take all my guilt away;
    O let me from this day
      Be wholly Thine.

2 May Thy rich grace impart
    Strength to my fainting heart,
      My zeal inspire;
    As Thou hast died for me,
    O may my love to Thee,
    Pure, warm, and changeless be—
      A living fire.

3 While life's dark maze I tread,
   And griefs around me spread,
      Be Thou my guide;
   Bid darkness turn to day,
   Wipe sorrow's tears away,
   Nor let me ever stray
      From Thee aside.

4 When ends life's transient dream,
   When death's cold, sullen stream
      Shall o'er me roll;
   Blest Saviour, then, in love,
   Fear and distrust remove;
   O bear me safe above—
      A ransomed soul.
                              Ray Palmer

363 *"Your joy no man taketh from you."* [ARLINGTON

When I can read my title clear
   To mansions in the skies,
I bid farewell to every fear,
   And wipe my weeping eyes.

2 Should earth against my soul engage,
   And hellish darts be hurled,
Then I can smile at Satan's rage,
   And face a frowning world.

3 Let cares like a wild deluge come,
   And storms of sorrow fall;
May I but safely reach my home,
   My God, my heaven, my all;—

4 There shall I bathe my weary soul
   In seas of heavenly rest;
And not a wave of trouble roll
   Across my peaceful breast.
                              Isaac Watts

364   *"The just shall live by faith."*   [MERIBAH

O Thou that hear'st the prayer of faith,
Wilt Thou not save a soul from death,
   That casts itself on Thee?
I have no refuge of my own,
But fly to what my Lord hath done
   And suffered once for me.

2 Slain in the guilty sinner's stead,
His spotless righteousness I plead,
   And His availing blood:
Thy merit, Lord, my robe shall be,
Thy merit shall atone for me
   And bring me near to God.

3 Then save me from eternal death,
The Spirit of adoption breathe,
   His consolations send:
By Him some word of life impart,
And sweetly whisper to my heart,—
   'Thy Maker is thy Friend.'

4 The king of terrors then would be
A welcome messenger to me,
   To bid me come away:
Unclogged by earth or earthly things,
I'd mount, I'd fly, with eager wings,
   To everlasting day.
               Augustus Montague Toplady

365   *"Faith, the evidence of things not seen."*   [SARDIS

'Tis by the faith of joys to come,
   We walk through deserts dark as night;
Till we arrive at heaven, our home,
   Faith is our guide, and faith our light.

2 The want of sight she well supplies;
   She makes the pearly gates appear;
   Far into distant worlds she pries,
   And brings eternal glories near.

3 Cheerful we tread the desert through,
   While faith inspires a heavenly ray;
   Though lions roar, and tempests blow,
   And rocks and dangers fill the way.

4 So Abra'm by divine command
   Left his own house to walk with God;
   His faith beheld the promised land
   And fired his zeal along the road.
                              Isaac Watts

366 *"A pillar of fire, to give them light."* [PROTECTION

LEAD, kindly Light, amid the encircling gloom,
     Lead Thou me on!
The night is dark, and I am far from home—
     Lead Thou me on!
Keep Thou my feet; I do not ask to see
The distant scene,—one step enough for me.

2 I was not ever thus, nor prayed that Thou
     Should lead me on,
   I loved to choose and see my path, but now
     Lead Thou me on!
   I loved the garish day, and, spite of fears,
   Pride ruled my will: remember not past years.

3 So long Thy power hath blest me, sure it still
     Will lead me on,
   O'er moor and fen, o'er crag and torrent, till
     The night is gone;
   And with the morn those angel faces smile
   Which I have loved long since, and lost awhile.
                              John Henry Newman

Christian Joy and Hope

367 *"We shall be like Him, for we shall see Him as He is."* [SELDON

WE walk by faith, and not by sight;
　No gracious words we hear
From Him who spake as never man,
　But we believe Him near.

2 We may not touch His hands and side,
　　Nor follow where He trod;
　But in His promise we rejoice,
　　And cry 'My Lord and God!'

3 Help Thou, O Lord, our unbelief;
　　And may our faith abound,
　To call on Thee when Thou art near,
　　And seek where Thou art found:

4 That when our life of faith is done,
　　In realms of clearer light
　We may behold Thee as Thou art,
　　With full and endless sight.
　　　　　　　　Henry Alford

368 *"Ye shall know the truth, and the truth shall make you free."* [BRADFORD

I KNOW that my Redeemer lives,
　And ever prays for me;
A token of His love He gives,
　A pledge of liberty.

2 I find Him lifting up my head;
　　He brings salvation near;
　His presence makes me free indeed,
　　And He will soon appear.

3 He wills that I should holy be;
　　What can withstand His will?
　The counsel of His grace in me
　　He surely shall fulfill.

4 Jesus, I hang upon Thy word;
   I steadfastly believe
   Thou wilt return, and claim me, Lord,
   And to Thyself receive.

5 When God is mine, and I am His,
   Of paradise possest,
   I taste unutterable bliss
   And everlasting rest.
                              Charles Wesley

369 *"Arise, shine; for thy Light is come."* [WILMOT
   LIGHT of those whose dreary dwelling
   Borders on the shades of death!
   Rise on us, Thyself revealing,—
   Dissipate the clouds beneath.

2 Thou, of heaven and earth Creator!
   In our deepest darkness rise;
   Scattering all the night of nature,
   Pouring day upon our eyes.

3 Still we wait for Thine appearing;
   Life and joy Thy beams impart,
   Chasing all our fears, and cheering
   Every poor benighted heart.

4 Save us, in Thy great compassion,
   O Thou mild, pacific Prince!
   Give the knowledge of salvation,
   Give the pardon of our sins.

5 By Thine all-restoring merit,
   Every burdened soul release;
   Every weary, wandering spirit
   Guide into Thy perfect peace.
                              Charles Wesley

370 *"The righteousness which is of God by faith."* [CREDO

No more, my God! I boast no more,
  Of all the duties I have done;
I quit the hopes I held before,
  To trust the merits of Thy Son.

2 Now, for the love I bear His name,
  What was my gain I count my loss;
My former pride I call my shame,
  And nail my glory to His cross.

3 Yes,—and I must and will esteem
  All things but loss for Jesus' sake;
O may my soul be found in Him,
  And of His righteousness partake!

4 The best obedience of my hands
  Dare not appear before Thy throne;
But faith can answer Thy demands,
  By pleading what my Lord has done.
                    Isaac Watts

371 *"Lord, lift Thou up the light of Thy countenance upon us."* [LEE

ETERNAL Sun of righteousness,
  Display Thy beams divine,
And cause the glory of Thy face
  Upon my heart to shine!

2 Light, in Thy light, O may I see,
  Thy grace and mercy prove,
Revived, and cheered, and blest by Thee,
  The God of pardoning love.

3 Lift up Thy countenance serene,
  And let Thy happy child
Behold, without a cloud between,
  The Father reconciled.

4 On me Thy promised peace bestow,
    The peace by Jesus given;—
  The joys of holiness below,
    And then the joys of heaven.
                    Charles Wesley

372   "*Walk as children of light.*"   [ABBE VOGLER
  O FOR a closer walk with God,
    A calm and heavenly frame!
  A light to shine upon the road
    That leads me to the Lamb!

2 Where is the blessedness I knew
    When first I saw the Lord?
  Where is the soul-refreshing view
    Of Jesus and His word?

3 What peaceful hours I once enjoyed!
    How sweet their memory still!
  But they have left an aching void
    The world can never fill.

4 Return, O holy Dove! return,
    Sweet Messenger of rest!
  I hate the sins that made Thee mourn,
    And drove Thee from my breast.

5 The dearest idol I have known,
    Whate'er that idol be,
  Help me to tear it from Thy throne,
    And worship only Thee!

6 So shall my walk be close with God,
    Calm and serene my frame;
  So purer light shall mark the road
    That leads me to the Lamb!
                    William Cowper

Christian Joy and Hope

[St. Crispin
373 *"Him that cometh to Me, I will in no wise cast out."*

Just as I am, without one plea
But that Thy blood was shed for me,
And that Thou bidd'st me come to Thee,
 O Lamb of God, I come!

2 Just as I am, and waiting not
To rid my soul of one dark blot,
To Thee whose blood can cleanse each spot,
 O Lamb of God, I come!

3 Just as I am, though tost about
With many a conflict, many a doubt,
Fightings and fears, within, without,
 O Lamb of God, I come!

4 Just as I am, poor, wretched, blind,
Sight, riches, healing of the mind,
Yea, all I need, in Thee to find,
 O Lamb of God, I come!

5 Just as I am, Thou wilt receive,
Wilt welcome, pardon, cleanse, relieve!
Because Thy promise I believe,
 O Lamb of God, I come!

6 Just as I am,—Thy love unknown
Has broken every barrier down,—
Now to be Thine, yea, Thine alone,
 O Lamb of God, I come!
                            Charlotte Elliott

[Seldon
374 *"Come ye, and let us walk in the light of the Lord."*

Walk in the light! so shalt thou know
 That fellowship of love
His Spirit only can bestow
 Who reigns in light above.

2 Walk in the light! and sin abhorred
    Shall not defile again;
  The blood of Jesus Christ the Lord
    Shall cleanse from every stain.

3 Walk in the light! and thou shalt find
    Thy heart made truly His,
  Who dwells in cloudless light enshrined,
    In whom no darkness is.

4 Walk in the light! and thou shalt own
    Thy darkness past away,
  Because in thee that light hath shone
    Which grows to perfect day.

5 Walk in the light! and e'en the tomb
    No fearful shade shall wear;
  Glory shall chase away its gloom,
    For Christ hath conquered there!

6 Walk in the light! and thine shall be
    A path, though thorny, bright;
  For God by grace shall dwell in thee,
    And God Himself is light!
                              Bernard Barton

375   "*I am the Light of the world.*   [PHRYGIA
  O ONE with God the Father
    In majesty and might,
  The brightness of His glory,
    Eternal Light of Light!
  O'er this our home of darkness
    Thy rays are streaming now;
  The shadows flee before Thee,
    The world's true Light art Thou.

2 Yet, Lord, we see but darkly:
   O heavenly Light, arise,
Dispel these mists that shroud us
   And hide Thee from our eyes!
We long to track the footprints
   That Thou Thyself hast trod;
We long to see the pathway
   That leads to Thee our God.

3 O Jesus, shine around us
   With radiance of Thy grace;
O Jesus, turn upon us
   The brightness of Thy face.
We need no star to guide us,
   As on our way we press,
If Thou Thy light vouchsafest,
   O Sun of righteousness!

376   *"He that hath ears to hear, let him hear."*   [CASSEL

I HEARD the voice of Jesus say,
   'Come unto Me and rest;
Lay down, thou weary one, lay down
   Thy head upon My breast!'
I came to Jesus as I was,
   Weary and worn and sad;
I found in Him a resting-place,
   And He has made me glad.

2 I heard the voice of Jesus say,
   'Behold! I freely give
The living water; thirsty one,
   Stoop down, and drink, and live!'
I came to Jesus, and I drank
   Of that life-giving stream;
My thirst was quenched, my soul revived,
   And now I live in Him.

3 I heard the voice of Jesus say,
   'I am this dark world's Light;
   Look unto Me, thy morn shall rise,
   And all thy day be bright.'
   I looked to Jesus, and I found
   In Him my Star, my Sun;
   And in that light of life I'll walk
   Till traveling days are done.
   Horatius Bonar

[RETREAT
377 *"In the secret of His tabernacle shall He hide me."*

FROM every stormy wind that blows,
From every swelling tide of woes,
There is a calm, a sure retreat;—
'Tis found beneath the mercy seat.

2 There is a place where Jesus sheds
   The oil of gladness on our heads;
   A place than all beside more sweet,—
   It is the blood-bought mercy seat.

3 There is a scene where spirits blend;
   Where friend holds fellowship with friend;
   Though sundered far, by faith they meet
   Around one common mercy-seat.

4 There, there on eagle wings we soar,
   And sin and sense molest no more;
   And heaven comes down, our souls to greet,
   And glory crowns the mercy-seat.

5 O may my hand forget her skill,
   My tongue be silent, cold, and still,
   This bounding heart forget to beat,
   If I forget the mercy-seat!
   Hugh Stowell

Christian Joy and Hope

378 [Chant

From the recesses of a lowly spirit,
Our humble prayer ascends; O Father, hear it,
Upsoaring on the wings of awe and meekness!
    Forgive its weakness!

2 We see Thy hand; it leads us, it supports us:
We hear Thy voice; it counsels and it courts us:
And then we turn away; and still Thy kindness
    Forgives our blindness.

3 O how long-suffering, Lord! but Thou delightest
To win with love the wandering; Thou invitest
By smiles of mercy, not by frowns or terrors,
    Man from his errors.

4 Father and Saviour! plant within each bosom
The seeds of holiness, and bid them blossom
In fragrance and in beauty bright and vernal,
    And spring eternal.

5 Then place them in Thine everlasting gardens,
Where angels walk and seraphs are the wardens;
Where every flower escaped through death's dark portal
    Becomes immortal.
John Bowring

379   "*Continuing instant in prayer.*"   [Prayer

Prayer is the soul's sincere desire,
    Unuttered, or exprest;
The motion of a hidden fire
    That trembles in the breast.

2 Prayer is the burden of a sigh,
   The falling of a tear;
   The upward glancing of the eye,
   When none but God is near.

3 Prayer is the simplest form of speech
   That infant lips can try;
   Prayer the sublimest strains that reach
   The Majesty on high.

4 Prayer is the contrite sinner's voice,
   Returning from his ways;
   While angels in their songs rejoice,
   And cry—'Behold, he prays.'

5 Prayer is the Christian's vital breath,
   The Christian's native air,
   His watchword at the gates of death;
   He enters heaven with prayer.

6 The saints, in prayer, appear as one
   In word, and deed, and mind;
   While with the Father and the Son
   Sweet fellowship they find.

7 Nor prayer is made by man alone:
   The Holy Spirit pleads;
   And Jesus, on the eternal throne,
   For sinners intercedes.

8 O Thou, by whom we come to God—
   The Life, the Truth, the Way;
   The path of prayer Thyself hast trod;
   Lord, teach us how to pray.
                        James Montgomery

380   *"Lord, teach us to pray."*   [DALTON

Lord, teach us how to pray aright,
  With reverence and with fear:
Though dust and ashes in Thy sight,
  We may, we must, draw near.

2 God of all grace, we come to Thee,
  With broken, contrite hearts;
Give what Thine eye delights to see,—
  Truth in the inward parts.

3 Give deep humility; the sense
  Of godly sorrow give;
A strong, desiring confidence
  To hear Thy voice and live;—

4 Patience, to watch, and wait, and weep,
  Though mercy long delay;
Courage, our fainting souls to keep,
  And trust Thee, though Thou slay.

5 Give these, and then Thy will be done:
  Thus strengthened with all might,
We, through Thy Spirit and Thy Son,
  Shall pray, and pray aright.
               James Montgomery

                                [CALVARY
381   *"I will make an everlasting covenant with you."*

They who seek the throne of grace,
Find that throne in every place:
If we live a life of prayer,
God is present every where.

2 In our sickness or our health,
In our want or in our wealth,
If we look to God in prayer,
God is present every where.

3 When our earthly comforts fail,
  When the foes of life prevail,
  'Tis the time for earnest prayer;—
  God is present every where.

4 Then, my soul, in every strait
  To thy Father come and wait;
  He will answer every prayer;
  God is present every where.

[PLEYEL'S HYMN

382 *"Unto every one of us is given grace according to the measure of the gift of Christ."*

FATHER, hear our humble claim:
We are met in Thy great name;
In the midst do Thou appear,
Manifest Thy presence here.

2 Lord, our fellowship increase;
  Knit us in the bond of peace;
  Join our hearts, O Father, join
  Each to each, and all to Thine.

3 Move and actuate and guide,
  Diverse gifts to each divide;
  Placed according to Thy will,
  Let us each his work fulfill.

4 Build us in one Spirit up,
  Called in one high calling's hope,
  One the Spirit, one the aim,
  One the pure baptismal flame:

5 One the faith, and one the Lord,
  Whom, by heaven and earth adored,
  We our God and Father call,—
  O'er all, through all, in us all.

Christian Joy and Hope

383 *"Bow down Thine ear, O Lord, hear me."* [Credo

When at Thy footstool, Lord, I bend,
　And plead with Thee for mercy there,
Think of the sinner's dying Friend,
　And for His sake receive my prayer.

2 O think not of my shame and guilt,
　　My thousand stains of deepest dye;
　Think of the blood which Jesus spilt,
　　And let that blood my pardon buy.

3 Think, Lord, how I am still Thine own,
　　The trembling creature of Thy hand;
　Think how my heart to sin is prone,
　　And what temptations round me stand.

4 O think not of my doubts and fears,
　　My strivings with Thy grace divine:
　Think upon Jesus' woes and tears,
　　And let His merits stand for mine.

5 Thine eye, Thine ear, they are not dull;
　　Thine arm can never shortened be;
　Behold me here; my heart is full;
　　Behold, and spare, and succor me!
　　　　　　　　Henry Francis Lyte

384 *"My soul, wait thou only upon God."* [Seldon

Author of good! to Thee we turn:
　Thine ever-wakeful eye
Alone can all our wants discern,
　Thine hand alone supply.

2 O let Thy love within us dwell,
　　Thy fear our footsteps guide;
　That love shall vainer loves expel,
　　That fear, all fears beside.

3 And since, by passion's force subdued,
    Too oft, with stubborn will,
  We blindly shun the latent good,
    And grasp the specious ill;—

4 Not what we wish, but what we want,
    Let mercy still supply:
  The good we ask not, Father, grant!
    The ill we ask, deny!
                              James Merrick

385 *"Whosoever shall call upon the name of the* [HEBER
       Lord shall be saved."

  APPROACH, my soul, the mercy-seat
    Where Jesus answers prayer;
  There humbly fall before His feet,
    For none can perish there.

2 Thy promise is my only plea,
    With this I venture nigh;
  Thou callest burdened souls to Thee,
    And such, O Lord, am I.

3 Bowed down beneath a load of sin,
    By Satan sorely prest,
  By war without and fears within,
    I come to Thee for rest.

4 Be Thou my shield and hiding-place,
    That, sheltered near Thy side,
  I may my fierce accuser face,
    And tell him Thou hast died!

5 O wondrous love! to bleed and die,
    To bear the cross and shame,
  That guilty sinners, such as I,
    Might plead Thy gracious name!
                              John Newton

386   *"God is our Refuge and Strength."*   [HEBER

My God, 'tis to Thy mercy-seat
    My soul for shelter flies:
'Tis here I find a safe retreat,
    When storms and tempests rise.

2 My cheerful hope can never die,
    If Thou, my God, art near;
Thy grace can raise my comforts high,
    And banish every fear.

3 My great Protector and my Lord,
    Thy constant aid impart;
And let Thy kind, Thy gracious word
    Sustain my trembling heart.

4 O never let my soul remove
    From this divine retreat;
Still let me trust Thy power and love,
    And dwell beneath Thy feet.
                        Anne Steele

387   *"If we ask anything according to His*   [INVITATION
        will, He heareth us."

Come, my soul, thy suit prepare,
Jesus loves to answer prayer:
He Himself has bid thee pray,
Therefore will not say thee nay.

2 Thou art coming to a King,
Large petitions with thee bring:
For His grace and power are such,
None can ever ask too much.

3 With my burden I begin:
Lord, remove this load of sin!
Let Thy blood, for sinners spilt,
Set my conscience free from guilt!

4 Lord, I come to Thee for rest;
   Take possession of my breast;
   There Thy blood-bought right maintain,
   And without a rival reign.

5 While I am a pilgrim here,
   Let Thy love my spirit cheer;
   As my Guide, my Guard, my Friend,
   Lead me to my journey's end!

6 Show me what I have to do;
   Every hour my strength renew;
   Let me live a life of faith,
   Let me die Thy people's death.
                           John Newton

388 *"Seek ye first the Kingdom of God, and* [ADMITTANCE
       His righteousness."

AND dost Thou say, 'Ask what thou wilt?'
   Lord, I would seize the golden hour:
I pray to be released from guilt,
   And freed from sin and Satan's power.

2 More of Thy presence, Lord, impart;
   More of Thine image let me bear;
   Erect Thy throne within my heart,
   And reign without a rival there.

3 Give me to read my pardon sealed,
   And from Thy joy to draw my strength;
   O, be Thy boundless love revealed,
   In all its hight, and breadth, and length.

4 Grant these requests—I ask no more;
   But to Thy care the rest resign;
   Sick, or in health, or rich, or poor,
   All shall be well, if Thou art mine.

389   *"And God said, Ask what I shall give thee."*   [SEASONS

BEHOLD the throne of grace!
    The promise calls us near:
There Jesus shows a smiling face,
    And waits to answer prayer.

2 That rich, atoning blood,
    Which sprinkled round we see,
Provides for those who come to God
    An all-prevailing plea.

3 Thine image, Lord! bestow,
    Thy presence and Thy love:
We ask to serve Thee here below,
    And reign with Thee above.

4 Teach us to live by faith,
    Conform our will to Thine,
Let us victorious be in death,
    And then in glory shine.
                      John Newton

390   *"Our fellowship is with the Father,*   [MADISON SQUARE
         and with His Son Jesus Christ."

OUR Heavenly Father calls,
    And Christ invites us near;
With both, our friendship shall be sweet,
    And our communion dear.

2 God pities all our griefs:
    He pardons every day;
Almighty to protect our souls,
    And wise to guide our way.

3 How large His bounties are!
    What various stores of good,
Diffused from our Redeemer's hand,
    And purchased with His blood!

4 Jesus, our living Head,
    We bless Thy faithful care;
  Our Advocate before the throne,
    And our Forerunner there.

5 Here fix, my roving heart!
    Here wait, my warmest love!
  Till the communion be complete,
    In nobler scenes above.
                    Philip Doddridge

                                [FEDERAL ST.
391 *"If ye shall ask anything in My name, I will do it."*
  JESUS! our best beloved Friend,
    On Thy redeeming name we call;
  Jesus! in love to us descend,
    Pardon and sanctify us all.

2 Our souls and bodies we resign,
    To fear and follow Thy commands;
  O take our hearts—our hearts are Thine;
    Accept the service of our hands.

3 Firm, faithful, watching unto prayer,
    Thy blessed will may we obey,
  Toil in Thy vineyard here and bear
    The heat and burden of the day.

4 Yet, Lord! for us a resting place,
    In heaven, at Thy right hand, prepare,
  And, till we see Thee face to face,
    Be all our conversation there.
                    James Montgomery

392 *"Blessed be the Lord my Strength."* [SWANWICK
  FOR ever blessed be the Lord,
    My Saviour and my Shield;
  He sends His Spirit with His word,
    To arm me for the field.

2 When sin and hell their force unite,
   He makes my soul His care,
Instructs me to the heavenly fight,
   And guards me through the war.

3 A Friend and Helper so divine
   Does my weak courage raise;
He makes the glorious victory mine,
   And His shall be the praise.
                              Isaac Watts

[RELIANCE

393   *"The Lord is my Light and my Salvation."*

GOD is my strong salvation,
   What foe have I to fear?
In darkness and temptation
   My Light, my Help is near;
Though hosts encamp around me,
   Firm to the fight I stand;
What terror can confound me,
   With God at my right hand?

2 Place on the Lord reliance,
   My soul, with courage wait;
His truth be thine affiance,
   When faint and desolate:
His might thine heart shall strengthen,
   His love thy joy increase;
Mercy thy days shall lengthen;
   The Lord will give thee peace.
                        James Montgomery

394   *"I know whom I have believed."*   [SWANWICK

I'M not ashamed to own my Lord,
   Or to defend His cause;
Maintain the honor of His word,
   The glory of His cross.

2 Jesus, my God!—I know His name—
   His name is all my trust;
   Nor will He put my soul to shame,
   Nor let my hope be lost.

3 Firm as His throne, His promise stands,
   And He can well secure
   What I've committed to His hands,
   Till the decisive hour.

4 Then will He own my worthless name
   Before His Father's face,
   And in the new Jerusalem
   Appoint my soul a place.
                               Isaac Watts

                                        [FEDERAL ST.
395 *"Who shall separate us from the love of Christ?"*

   O HOLY Saviour, Friend unseen,
   The faint, the weak, on Thee may lean:
   Help me throughout life's varying scene,
       By faith to cling to Thee!

2 Though faith and hope awhile be tried,
   I ask not, need not, aught beside:
   How safe, how calm, how satisfied,
       The souls that cling to Thee!

3 They fear not life's rough storms to brave,
   Since Thou art near, and strong to save:
   Nor shudder e'en at death's dark wave;
       Because they cling to Thee!

4 Blest is my lot, whate'er befall:
   What can disturb me, who appall,
   While as my strength, my rock, my all,
       Saviour! I cling to Thee!
                          Charlotte Elliott

Christian Duty and Trial

396   [PLEYEL'S HYMN
"Lord, who shall abide in Thy tabernacle?"

Who, O Lord, when life is o'er,
Shall to heavenly mansions soar?
Who, an ever-welcome guest,
In Thy holy place shall rest?

2   He whose heart Thy love has warmed;
He whose will, to Thine conformed,
Bids his life unsullied run;
He whose words and thoughts are one;

3   He who shuns the sinner's road,
Loving those who love their God;
Who, with hope, and faith unfeigned,
Treads the path by Thee ordained;

4   He who trusts in Christ alone,
Not in aught himself hath done:
He, great God, shall be Thy care,
And Thy choicest blessings share.

James Merrick

397   [BEETHOVEN
"I will run the way of Thy commandments."

Be with me, Lord, where'er I go;
Teach me what Thou wouldst have me do;
Suggest whate'er I think or say;
Direct me in Thy narrow way.

2 Prevent me lest I harbor pride,
   Lest I in mine own strength confide;
   Show me my weakness, let me see
   I have my power, my all from Thee.

3 Enrich me always with Thy love;
   My kind protection ever prove:
   Thy signet put upon my breast,
   And let Thy Spirit on me rest.

4 O may I never do my will,
   But Thine and only Thine fulfill:
   Let all my time and all my ways
   Be spent and ended to Thy praise.
                             John Cennick

398 *"And they forsook all, and followed Him."* [QUARTET

Jesus calls us, o'er the tumult
   Of our life's wild, restless sea;
   Day by day His sweet voice soundeth,
   Saying, Christian, follow Me!

2 Jesus calls us—from the worship
   Of the vain world's golden store;
   From each idol that would keep us,—
   Saying, Christian, love Me more!

3 In our joys and in our sorrows,
   Days of toil and hours of ease,
   Still He calls, in cares and pleasures,
   Christian, love Me more than these!

4 Jesus calls us! by Thy mercies,
   Saviour, may we hear Thy call;
   Give our hearts to Thy obedience,
   Serve and love Thee best of all!

399   *"Make me to go in the path of Thy commandments."*   [MIDNIGHT

O THAT the Lord would guide my ways
   To keep His statutes still!
O that my God would grant me grace
   To know and do His will!

2 O send Thy Spirit down to write
   Thy law upon my heart!
Nor let my tongue indulge deceit,
   Nor act the liar's part.

3 From vanity turn off mine eyes;
   Let no corrupt design,
Nor covetous desire, arise
   Within this soul of mine.

4 Order my footsteps by Thy word,
   And make my heart sincere;
Let sin have no dominion, Lord,
   But keep my conscience clear.

5 Make me to walk in Thy commands,—
   'Tis a delightful road;
Nor let my head, or heart, or hands,
   Offend against my God.
                        Isaac Watts

400   *"Hearkening unto the voice of His word."*   [PHRYGIA

'SPEAK, for Thy servant heareth,'—
   Thus give us grace, O Lord,
To listen and to answer
   Whene'er Thy voice is heard:
Whether we wait expectant
   Its sound to guide us home,
Or all unsought, unwelcome,
   Its sudden warning come.

2 Above the whirl of traffic,
    Above the stir of life,
  Amid the songs of pleasure,
    And o'er the din of strife,
  May never cease within us
    Thy whispers soft and clear,
  Nor ready hearts replying,
    'Speak, Lord, Thy servants hear.'

3 And in the latest conflict,
    When strength and faith are low,
  And all our schemes of comfort
    Are baffled by the foe:
  Amid life's feeble throbbings,
    Yet nearer and more near
  May Thy sweet tones of solace
    Speak, and Thy servants hear.
              Henry Alford

401   "*Be ye also ready.*"   [LABAN

A CHARGE to keep I have,
    A God to glorify,
  A never-dying soul to save,
    And fit it for the sky;—

2 To serve the present age,
    My calling to fulfill:
  O may it all my powers engage
    To do my Master's will.

3 Arm me with jealous care,
    As in Thy sight to live;
  And O, Thy servant, Lord, prepare
    A strict account to give.

4 Help me to watch and pray,
    And on Thyself rely;
  Assured, if I my trust betray,
    I shall for ever die.
              Charles Wesley

402 *"Now they do it to obtain a corruptible* [LICHTENSTEIN
crown, but we an incorruptible."

SOLDIERS who to Christ belong,
Trust ye in His word, be strong;
For His promises are sure,
His rewards for aye endure.

2 His no crowns that pass away;
His no palm that sees decay;
His the joy that shall not fade;
His the light that knows no shade.

3 Here on earth ye can but clasp
Things that perish in the grasp;
Lift your hearts then to the skies,
God Himself shall be your prize.

4 Praise we now with saints at rest
Father, Son, and Spirit blest;
For His promises are sure,
His rewards shall aye endure.

403 *"Be thou faithful unto death, and I will* [WATERFORD
give thee a crown of life."

STAND up, stand up for Jesus,
Ye soldiers of the cross;
Lift high His royal banner,
It must not suffer loss:
From victory unto victory
His army shall He lead,
Till every foe is vanquished,
And Christ is Lord indeed.

2 Stand up, stand up for Jesus,
The trumpet call obey;
Forth to the mighty conflict
In this His glorious day:

'Ye that are men, now serve Him'
Against unnumbered foes;
Let courage rise with danger,
And strength to strength oppose.

3 Stand up, stand up for Jesus,
  The strife will not be long;
This day the noise of battle,
  The next the victor's song:
To Him that overcometh,
  A crown of life shall be;
He with the King of glory
  Shall reign eternally.   *George Duffield*

404 *"Be strong in the Lord, and in the power of* [LABAN
  His might."

Soldiers of Christ, arise,
  And put your armor on,
Strong in the strength which God supplies
  Through His Eternal Son.

2 Strong in the Lord of Hosts,
    And in His mighty power,
  Who in the strength of Jesus trusts,
    Is more than conqueror.

3 Stand, then, in His great might,
    With all His strength endued;
  And take, to arm you for the fight,
    The panoply of God:—

4 That having all things done,
    And all your conflicts past,
  Ye may o'ercome through Christ alone,
    And stand entire at last.

5 From strength to strength go on,
    Wrestle, and fight, and pray;
  Tread all the powers of darkness down,
    And win the well-fought day.   *C. Wesley*

Christian Duty and Trial

405 *"Take ye heed; watch and pray."* [LABAN

My soul, be on thy guard;
  Ten thousand foes arise;
The hosts of sin are pressing hard
  To draw thee from the skies.

2 O watch, and fight, and pray;
  The battle ne'er give o'er;
Renew it boldly every day,
  And help divine implore.

3 Ne'er think the victory won,
  Nor lay thine armor down:
Thine arduous work will not be done,
  Till thou obtain thy crown.

4 Fight on, my soul, till death
  Shall bring thee to thy God;
He'll take thee, at thy parting breath,
  To His divine abode.

George Heath

406 *"Fight the good fight of faith."* [CAMBRIDGE

Am I a soldier of the cross,
  A follower of the Lamb?
And shall I fear to own His cause,
  Or blush to speak His name?

2 Are there no foes for me to face?
  Must I not stem the flood?
Is this vile world a friend to grace,
  To help me on to God?

3 Sure I must fight, if I would reign;
  Increase my courage, Lord:
I'll bear the toil, endure the pain,
  Supported by Thy word.

4 Thy saints in all this glorious war
   Shall conquer, though they die;
   They view the triumph from afar,
   And seize it with their eye.

5 When that illustrious day shall rise,
   And all Thy armies shine
   In robes of victory through the skies,
   The glory shall be Thine.
                       Isaac Watts

407 "*They that wait upon the Lord shall renew their strength.*" [ARMOR

  AWAKE our souls, away our fears,
    Let every trembling thought be gone;
  Awake and run the heavenly race,
    And put a cheerful courage on.

2 True, 'tis a strait and thorny road,
    And mortal spirits tire and faint;
  But they forget the mighty God,
    That feeds the strength of every saint :—

3 The mighty God, whose matchless power
    Is ever new and ever young,
  And firm endures, while endless years
    Their everlasting circles run.

4 From Thee, the overflowing Spring,
    Our souls shall drink a fresh supply,
  While such as trust their native strength
    Shall melt away, and droop, and die.

5 Swift as an eagle cuts the air,
    We'll mount aloft to Thine abode;
  On wings of love our souls shall fly,
    Nor tire amid the heavenly road.
                       Isaac Watts

Christian Duty and Trial

408 *"So run, that ye may obtain."* [CAMBRIDGE

Awake, my soul, stretch every nerve,
   And press with vigor on;
A heavenly race demands thy zeal,
   And an immortal crown.

2 A cloud of witnesses around
   Hold thee in full survey;
Forget the steps already trod,
   And onward urge thy way.

3 'Tis God's all-animating voice,
   That calls thee from on high:
'Tis His own hand presents the prize
   To thine uplifted eye.

4 Blest Saviour, introduced by Thee,
   Have I my race begun;
And, crowned with victory, at Thy feet
   I'll lay my honors down.
                              Philip Doddridge

409 *"Whatsoever is not of faith is sin."* [MEAR

O it is hard to work for God,
   To rise and take His part
Upon this battle-field of earth,
   And not sometimes lose heart!

2 He hides Himself so wondrously,
   As though there were no God;
He is least seen when all the powers
   Of ill are most abroad.

3 Thrice blest is he to whom is given
   The instinct that can tell
That God is on the field, when He
   Is most invisible.

4 Then learn to scorn the praise of men,
    And learn to lose with God;
    For Jesus won the world through shame,
    And beckons thee His road.

5 For right is right, since God is God,
    And right the day must win:
    To doubt would be disloyalty,
    To falter would be sin.
              Frederick William Faber

410 [MISSIONARY CHANT
"Let us labor, therefore, to enter into that rest."

Go, labor on; spend and be spent,
    Thy joy to do the Father's will;
    It is the way the Master went;
    Should not the servant tread it still?

2 Go, labor on; 'tis not for naught;
    Thine earthly loss is heavenly gain;
    Men heed thee, love thee, praise thee not;
    The Master praises:—what are men?

3 Go, labor on, while it is day;
    The world's dark night is hastening on;
    Speed, speed thy work, cast sloth away;
    It is not thus that souls are won.

4 Toil on, faint not, keep watch, and pray;
    Be wise the erring soul to win;
    Go forth into the world's highway,
    Compel the wanderer to come in.

5 Toil on, and in thy toil rejoice;
    For toil comes rest, for exile home;
    Soon shalt thou hear the Bridegroom's voice,
    The midnight cry, 'Behold, I come!'
              Horatius Bonar

411   *"Put on the whole armor of God."*   [Armor

    Awake, my soul! lift up thine eyes;
    See where thy foes against thee rise,
    In long array, a numerous host;
    Awake, my soul! or thou art lost.

2 Sea where rebellious passions rage,
    And fierce desires and lusts engage;
    The meanest foe of all the train
    Has thousands and ten thousands slain.

3 Thou treadest on enchanted ground;
    Perils and snares beset thee round;
    Beware of all, guard every part,
    But most the traitor in thy heart.

4 Put on the armor, from above,
    Of heavenly truth and heavenly love,
    The terror and the charm repel,
    The powers of earth and powers of hell.
                     Anna Lætitia Barbauld

                                                 [Armor
412 *"Endure hardness, as a good soldier of Jesus Christ."*

    Stand up, my soul, shake off thy fears,
      And gird the gospel armor on;
    March to the gates of endless joy,
      Where Jesus, thy great Captain's gone.

2 Hell and thy sins resist thy course;
      But hell and sin are vanquished foes;
    Thy Jesus nailed them to the cross,
      And sung the triumph when He rose.

3 Then let my soul march boldly on,—
      Press forward to the heavenly gate;
    There peace and joy eternal reign,
      And glittering robes for conquerors wait.

4 There shall I wear a starry crown,
  And triumph in almighty grace,
  While all the armies of the skies
  Join in my glorious Leader's praise.
                                        Isaac Watts

413 *"Blessed are those servants whom the Lord* [LABAN
       when He cometh shall find watching."

Ye servants of the Lord,
  Each in his office wait,
Observant of His heavenly word,
  And watchful at His gate.

2 Let all your lamps be bright,
    And trim the golden flame;
  Gird up your loins, as in His sight,
    For awful is His name.

3 Watch; 'tis your Lord's command;
    And, while we speak, He's near;
  Mark the first signal of His hand,
    And ready all appear.

4 O happy servant he,
    In such a posture found!
  He shall his Lord with rapture see,
    And be with honor crowned.
                                        Philip Doddridge

414 *"I can do all things through Christ which* [HAYDN
       strengtheneth me."

Jesus, my Strength, my Hope,
  On Thee I cast my care,
With humble confidence look up,
  And know Thou hear'st my prayer.
Give me on Thee to wait
  Till I can all things do,
On Thee, Almighty to create!
  Almighty to renew!

2 I want a sober mind,
   A self-renouncing will,
That tramples down and casts behind
   The baits of pleasing ill:
A soul inured to pain,
   To hardship, grief, and loss;
Bold to take up, firm to sustain,
   The consecrated cross.

3 I want a godly fear,
   A quick-discerning eye,
That looks to Thee when sin is near,
   And sees the tempter fly;
A spirit still prepared,
   And armed with jealous care,
For ever standing on its guard,
   And watching unto prayer.

4 I want a true regard,
   A single, steady aim,
Unmoved by threatening or reward,
   To Thee and Thy great name;
A jealous, just concern
   For Thine immortal praise;
A pure desire that all may learn
   And glorify Thy grace.

5 I rest upon Thy word;
   Thy promise is for me;
My succor and salvation, Lord,
   Shall surely come from Thee,
But let me still abide,
   Nor from my hope remove,
Till Thou my patient spirit guide
   Into Thy perfect love!

Charles Wesley

Christian Duty and Trial

415 [ELBERFELD]
"Behold, we have forsaken all and followed Thee."

Jesus, I my cross have taken,
　All to leave and follow Thee:
Destitute, despised, forsaken,
　Thou, from hence, my all shalt be:
Perish every fond ambition,
　All I've sought, or hoped, or known:
Yet how rich is my condition!
　God and heaven are still my own!

2 Take, my soul, thy full salvation;
　Rise o'er sin, and fear, and care;
Joy to find in every station,
　Something still to do or bear:
Think what Spirit dwells within thee!
　What a Father's smile is thine!
What a Saviour died to win thee!
　Child of heaven, shouldst thou repine?

3 Haste thee on from grace to glory,
　Armed by faith, and winged by prayer;
Heaven's eternal day 's before thee,
　God's own hand shall guide thee there!
Soon shall close thine earthly mission,
　Swift shall pass thy pilgrim days;
Hope soon change to glad fruition,
　Faith to sight, and prayer to praise!
　　　　　　　　Henry Francis Lyte

416 [MISSIONARY CHANT]
"Denying ungodliness and worldly lusts, we should live soberly, righteously, and godly, in this present world."

So let our lips and lives express
The holy gospel we profess;
So let our works and virtues shine,
To prove the doctrine all divine.

2 Thus shall we best proclaim abroad
 The honors of our Saviour God;
 When His salvation reigns within,
 And grace subdues the power of sin.

3 Our flesh and sense must be denied,
 Passion and envy, lust and pride:
 While justice, temperance, truth, and love,
 Our inward piety approve.

4 Religion bears our spirits up,
 While we expect that blessed hope,
 The bright appearance of the Lord,
 And faith stands leaning on His word.
Isaac Watts

[RHEINECK

417 *"If any man will come after Me, let him deny himself, and take up his cross, and follow Me."*

Didst Thou, my Saviour, suffer shame,
 And bear the cross for me?
And shall I fear to own Thy name,
 Or Thy disciple be?

2 Forbid it, Lord, that I should dread
 To suffer shame or loss;
 O let me in Thy footsteps tread,
 And glory in Thy cross.

3 Inspire my soul with life divine,
 And make me truly bold;
 Let knowledge, faith, and meekness shine,
 Nor love nor zeal grow cold.

4 Let mockers scoff—the world defame,
 And treat me with disdain;
 Still may I glory in Thy name,
 And count reproach my gain.
Kirkham

Christian Duty and Trial

418   *"Thou art my Refuge and my Portion in the land of the living."*   [MARTYN

Jesus, lover of my soul,
  Let me to Thy bosom fly,
While the nearer waters roll,
  While the tempest still is high!
Hide me, O my Saviour, hide,
  Till the storm of life is past;
Safe into the haven guide;
  O receive my soul at last!

2 Other refuge have I none;
  Hangs my helpless soul on Thee;
Leave, ah! leave me not alone,
  Still support and comfort me!
All my trust on Thee is stayed,
  All my help from Thee I bring:
Cover my defenceless head
  With the shadow of Thy wing!

3 Thou, O Christ, art all I want;
  More than all in Thee I find;
Raise the fallen, cheer the faint,
  Heal the sick, and lead the blind!
Just and holy is Thy name,—
  I am all unrighteousness;
False and full of sin I am,—
  Thou art full of truth and grace.

4 Plenteous grace with Thee is found—
  Grace to pardon all my sin;
Let the healing streams abound,
  Make and keep me pure within:
Thou of life the fountain art,
  Freely let me take of Thee;
Spring Thou up within my heart,—
  Rise to all eternity.

Charles Wesley

419 *"Search me, O God, and know my heart."* [CREDO

O Thou, to whose all-searching sight
The darkness shineth as the light,
Search, prove my heart—it pants for Thee;
O, burst these bonds and set it free!

2 Wash out its stains, refine its dross;
Nail my affections to the cross;
Hallow each thought; let all within
Be clean, as Thou, my Lord, art clean.

3 If in this darksome wild I stray,
Be Thou my light—be Thou my way;
No foes nor danger will I fear,
While Thou, my Saviour God, art near.

4 Saviour, where'er Thy steps I see,
Dauntless, untired, I follow Thee:
O let Thy hand support me still,
And lead me to Thy holy hill.

5 If rough and thorny be the way,
My strength proportion to my day,
Till toil, and grief, and pain shall cease,
Where all is calm, and joy, and peace.
Gerhard Tersteegen

420 *"To me to live is Christ, and to die is gain."* [HEROLD

Christ, of all my hopes the ground,
  Christ, the spring of all my joy,
Still in Thee may I be found,
  Still for Thee my powers employ.

2 Fountain of o'erflowing grace,
  Freely from Thy fulness give;
Till I close my earthly race,
  May I prove it 'Christ to live!'

3 Firmly trusting in Thy blood,
   Nothing shall my heart confound;
   Safely shall I pass the flood,
   Safely reach Immanuel's ground.

4 When I touch the blessed shore,
   Back the closing waves shall roll;
   Death's dark stream shall never more
   Part from Thee my ravished soul.

5 Thus, O thus, an entrance give
   To the land of cloudless sky;
   Having known it 'Christ to live,'
   Let me know it 'Gain to die.'
                        Ralph Wardlaw

421 *"What things were gain to me, those I counted* [GRACE
    loss for Christ."

AND must I part with all I have,
   My dearest Lord, for Thee?
   It is but right! since Thou hast done
   Much more than this for me.

2 Yes, let it go!—One look from Thee
   Will more than make amends
   For all the losses I sustain
   Of credit, riches, friends.

3 Ten thousand worlds, ten thousand lives,
   How worthless they appear,
   Compared with Thee, supremely good!
   Divinely bright and fair!

4 Thy favor, Lord, is endless life;—
   Let me that life obtain,
   Then I renounce all earthly joys,
   And glory in my gain.
                        Benjamin Beddome

422 *"Looking unto Jesus, the Author and Finisher of our faith."* [WATERFORD

O Lamb of God, still keep me
  Near to Thy wounded side;
'Tis only there in safety
  And peace I can abide.
What foes and snares surround me,
  What doubts and fears within!
The grace that sought and found me,
  Alone can keep me clean.

2 'Tis only in Thee hiding,
  I know my life secure;
Only in Thee abiding,
  The conflict can endure:
Thine arm the victory gaineth
  O'er every hateful foe;
Thy love my heart sustaineth
  In all its care and woe.

3 Soon shall my eyes behold Thee
  With rapture face to face;
One half hath not been told me
  Of all Thy power and grace;
Thy beauty, Lord, and glory,
  The wonders of Thy love,
Shall be the endless story
  Of all Thy saints above.
      James George Deck

423 *"If thou seek Him, He will be found of thee."* [CHANT

Nearer, my God, to Thee!
  Nearer to Thee,
E'en though it be a cross
  That raiseth me;
Still all my song shall be,
Nearer, my God, to Thee,
  Nearer to Thee.

2 Though like the wanderer,
    The sun gone down,
  Darkness be over me,
    My rest a stone;
  Yet in my dreams I'd be
  Nearer, my God, to Thee,
    Nearer to Thee!

3 There let the way appear
    Steps unto Heaven;
  All that Thou sendest me
    In mercy given;
  Angels to beckon me
  Nearer, my God, to Thee,
    Nearer to Thee!

4 Then with my waking thoughts
    Bright with Thy praise,
  Out of my stony griefs
    Bethel I'll raise;
  So by my woes to be
  Nearer, my God, to Thee,
    Nearer to Thee!

5 Or if on joyful wing
    Cleaving the sky,
  Sun, moon, and stars forgot,
    Upward I fly,
  Still all my song shall be,
  Nearer, my God, to Thee,
    Nearer to Thee!
                    Sarah Flower Adams

424 *"A man can receive nothing, except it be given him from heaven."* [AYNHOE

IF, through unruffled seas,
  Toward heaven we calmly sail,
With grateful hearts, O God, to Thee,
  We'll own the favoring gale.

2 But should the surges rise,
  And rest delay to come,
Blest be the sorrow—kind the storm,
  Which drives us nearer home.

3 Soon shall our doubts and fears
  All yield to Thy control:
Thy tender mercies shall illume
  The midnight of the soul.

4 Teach us, in every state,
  To make Thy will our own;
And when the joys of sense depart
  To live by faith alone.

425 *"All things are for your sakes."* [DURING

SINCE all the coming scenes of time
  God's watchful eye surveys,
O who so wise to choose our lot
  And regulate our ways?

2 Since none can doubt His equal love,
  Immeasurably kind,
To His unerring gracious will
  Be every wish resigned.

3 Good when He gives, supremely good;
  Nor less when He denies;
E'en crosses, from His sovereign hand,
  Are blessings in disguise.
                              James Hervey

426   "*Thy will be done.*"   [DUNDEE

Thy holy will, my God, be mine;
    I yield my all to Thee;
No more shall thought or wish repine,
    Whate'er my lot shall be.

2 Thy wisdom is a mighty deep,
    Beyond my thought Thy grace;
My soul shall lay her fears asleep,
    Secure in Thine embrace.

3 When clouds and darkness rule the hour,
    Thy bow on high I see;
And e'en the rending tempest's power
    Shall work but good for me.

4 At every step mine eyes shall turn
    To watch Thy guiding hand;
My dearest wish shall be to learn
    And do Thy pure command.

5 On Thee I rest my trusting soul;
    Thou wilt not let me fall;
Though surging billows o'er me roll,
    I shall be safe through all.

6 Grant me, my God, at last to hear,
    Well pleased, the call to die;
And 'mid the shades, with vision clear,
    To see my Saviour nigh.

7 Then when Thy glory breaks on me,
    All radiant as the sun,
Be this the joy of heaven,—to see
    Thy will for ever done.

Ray Palmer

427   "*My times are in Thy hand.*"   [RESIGNATION

SOVEREIGN Ruler of the skies,
Ever gracious, ever wise,
All my times are in Thy hand,
All events at Thy command.

2 Times of sickness, times of health,
Times of penury and wealth;
Times of trial and of grief,
Times of triumph and relief.

3 Times the tempter's power to prove,
Times to taste a Saviour's love;
All must come, and last, and end,
As shall please my heavenly Friend.

4 O Thou Gracious, Wise, and Just!
In Thy hands my life I trust:
Have I something dearer still?
I resign it to Thy will.

5 May I always own Thy hand;
Still to the surrender stand;
Know that Thou art God alone;
I and mine are all Thy own.
John Ryland

[LICHTENSTEIN
428   "*Except ye be converted, and become as little children, ye shall not enter into the kingdom.*"

QUIET, Lord, my froward heart,
  Make me teachable and mild,
Upright, simple, free from art,
  Make me as a weaned child,
From distrust and envy free,
Pleased with all that pleases Thee.

2 What Thou shalt to-day provide,
   Let me as a child receive;
What to-morrow may betide
   Calmly to Thy wisdom leave:
'Tis enough that Thou wilt care;
Why should I the burden bear?

3 As a little child relies
   On a care beyond his own,
Knows he's neither strong nor wise,
   Fears to stir a step alone;
Let me thus with Thee abide,
As my Father, Guard, and Guide.
John Newton

429   "*Rejoicing in hope.*"   [THACHER

BLEST be Thy love, dear Lord,
   That taught us this sweet way,
Only to love Thee for Thyself,
   And for that love obey.

2 O Thou, our souls' chief Hope!
   We to Thy mercy fly;
Where'er we are, Thou canst protect,
   Whate'er we need, supply.

3 Whether we sleep or wake,
   To Thee we both resign;
By night we see, as well as day,
   If Thou upon us shine.

4 Whether we live or die,
   Both we submit to Thee;
In death we live, as well as life,
   If Thine in death we be.
John Austin

430   *"I seek not mine own will."*   [LUDWIG

THY way, not mine, O Lord,
  However dark it be!
Lead me by Thine own hand,
  Choose out the path for me.

2 I dare not choose my lot:
  I would not, if I might;
Choose Thou for me, my God,
  So shall I walk aright.

3 The kingdom that I seek
  Is Thine: so let the way
That leads to it be Thine,
  Else I must surely stray.

4 Not mine, not mine the choice,
  In things or great or small;
Be Thou my guide, my strength,
  My wisdom, and my all.
                    Horatius Bonar.

431   *"I will not leave you comfortless."*   [MANNA

O LOVE Divine, that stooped to share
  Our sharpest pang, our bitterest tear,
On Thee we cast each earth-born care,
  We smile at pain while Thou art near!

2 Though long the weary way we tread,
  And sorrow crowns each lingering year,
No path we shun, no darkness dread,
  Our hearts still whispering, Thou art near!

3 When drooping pleasure turns to grief,
  And trembling faith is changed to fear,
The murmuring wind, the quivering leaf,
  Shall softly tell us Thou art near!

4 On Thee we fling our burdening woe,
  O Love Divine, for ever dear,
  Content to suffer while we know,
  Living and dying, Thou art near!
                    Oliver Wendell Holmes

432   "*The will of the Lord be done.*"   [SARUM

My God and Father, while I stray
Far from my home, on life's rough way,
O teach me from my heart to say,
  Thy will be done!

2 Though dark my path and sad my lot,
  Let me be still and murmur not,
  Or breathe the prayer divinely taught,
    Thy will be done!

3 Though Thou hast called me to resign
  What most I prized, it ne'er was mine,
  I have but yielded what was Thine;
    Thy will be done!

4 Let but my fainting heart be blest
  With Thy sweet Spirit for its guest,
  My God, to Thee I leave the rest;
    Thy will be done!

5 Renew my will from day to day;
  Blend it with Thine; and take away
  All that now makes it hard to say,
    Thy will be done!

6 Then, when on earth I breathe no more,
  The prayer, oft mixed with tears before,
  I'll sing upon a happier shore,
    Thy will be done!
                    Charlotte Elliott

Christian Duty and Trial

433 *"Not as I will, but as Thou wilt."* [NAOMI

I WORSHIP Thee, sweet Will of God!
  And all Thy ways adore,
And every day I live, I seem
  To love Thee more and more.

2 I have no cares, O blessed Will,
  For all my cares are Thine;
I live in triumph, Lord, for Thou
  Hast made Thy triumphs mine.

3 He always wins who sides with God,
  To him no chance is lost;
God's will is sweetest to him when
  It triumphs at his cost.

4 Ill that He blesses, is our good,
  And unblest good is ill;
And all is right that seems most wrong,
  If it be His sweet will.
  Frederick William Faber

434 *"He careth for you."* [DENNIS

How gentle God's commands!
  How kind His precepts are!
'Come, cast your burdens on the Lord,
  And trust His constant care.'

2 Beneath His watchful eye
  His saints securely dwell;
That hand which bears all nature up
  Shall guard His children well.

3 Why should this anxious load
  Press down your weary mind?
Haste to your heavenly Father's throne,
  And sweet refreshment find.

4 His goodness stands approved
    Through each succeeding day:
    I'll drop my burden at His feet,
    And bear a song away.
                    Philip Doddridge

435   *"Commit thy way unto the Lord."*   [DENNIS
Commit thou all thy griefs
    And ways into His hands,
    To His sure truth and tender care,
    Who earth and heaven commands.

2 Who points the clouds their course,
    Whom winds and seas obey,
    He shall direct thy wandering feet,
    He shall prepare thy way.

3 Thou on the Lord rely;
    So safe shalt thou go on;
    Fix on His work thy steadfast eye,
    So shall thy work be done.

4 No profit canst thou gain
    By self-consuming care;
    To Him commend thy cause; His ear
    Attends the softest prayer.

5 Give to the winds thy fears,
    Hope and be undismayed;
    God hears thy sighs and counts thy tears,
    God shall lift up thy head.

6 What though thou rulest not?
    Yet heaven and earth and hell
    Proclaim, God sitteth on the throne
    And ruleth all things well!
                    Paul Gerhardt

436 *"The ways of the Lord are right."* [OBEDIENCE]

WHATE'ER my God ordains is right,
  Holy His will abideth;
I will be still, whate'er He doth,
  And follow where He guideth.
He is my God, though dark my road;
  He holds me that I shall not fall,
  Wherefore to Him I leave it all.

2 Whate'er my God ordains is right,
  He never will deceive me:
He leads me by the proper path,
  I know He will not leave me,
And take content what He hath sent:
  His hand can turn my grief away,
  And patiently I wait His day.

3 Whate'er my God ordains is right,
  Here shall my stand be taken:
Though sorrow, need, or death be mine,
  Yet am I not forsaken:
My Father's care is round me there:
  He holds me that I shall not fall,
  And so to Him I leave it all.
                                Samuel Rodigast

[NAOMI]
437 *"My meat is to do the will of Him that sent me."*

FATHER! whate'er of earthly bliss
  Thy sovereign hand denies,
Accepted at Thy throne of grace,
  Let this petition rise:—

2 'Give me a calm, a thankful heart,
  From every murmur free!
The blessings of Thy grace impart,
  And let me live to Thee.

3 'Let the sweet hope that Thou art mine
My path of life attend:
Thy presence through my journey shine,
And bless my journey's end.'
Anne Steele

438 *"If any man sin, we have an Advocate with the Father."* [ASHFORD

O Thou, the contrite sinners' Friend,
Who loving, lov'st them to the end,
On this alone my hopes depend,
That Thou wilt plead for me!

2 When, weary in the Christian race,
Far off appears my resting-place,
And fainting I mistrust Thy grace,
Then, Saviour, plead for me!

3 When I have erred and gone astray
Afar from Thine and wisdom's way,
And see no glimmering guiding ray,
Still, Saviour, plead for me!

4 When Satan, by my sins made bold,
Strives from Thy cross to loose my hold,
Then with Thy pitying arms enfold,
And plead, O plead for me!

5 And when my dying hour draws near,
Darkened with anguish, guilt, and fear,
Then to my fainting sight appear,
Pleading in heaven for me!

6 When the full light of heavenly day
Reveals my sins in dread array,
Say Thou hast washed them all away;
O say Thou plead'st for me!
Charlotte Elliott

439 "*Casting all your care upon Him.*" [DIR, DIR JEHOVAH

THRICE happy he whose tranquil mind,
  Whate'er, O Lord, his lot may be,
His truest source of peace can find
  In casting all his care on Thee:

2 Who ever strives from day to day,
    With earnest faith through toil and pain,
  To tread the strait and narrow way
    Till Thou shalt claim Thine own again;

3 Content to live, content to die,
    Content, O Lord, through good or ill;
  Content—without the asking why—
    Whate'er befal, to do Thy will.

4 So may we strive, and striving win
    The prize of those who die forgiven,
  Content to live, till freed from sin
    We reach Thy mansions, King of heaven.
                              Godfrey Thring

[WINCHESTER
440 "*He hath borne our griefs, and carried our sorrows.*"

WHERE high the heavenly temple stands,
The house of God not made with hands,
A great High Priest our nature wears,
The guardian of mankind appears.

2 He who for man their Surety stood,
  And poured on earth His precious blood,
  Pursues in heaven His mighty plan,
  The Saviour and the Friend of man.

3 Though now ascended up on high,
  He bends to earth a brother's eye;
  Partaker of the human name,
  He knows the frailty of our frame.

4 Our fellow-sufferer yet retains
  A fellow-feeling of our pains;
  And still remembers, in the skies,
  His tears, His agonies, and cries.

5 With boldness, therefore, at the throne,
  Let us make all our sorrows known;
  And ask the aid of heavenly power
  To help us in the evil hour.
                                John Logan

441   *"What I do, thou knowest not now."*   [MEAR

  GOD moves in a mysterious way
    His wonders to perform;
  He plants His footsteps in the sea,
    And rides upon the storm.

2 Deep in unfathomable mines
    Of never-failing skill,
  He treasures up His bright designs,
    And works His sovereign will.

3 Judge not the Lord by feeble sense,
    But trust Him for His grace;
  Behind a frowning Providence
    He hides a smiling face.

4 His purposes will ripen fast,
    Unfolding every hour;
  The bud may have a bitter taste,
    But sweet will be the flower.

5 Blind unbelief is sure to err,
    And scan His work in vain;
  God is His own interpreter,
    And He will make it plain.
                             William Cowper

442   *"Lo, I am with you alway."*   [DIR, DIR JEHOVAH

W HEN gathering clouds around I view,
And days are dark and friends are few,
On Him I lean, who not in vain
Experienced every human pain;
He sees my wants, allays my fears,
And counts and treasures up my tears.

2 If aught should tempt my soul to stray
From heavenly wisdom's narrow way;
To fly the good I would pursue,
Or do the sin I would not do;
Still He, who felt temptation's power,
Shall guard me in that dangerous hour.

3 If vexing thoughts within me rise,
And, sore dismayed, my spirit dies;
Still He, who once vouchsafed to bear
The sickening anguish of despair,
Shall sweetly soothe, shall gently dry,
The throbbing heart, the streaming eye.

4 And O! when I have safely past
Through every conflict but the last;
Still, still unchanging, watch beside
My painful bed, for Thou hast died!
Then point to realms of cloudless day,
And wipe the latest tear away!
Sir Robert Grant

[CONTENTMENT

443   *"Into Thine hand I commit my spirit."*

MY spirit on Thy care,
  Blest Saviour, I recline;
Thou wilt not leave me to despair,
  For Thou art Love divine.

2 In Thee I place my trust,
  On Thee I calmly rest;
  I know Thee good, I know Thee just,
  And count Thy choice the best.

3 Whate'er events betide,
  Thy will they all perform;
  Safe in Thy breast my head I hide,
  Nor fear the coming storm.

4 Let good or ill befal,
  It must be good for me;
  Secure of having Thee in all,
  Of having all in Thee.
    Henry Francis Lyte

[WINDHAM
444 *"And sin, when it is finished, bringeth forth death."*

BROAD is the road that leads to death,
  And thousands walk together there;
  But wisdom shows a narrow path,
  With here and there a traveler.

2 Deny thyself and take thy cross,
  Is the Redeemer's great command !
  Nature must count her gold but dross,
  If she would gain this heavenly land.

3 The fearful soul that tires and faints,
  And walks the ways of God no more,
  Is but esteemed almost a saint,
  And makes his own destruction sure.

4 Lord, let not all my hopes be vain;
  Create my heart entirely new:
  Which hypocrites could ne'er attain,
  Which false apostates never knew.
    Isaac Watts

445 *"The Lord of hosts is with us."* [EIN FESTE BURG

A MIGHTY fortress is our God,
A bulwark never failing:
Our Helper He amid the flood
Of mortal ills prevailing.
   For still our ancient foe
   Doth seek to work our woe;
   His craft and power are great,
   And, armed with cruel hate,
On earth is not his equal.

2 Did we in our own strength confide,
Our striving would be losing,—
Were not the right Man on our side,
The Man of God's own choosing.
   Dost ask who that may be?
   Christ Jesus, it is He,
   Lord Sabaoth His name,
   From age to age the same,
And He must win the battle.

3 And though this world, with devils filled,
Should threaten to undo us,
We will not fear, for God hath willed
His truth to triumph through us.
   The Prince of darkness grim,
   We tremble not for him,
   His rage we can endure,
   For lo! his doom is sure,
One little word shall fell him.

4 That word above all earthly powers,
No thanks to them, abideth,
The Spirit and the gifts are ours
Through Him who with us sideth.

Let goods and kindred go,
This mortal life also;
The body they may kill,
God's truth abideth still,
His kingdom is for ever.   *Martin Luther*

446 [PORTUGUESE HYMN
"*None of them that trust in Him shall be desolate.*"

How firm a foundation, ye saints of the Lord,
Is laid for your faith in His excellent word;
What more can He say than to you He hath said,—
To you who for refuge to Jesus have fled?

2 Fear not, He is with thee, O be not dismayed;
For He is thy God, and will give thee His aid;
He'll strengthen thee, help thee, and cause thee to stand,
Upheld by His gracious, omnipotent hand.

3 When through the deep waters He calls thee to go,
The rivers of sorrow shall ne'er overflow;
His presence shall guide thee, His mercy shall bless,
And sanctify to thee thy deepest distress.

4 When through fiery trials thy pathway is laid,
His grace all-sufficient shall lend thee its aid;
The flame shall not hurt thee; He does but design
Thy dross to consume, and thy gold to refine.

5 His people through life shall abundantly prove
His sovereign, eternal, unchangeable love;
When age with gray hairs shall their temples adorn,
Like lambs they shall still in His bosom · be borne.

6 The soul that on Jesus hath leaned for repose,
   He will not—He will not desert to its foes;
   That soul—though all hell should endeavor to
      shake,
   He'll never—no, never—no, never forsake.
                                        George Keith

                                        [RHEINECK
447 *"Preserve me, O God: for in Thee do I put my trust."*

   DEAR Refuge of my weary soul,
      On Thee, when sorrows rise—
   On Thee, when waves of trouble roll,
      My fainting hope relies.

 2 To Thee I tell each rising grief,
      For Thou alone canst heal;
   Thy word can bring a sweet relief
      For every pain I feel.

 3 But O! when gloomy doubts prevail,
      I fear to call Thee mine;
   The springs of comfort seem to fail,
      And all my hopes decline.

 4 Yet, gracious God, where shall I flee?
      Thou art my only trust;
   And still my soul would cleave to Thee,
      Though prostrate in the dust.

 5 Thy mercy-seat is open still;
      Here let my soul retreat,
   With humble hope attend Thy will,
      And wait beneath Thy feet.
                                        Anne Steele

Time, Death, and Judgment

448 *"The day of the Lord so cometh as a thief* [ARIMATHEA
in the night."

WHILE, with ceaseless course, the sun
   Hasted through the former year,
Many souls their race have run,
   Never more to meet us here:
Fixed in an eternal state,
   They have done with all below;
We a little longer wait,
   But how little—none can know.

2 As the winged arrow flies
   Speedily the mark to find;
As the lightning from the skies
   Darts, and leaves no trace behind,—
Swiftly thus our fleeting days
   Bear us down life's rapid stream:
Upward, Lord, our spirits raise!
   All below is but a dream.

3 Thanks for mercies past receive;
   Pardon of our sins renew;
Teach us, henceforth, how to live
   With eternity in view:
Bless Thy word to young and old;
   Fill us with a Saviour's love:
And when life's short tale is told,
   May we dwell with Thee above.
John Newton

449   *"Hitherto hath the Lord helped us."*   [MENDON

    GREAT God, we sing that mighty hand
    By which supported still we stand;
    The opening year Thy mercy shows;
    Let mercy crown it till it close.

2 By day, by night, at home, abroad,
    Still are we guarded by our God;
    By His incessant bounty fed,
    By His unerring counsel led.

3 With grateful hearts the past we own;
    The future, all to us unknown,
    We to Thy guardian care commit,
    And peaceful leave before Thy feet.

4 In scenes exalted or deprest,
    Thou art our joy, and Thou our rest;
    Thy goodness all our hopes shall raise,
    Adored through all our changing days.

5 When death shall interrupt these songs,
    And seal in silence mortal tongues,
    Our Helper, God, in whom we trust,
    In better worlds our souls shall boast.
                     Philip Doddridge

450   *"So teach us to number our days that we may* [DALLAS
        apply our hearts unto wisdom."

    FOR Thy mercy and Thy grace,
      Faithful through another year,
    Hear our song of thankfulness,
      Father, and Redeemer, hear!

2 In our weakness and distress,
      Rock of strength! be Thou our stay!
    In the pathless wilderness
      Be our true and living way!

Time, Death, and Judgment

3 Who of us death's awful road
  In the coming year shall tread?
With Thy rod and staff, O God,
  Comfort Thou his dying head!

4 Keep us faithful, keep us pure,
  Keep us evermore Thine own!
Help, O help us to endure!
  Fit us for the promised crown!

3 So within Thy palace gate
  We shall praise, on golden strings,
Thee, the only Potentate,
  Lord of lords, and King of kings!
                              Henry Downton

                                    [TALLIS
451 *"Now is our salvation nearer than when we believed."*

AWAKE, ye saints, and raise your eyes,
  And raise your voices high;
Awake and praise that sovereign love,
  That shows salvation nigh.

2 On all the wings of time it flies,
  Each moment brings it near;
Then welcome each declining day!
  Welcome each closing year!

3 Not many years their round shall run,
  Nor many mornings rise,
Ere all its glories stand revealed
  To our admiring eyes.

4 Ye wheels of nature, speed your course!
  Ye mortal powers, decay!
Fast as ye bring the night of death,
  Ye bring eternal day!
                              Philip Doddridge

Time, Death, and Judgment

452   *"Thou crownest the year with Thy goodness."*   [MENDON

On God the race of man depends,
Far as the earth's remotest ends,
Where the Creator's name is known
By nature's feeble light alone.

2 At His command the morning ray
Smiles in the east, and leads the day;
He guides the sun's declining wheels
Over the tops of western hills.

3 Seasons and times obey His voice;
The evening and the morn rejoice
To see the earth made soft with showers,
Laden with fruit, and drest in flowers.

4 Thy works pronounce Thy power divine;
O'er every field Thy glories shine;
Through every month Thy gifts appear;
Great God! Thy goodness crowns the year!
Isaac Watts

453   *"Awake to righteousness, and sin not."*   [DUNDEE

Thee we adore, Eternal Name!
  And humbly own to Thee,
How feeble is our mortal frame,
  What dying worms are we!

2 The year rolls round, and steals away
  The breath that first it gave;
Whate'er we do, whate'er we be,
  We're traveling to the grave.

3 Great God! on what a slender thread
  Hang everlasting things!
The eternal state of all the dead
  Upon life's feeble strings.

4 Infinite joy, or endless wo,
   Attends on every breath,
   And yet, how unconcerned we go
   Upon the brink of death!

5 Waken, O Lord, our drowsy sense,
   To walk this dangerous road;
   And if our souls are hurried hence,
   May they be found with God.
                            Isaac Watts

[ETERNITY

454 *"Blessed are the dead which die in the Lord."*

O FOR the death of those
   Who slumber in the Lord!
O be like theirs my last repose,
   Like theirs my last reward!

2 Their bodies in the ground,
   In silent hope may lie,
   Till the last trumpet's joyful sound
   Shall call them to the sky.

3 Their ransomed spirits soar
   On wings of faith and love,
   To meet the Saviour they adore,
   And reign with Him above.

4 With us their names shall live
   Through long succeeding years,
   Embalmed with all our hearts can give,
   Our praises and our tears.

5 O for the death of those
   Who slumber in the Lord!
   O be like theirs my last repose,
   Like theirs my last reward!

[WALDSTEIN

455 *"Just and true are Thy ways, Thou King of saints."*

BLESSING, honor, thanks, and praise,
    Pay we, gracious God, to Thee·
Thou in Thine abundant grace
    Givest us the victory.
True and faithful to Thy word,
    Thou hast glorified Thy Son:
Jesus Christ our dying Lord
    Hath for us the victory won.

2 Happy are the faithful dead,
    In the Lord who sweetly die;
They from all their toils are freed,
    In God's keeping safely lie:
These the Spirit hath declared
    Blest, unutterably blest;
Jesus is their great reward,
    Jesus is their endless rest.

3 Followed by their works they go
    Where their Head is gone before,
Reconciled by grace below;
    Grace has opened mercy's door:
Fuller joys ordained to know,
    Waiting for the last great day,
When the archangel's trump shall blow,
    'Rise, to judgment come away.'

4 Absent from our loving Lord
    We shall not continue long:
Join we then with one accord
    In the new, the joyful song:
Blessing, honor, thanks, and praise,
    Triune God, we pay to Thee,
Who in Thine abundant grace
    Givest us the victory.

Charles Wesley

456 *"Blessed and holy is he that hath part in the first resurrection."* [Deux points

O stay thy tears; for they are blest,
  Whose days are past, whose toil is done:
Here, midnight care disturbs our rest,
  Here, sorrow dims the noonday sun.

2 How blest are they whose transient years
    Pass like an evening meteor's flight!
  Not dark with guilt, nor dim with tears;
    Whose course is short, unclouded, bright.

3 O cheerless were our lengthened way,
    Did Heaven's own light not break the gloom,
  Stream downward from eternal day,
    And cast a glory round the tomb.

4 O stay thy tears; the blest above
    Have hailed a spirit's heavenly birth,
  Sung a new song of joy and love;
    And why should anguish reign on earth?
                              Andrews Norton

457 *"Thy brother shall rise again."* [Mozart

Brother, though from yonder sky
Cometh neither voice nor cry,
Yet we know from thee to-day
Every pain hath past away.

2 Not for thee shall tears be given,
  Child of God and heir of heaven!
  For He gave thee sweet release;
  Thine the Christian's death of peace.

3 Well we know thy living faith
  Had the power to conquer death;
  As a living rose may bloom
  By the border of the tomb.

4 Brother, in that solemn trust
We commend thee, dust to dust;
In that faith we wait till, risen,
Thou shalt meet us all in heaven.
James Henry Bancroft

458 *"Them also which sleep in Jesus will God bring* [REST
with Him." with Him."

ASLEEP in Jesus! blessed sleep,
From which none ever wakes to weep,
A calm and undisturbed repose,
Unbroken by the last of foes!

2 Asleep in Jesus! O how sweet
To be for such a slumber meet!
With holy confidence to sing
That death hath lost his venomed sting.

3 Asleep in Jesus! peaceful rest,
Whose waking is supremely blest;
No fear, no woe, shall dim that hour
That manifests the Saviour's power.

4 Asleep in Jesus! O for me
May such a blissful refuge be,
Securely shall my ashes lie,
Waiting the summons from on high!
Margaret Mackay

459 *"Death is swallowed up in victory."* [ETERNITY

IT is not death to die,
  To leave this weary road,
And, 'mid the brotherhood on high,
  To be at home with God.

2 It is not death to bear
  The wrench that sets us free
From dungeon-chain, to breathe the air
  Of boundless liberty.

3 It is not death to fling
  Aside this sinful dust,
  And rise on strong, exulting wing
  To live among the just.

4 Jesus, Thou Prince of life!
  Thy chosen cannot die;
  Like Thee, they conquer in the strife,
  To reign with Thee on high.
                    Cæsar Malan

460   "*The Lord hath need of him.*"   [NUREMBERG

  CHRIST will gather in His own
  To the place where He is gone,
  Where their heart and treasure lie,
  Where our life is hid on high.

2 Day by day the voice saith, 'Come,
  Enter thine eternal home;'
  Asking not if we can spare
  This dear soul it summons there.

3 Had He asked us, well we know
  We should murmur, 'Spare this blow!'
  Yes, with streaming tears should pray,
  'Lord, we love him, let him stay.'

4 But the Lord doth naught amiss,
  And, since He hath ordered this,
  We have naught to do but still
  Rest in silence on His will.

5 Many a heart no longer here
  Ah! was all too inly dear;
  Yet, O Love! 'tis Thou dost call,
  Thou wilt be our all in all.
                    Nicholas Louis Zinzendorf

461 *"It is appointed unto men once to die, but after this the judgment."* [Gounod

BEHOLD the path that mortals tread
Down to the regions of the dead!
Nor will the fleeting moments stay,
Nor can we measure back our way. .

2 Our kindred and our friends are gone;
Know, O my soul, this doom thine own;
Feeble as theirs my mortal frame,
The same my way, my house the same.

3 And must I, from the cheerful light,
Pass to the grave's perpetual night,—
From scenes of duty, means of grace,
Must I to God's tribunal pass?

4 Awake, my soul, thy way prepare,
And lose, in this, each mortal care;
With steady feet that path be trod,
Which through the grave conducts to God.

462 [Judgment Hymn
"The dead shall hear the voice of the Son of God."

THE last loud trumpet's wondrous sound
Shall through the rending tombs rebound,
And wake the nations under ground.
The Judge ascends His awful throne,
He makes each secret sin be known,
And all with shame confess their own.

2 Thou who for me didst feel such pain,
Whose precious blood the cross did stain,
Let not those agonies be vain!
Forget not what my ransom cost,
Nor let my dear-bought soul be lost,
In storms of guilty terror tost.

3 Give my exalted soul a place
  Among Thy chosen, faithful race,
  The sons of God, and heirs of grace:
  Prostrate my contrite heart I bend;
  My God, my Father, and my Friend,
  Do not forsake me in mine end!
          Wentworth Dillon, Earl of Roscommon

463 *"Lord, remember me when Thou comest into Thy kingdom."* [TALLIS

There is an hour, when I must part
  With all I hold most dear;
  And life, with its best hopes, will then
  As nothingness appear.

2 There is an hour, when I must sink
  Beneath the stroke of death,
  And yield to Him, who gave it first,
  My struggling vital breath.

3 There is an hour, when I must stand
  Before the judgment seat,
  And all my sins, and all my foes,
  In awful vision meet.

4 There is an hour, when I must look
  On one eternity,
  And nameless woe, or blissful life,
  . My endless portion be.

5 O Saviour, then, in all my need,
  Be near, be near to me;
  And let my soul, in steadfast faith,
  Find life and heaven in Thee!
          Andrew Reed

464 "*The trumpet shall sound, and the dead shall be raised.*" [Dies Iræ

Day of judgment, day of wonders!
Hark!—the trumpet's awful sound,
Louder than a thousand thunders,
Shakes the vast creation round:
  How the summons
Will the sinner's heart confound!

2 See the Judge, our nature wearing,
Clothed in majesty divine!
You, who long for His appearing,
Then shall say,—'This God is mine!'
  Gracious Saviour,
Own me in that day for Thine.

3 At His call, the dead awaken,
Rise to life from earth and sea;
All the powers of nature shaken
By His looks, prepare to flee:
  Careless sinner,
What will then become of thee?

4 But to those who have confessed,
Loved and served the Lord below,
He will say,—'Come near, ye blessed!
See the kingdom I bestow: ·
  You for ever
Shall My love and glory know.'
John Newton

465 [Wer nur den lieben Gott
"*Even so, come, Lord Jesus.*"

When Jesus came to earth of old
He came in weakness and in woe;
He wore no form of angel mold,
But took our nature, poor and low.

2 But when He cometh back once more,
    There shall be set the great white throne,
  And earth and heaven shall flee before
    The face of Him that sits thereon.

3 O Son of God, in glory crowned,
    The Judge ordained of quick and dead!
  O Son of Man, so pitying found
    For all the tears Thy people shed!

4 Be with us in this darkened place,
    This weary, restless, dangerous night;
  And teach, O teach us, by Thy grace
    To struggle onward into light!

5 And since, in God's recording book,
    Our sins are written, every one,
  The crime, the wrath, the wandering look,
    The good we knew, and left undone:

6 Lord, ere the last dread trump be heard,
    And ere before Thy face we stand,
  Look Thou on each accusing word,
    And blot it with Thy bleeding hand!

7 And by the love that brought Thee here,
    And by the cross, and by the grave,
  Give perfect love for conscious fear,
    And in the day of judgment save!

8 And lead us on, while here we stray,
    And make us love our heavenly home,
  Till from our hearts we love to say,
    'Even so, Lord Jesus, quickly come!'

Cecil Frances Alexander

Time, Death, and Judgment

466   *"Of that day and that hour knoweth no man."*   [ETERNITY

    Thou Judge of quick and dead,
      Before whose bar severe,
    With holy joy, or guilty dread,
      We all shall soon appear;
    Our cautioned souls prepare
      For that tremendous day;
    And fill us now with watchful care,
      And stir us up to pray.

2   To damp our earthly joys,
      To wake our gracious fears,
    For ever let the archangel's voice
      Be sounding in our ears,—
    The solemn midnight cry,—
      'Ye dead, the Judge is come!
    Arise, and meet Him in the sky,
      And meet your instant doom!'

3   O may we thus be found,
      Obedient to Thy word;
    Attentive to the trumpet's sound,
      And looking for our Lord!
    O may we thus insure
      Our lot among the blest;
    And watch a moment to secure
      An everlasting rest!

Charles Wesley

467   *"The Lord reigneth, He is clothed with majesty."*   [DEDICATION

    Eternal God! Eternal King!
    Ruler of heaven and earth beneath!
  From Thee our hopes, our comforts spring;
    In Thee we live, and move, and breathe.

2 Thy sway is known below, above,
   And full of majesty Thy voice;
   And as it speaks, in wrath or love,
   The nations tremble or rejoice.

3 The final, awful hour is near,
   Time paces on with ceaseless tread,
   When opening graves that voice shall hear,
   And render up the sleeping dead.

4 O in that great, decisive day,
   May we be found in Christ, and stand—
   While flaming worlds shall melt away—
   Accepted, owned, at Thy right hand!
                              Henry March

468   "*Every eye shall see Him.*"   [BOYLSTON

AND will the Judge descend,
   And must the dead arise,
   And not a single soul escape
   His all-discerning eyes?

2 How will my heart endure
   The terrors of that day,
   When earth and heaven before His face
   Astonished shrink away!

3 But ere that trumpet shakes
   The mansions of the dead,
   Hark, from the gospel's gentle voice
   What joyful tidings spread!

4 Ye sinners, seek His grace
   Whose wrath ye cannot bear;
   Fly to the shelter of His cross,
   And find salvation there.

5 So shall that curse remove,
By which the Saviour bled;
And the last awful day shall pour
His blessings on your head.
Philip Doddridge

469 *"Watch therefore, for ye know neither* [ISOLATION
the day nor the hour."

Lo! on a narrow neck of land,
'Twixt two unbounded seas I stand!
Yet how insensible!
A point of time, a moment's space,
Removes me to yon heavenly place,
Or—shuts me up in hell!

2 O God! mine inmost soul convert,
And deeply on my thoughtful heart
Eternal things impress;
Give me to feel their solemn weight,
And save me ere it be too late;
Wake me to righteousness.

3 Before me place, in dread array,
The pomp of that tremendous day,
When Thou with clouds shalt come
To judge the nations at Thy bar;
And tell me, Lord! shall I be there
To meet a joyful doom?

4 Be this my one great business here,
With holy trembling, holy fear,
To make my calling sure!
Thine utmost counsel to fulfill,
And suffer all Thy righteous will,
And to the end endure!
Charles Wesley

470 "*For He cometh, for He cometh to judge the earth.*" [TREMO

THE Lord will come! the earth shall quake;
The hills their fixed seat forsake;
And, withering, from the vault of night
The stars withdraw their feeble light.

2 The Lord will come! but not the same
As once in lowly form He came,—
A quiet Lamb to slaughter led,—
The bruised, the suffering, and the dead.

3 The Lord will come! a dreadful form,
With wreath of flame, and robe of storm,
On cherub wings, and wings of wind,
Anointed Judge of human-kind!

4 Then sinners to the rocks complain,
And seek the mountain's cleft in vain!
But faith, victorious o'er the tomb,
Shall sing for joy,—'The Lord is come.'

Reginald Heber

471 "*Into Thine hand I commit my spirit.*" [COBURG

WHEN my last hour is close at hand,
  My last sad journey taken,
Do Thou, Lord Jesus, by me stand;
  Let me not be forsaken:
O Lord! my spirit I resign
Into Thy loving hands divine;
  'Tis safe within Thy keeping.

2 Countless as sands upon the shore,
  My sins may then appal me;
Yet, though my conscience vex me sore,
  Despair shall not enthral me;
For as I draw my latest breath,
I'll think, Lord Christ, upon Thy death,
  And there find consolation!

472   "*They that sow in tears shall reap in joy.*"   [BOYLSTON

    THE harvest dawn is near,
      The year delays not long;
    And he who sows with many a tear,
      Shall reap with many a song.

2 Sad to his toil he goes,
      His seed with weeping leaves;
    But he shall come, at twilight's close,
      And bring his golden sheaves.
                      George Burgess

473   "*Whatsoever a man soweth, that shall he also reap.*"   [WER NUR DEN LIEBEN GOTT

    FATHER!—if I may call Thee so,—
      I tremble with my one desire:
    Lift up this heavy load of wo,
      Nor let me in my sins expire!

2 I tremble lest the wrath divine,
      Which bruises now my sinful soul,
    Should bruise and break this soul of mine,
      Long as eternal ages roll.

3 Thy wrath I fear, Thy wrath alone,
      This endless exile, Lord, from Thee!
    O save! O give me to Thy Son,
      Who trembled, wept, and bled for me!

474   "*I know that my Redeemer liveth.*"   [CHRISTMAS

    MY faith shall triumph o'er the grave,
      And trample on the tomb;
    I know that my Redeemer lives,
      And on the clouds shall come.

2 I know that He shall soon appear
   In power and glory meet;
   And death, the last of all His foes,
   Lie vanquished at His feet.

3 Then, though the grave my flesh devour,
   And hold me for its prey,
   I know my sleeping dust shall rise
   On the last judgment-day.

4 I, in my flesh, shall see my God,
   When He on earth shall stand;
   I shall with all His saints ascend
   To dwell at His right hand.

5 Then shall He wipe all tears away,
   And hush the rising groan;
   And pains and sighs and griefs and fears
   Shall ever be unknown.

[MADISON SQUARE

475 *"The night is far spent, the day is at hand."*

ONE sweetly solemn thought
   Comes to me o'er and o'er,—
I'm nearer to my home to-day
   Than e'er I was before.

2 Nearer my Father's house,
   Where many mansions be;
   Nearer the Saviour's great white throne,
   Nearer the crystal sea!

3 Nearer the bound of life,
   Where burdens we lay down;
   Nearer to leave the heavy cross,
   Nearer to wear the crown.

4 But, lying dark between,
   And winding through the night,
   There rolls the dim and unknown stream
   That leads at last to light.

5 O if my mortal feet
   Have almost gained the brink!
   And I to-day am nearer home,
   Nearer than now I think!

6 Father, perfect my trust!
   And let me feel in death
   My spirit's feet are firmly set
   Upon the rock of faith!
                      Phœbe Cary

476   "*The Lord is at hand.*"   [SICILY]

O'ER the distant mountains breaking,
   Comes the reddening dawn of day;
Rise, my soul, from sleep awaking,
   Rise, and sing, and watch, and pray:
      'Tis thy Saviour,
On His bright, returning way.

2 O Thou long-expected! weary
   Waits my anxious soul for Thee;
Life is dark and earth is dreary
   Where the light I do not see:
      O my Saviour,
   When wilt Thou return to me?

3 Long, too long, in sin and sadness,
   Far away from Thee I pine;
When, O when, shall I the gladness
   Of Thy Spirit feel in mine?
      O my Saviour,
   When shall I be wholly Thine?

4 Nearer is my soul's salvation,
  Spent the night, the day at hand;
Keep me in my lowly station,
  Watching for Thee, till I stand,
    O my Saviour,
  In Thy bright and promised land!

5 With my lamp well-trimmed and burning,
  Swift to hear, and slow to roam,
Watching for Thy glad returning
  To restore me to my home,
    Come, my Saviour,
  O my Saviour, quickly come!
                    John Samuel Bewley Monsell

477   "*Dies iræ, dies illa.*"   [DEUX POINTS

THAT day of wrath! that dreadful day,
When heaven and earth shall pass away!
What power shall be the sinner's stay?
How shall he meet that dreadful day?

2 When, shriveling like a parched scroll,
The flaming heavens together roll,
And louder yet, and yet more dread,
Swells the high trump that wakes the dead!

3 O, on that day, that wrathful day,
When man to judgment wakes from clay,
Be Thou, O Christ, the sinner's stay,
Though heaven and earth shall pass away.
                    Walter Scott

                              [MADISON SQUARE
478   "*A little while, and ye shall see Me.*"

A FEW more years shall roll,
  A few more seasons come,
And we shall be with those that rest
  Asleep within the tomb.

2 A few more struggles here,
 A few more partings o'er,
 A few more toils, a few more tears,
 And we shall weep no more.

3 'Tis but a little while,
 And He shall come again,
 Who died that we might live, who lives
 That we with Him may reign.

4 Then, O my Lord, prepare
 My soul for that glad day;
 O wash me in Thy precious blood
 And take my sins away!
Horatius Bonar

[MERIBAH

479 *"Behold, the Judge standeth before the door."*

WHEN Thou, my righteous Judge, shall come
To fetch Thy ransomed people home,
 Shall I among them stand?
Shall such a worthless worm as I,
Who sometimes am afraid to die,
 Be found at Thy right hand?

2 Blest Saviour! grant it by Thy grace;
Be Thou, dear Lord, my hiding-place,
 In this the accepted day;
Thy pardoning voice O let me hear,
To still my unbelieving fear,
 Nor let me fall, I pray.

3 Among Thy saints let me be found,
Whene'er the archangel's trump shall sound,
 To see Thy smiling face;
Then in triumphant strains I'll sing,
While heaven's resounding mansions ring
 With shouts of sovereign grace.
Selina, Countess of Huntingdon

480 *"Behold, the Bridegroom cometh: go ye out to meet Him."* [JUDGMENT HYMN

Great God! what do I see and hear?—
  The end of things created!
Behold the Judge of man appear,
  On clouds of glory seated!
The trumpet sounds—the graves restore
The dead which they contained before!
  Prepare, my soul! to meet Him.

2 The dead in Christ shall first arise,
    To greet the archangel's warning,
  To meet the Saviour in the skies
    On this auspicious morning:
  No gloomy fears their souls dismay,
  His presence sheds eternal day
    On those prepared to meet Him.

3 Great God! what do I see and hear?—
    The end of things created!
  Behold the Judge of man appear,
    On clouds of glory seated!
  Beneath His cross I view the day
  When heaven and earth shall pass away,
    And thus prepare to meet Him!

William Bengo Collyer

481 *"The Lord grant unto him that he may find mercy of the Lord in that day."* [JUDGMENT HYMN

Most surely at the appointed time,
  The Lord, the Judge, descendeth:
In might and majesty sublime
  His course to earth He bendeth.
What sinner then shall mock His ire,
When all around is wrapt in fire,
  As in His word is written!

2 The trumpet then all ears shall hear,
    At nature's dissolution:
  All at the summons shall appear,
    Each to his retribution.
  Then death himself in fear shall die,
  When all around the voice shall fly,
    That man to life recalleth.

3 Ah! what shall I, a sinner, say,
    With Thee in judgment pleading!
  Or who shall stand for me that day,
    For mercy interceding?
  Thou, Lord, mine Advocate shalt be,
  Who, sinners from the curse to free,
    Didst come, the world's Redeemer!
                    Arthur Tozer Russell

482   *"Surely I come quickly."*   [MOUNT ZION

  Lo! He comes, with clouds descending,
    Once for favored sinners slain:
  Thousand thousand saints attending
    Swell the triumph of His train:
      Hallelujah!
    God appears, on earth to reign!

2 Every eye shall now behold Him,
    Robed in dreadful majesty;
  Those who set at naught and sold Him,
    Pierced and nailed Him to the tree,
      Deeply wailing,
    Shall the true Messiah see.

3 Now redemption, long expected,
    See in solemn pomp appear!
  All His saints, by man rejected,
    Now shall meet Him in the air;
      Hallelujah!
    See the day of God appear!

4 Answer Thine own Bride and Spirit;
   Hasten, Lord, the general doom;
   The new Heaven and earth to inherit
   Take Thy pining exiles home:
      All creation
   Travails, groans, and bids Thee come!

5 Yea, Amen! let all adore Thee,
   High on Thine eternal throne:
   Saviour, take the power and glory;
   Claim the kingdom for Thine own:
      O come quickly,
   Everlasting God, come down!
                    Charles Wesley

Heaven

483   *"A city which hath foundations, whose Builder and Maker is God."*   [Glory

Jerusalem, my happy home,
    Name ever dear to me!
When shall my labors have an end,
    In joy and peace and thee?

2 When shall these eyes thy heaven-built walls
    And pearly gates behold?
Thy bulwarks with salvation strong,
    And streets of shining gold?

3 There happier bowers than Eden's bloom,
    Nor sin nor sorrow know;
Blest seats! through rude and stormy scenes
    I onward press to you.

4 Why should I shrink from pain and woe,
    Or feel at death dismay?
I've Canaan's goodly land in view,
    And realms of endless day.

5 Apostles, martyrs, prophets, there
    Around my Saviour stand;
And soon my friends in Christ below
    Will join the glorious band.

6 Jerusalem, my happy home!
    My soul still pants for thee:
Then shall my labors have an end,
    When I thy joys shall see.

484 *"Here have we no continuing city, but we seek one to come."* [HEIDELBERG

BRIEF life is here our portion,
　Brief sorrow, short-lived care;
The life that knows no ending,
　The tearless life, is There.

2 O happy retribution!
　Short toil, eternal rest!
For mortals and for sinners
　A mansion with the blest!

3 There grief is turned to pleasure:
　Such pleasure as below
No human voice can utter,
　No human heart can know.

4 And now we fight the battle,
　But then shall wear the crown
Of full and everlasting
　And passionless renown.

5 But He whom now we trust in
　Shall then be seen and known,
And they who know and see Him
　Shall have Him for their own.

6 The morning shall awaken,
　And shadows shall decay,
And each true-hearted servant
　Shall shine as doth the day.

7 And God, our King and Portion,
　In fulness of His grace,
We then shall see for ever
　And worship face to face.
　　　　　　John Mason Neale

485   *"They desire a better country, that is an heavenly."*   [HEIDELBERG]

    For thee, O dear, dear country,
      Mine eyes their vigils keep;
    For very love, beholding
      Thy happy name, they weep.

2 O one, O only mansion!
     O Paradise of joy!
   Where tears are ever banished,
     And smiles have no alloy.

3 Thine ageless walls are bonded
     With amethyst unpriced;
   The saints build up its fabric,
     The corner-stone is Christ.

4 O sweet and blessed country,
     The home of God's elect!
   O sweet and blessed country,
     That eager hearts expect!

5 Jesus, in mercy bring us
     To that dear land of rest;
   Who art with God the Father
     And Spirit ever blest.
                     John Mason Neale

486   *"The throne of God and the Lamb."*   [HEIDELBERG]

    Jerusalem the golden,
      With milk and honey blest,
    Beneath thy contemplation
      Sink heart and voice opprest.

2 They stand, those halls of Zion,
     Conjubilant with song,
   And bright with many an angel,
     And all the martyr throng.

3 The Prince is ever in them;
  The daylight is serene;
  The pastures of the blessed
  Are decked in glorious sheen.

4 There is the throne of David;
  And there, from care released,
  The song of them that triumph,
  The shout of them that feast.

5 And they who with their Leader
  Have conquered in the fight,
  For ever and for ever
  Are clad in robes of white.
                    John Mason Neale

                              [LEDFORTH
487 "*Behold, I come quickly, and My reward is with Me.*"
  O PARADISE! O Paradise!
    Who doth not crave for rest?
  Who would not seek the happy land,
    Where they that loved are blest;
      Where loyal hearts and true
        Stand ever in the light,
      All rapture through and through,
        In God's most holy sight!

2 O Paradise! O Paradise!
    'Tis weary waiting here:
  I long to be where Jesus is,
    To feel, to see Him near;
    (Chorus)

3 O Paradise! O Paradise!
    I want to sin no more;
  I want to be as pure on earth
    As on Thy spotless shore!
    (Chorus)   *Frederick William Faber*

488 *"And so shall we ever be with the Lord."* [ONWARD

 'For ever with the Lord!'
  Amen! so let it be!
 Life from the dead is in that word,
  And immortality!

2 Here in the body pent,
  Absent from Him I roam,
 Yet nightly pitch my moving tent
  A day's march nearer home.

3 My Father's house on high,
  Home of my soul! how near,
 At times, to faith's foreseeing eye,
  Thy golden gates appear!

4 Ah! then my spirit faints
  To reach the land I love,
 The bright inheritance of saints,
  Jerusalem above!

5 'For ever with the Lord!'
  Saviour, if 'tis Thy will,
 The promise of that faithful word
  E'en here to me fulfill.

6 So when my latest breath
  Shall rend the veil in twain,
 By death I shall escape from death,
  And life eternal gain.

7 Knowing as I am known,
  How shall I love that word,
 And oft repeat before the throne,—
  'For ever with the Lord!'
     James Montgomery

Heaven

489 [Glory
"The city of the living God, the heavenly Jerusalem."

O MOTHER dear, Jerusalem;
   When shall I come to thee?
When shall my sorrows have an end?
   Thy joys when shall I see?

2 O happy harbor of God's saints!
   O sweet and pleasant soil!
In thee no sorrow can be found,
   Nor grief, nor care, nor toil.

3 No dimming cloud o'ershadows thee,
   No gloom nor darksome night;
But every soul shines as the sun,
   For God Himself gives light.

4 Thy walls are made of precious stones,
   Thy bulwarks diamond-square,
Thy gates are all of orient pearl;
   O God, if I were there!

5 O passing happy were my state,
   Might I be worthy found
To wait upon my God and King,
   His praises there to sound!
David Dickson

490 *"If ye then be risen with Christ, seek those* [ERNAN
things which are above."

DESCEND from heaven, Immortal Dove;
   Stoop down and take us on Thy wings;
And mount, and bear us far above
   The reach of these inferior things.

2 O for a sight, a pleasing sight,
   Of our Almighty Father's throne!
There sits our Saviour, crowned with light,
   Clothed in a body like our own.

3 Adoring saints around Him stand,
   And thrones and powers before Him fall;
  The God shines gracious through the man,
   And sheds sweet glories on them all.

4 When shall the day, dear Lord, appear,
   That I shall mount, to dwell above;
  And stand, and bow, and worship there,
   And view Thy face, and sing, and love?
Isaac Watts

491   [CHRISTMAS
"He that overcometh shall inherit all things."

GIVE me the wings of faith, to rise
   Within the veil, and see
The saints above—how great their joys!
   How bright their glories be!

2 Once they were mourning here below,
   And wet their couch with tears;
  They wrestled hard, as we do now,
   With sins, and doubts, and fears.

3 I ask them whence their victory came;
   They, with united breath,
  Ascribe their conquest to the Lamb,
   Their triumph to His death.

4 They marked the footsteps that He trod,—
   His zeal inspired their breast;
  And, following their incarnate God,
   Possess the promised rest.

5 Our glorious Leader claims our praise
   For His own pattern given,
  While the long cloud of witnesses
   Shows the same path to heaven.
Isaac Watts

492 *"The Lamb is the light thereof."* [JERUSALEM

O HEAVENLY Jerusalem,
  Of everlasting halls,
Thrice blessed are the people
  Thou storest in Thy walls.

2 Thou art the golden mansion,
    Where saints for ever sing;
  The seat of God's own chosen,
    The palace of the King.

3 There God for ever sitteth,
    Himself of all the crown;
  The Lamb, the light that shineth
    And never goeth down.

4 Naught to this seat approacheth,
    Their sweet peace to molest;
  They sing their God for ever,
    Nor day nor night they rest.

5 Sure hope doth thither lead us;
    Our longings thither tend:
  May short-lived toil ne'er daunt us
    For joys that cannot end.

6 To Christ the Sun that lightens
    His church above, below,—
  To Father, and to Spirit,
    All things created bow.
                    Isaac Williams

[THREE ANGELS
493 *"The things which are not seen are eternal."*

O COULD our thoughts and wishes fly,
  Above these gloomy shades,
To those bright worlds beyond the sky
  Which sorrow ne'er invades!

2 There joys, unseen by mortal eyes
    Or reason's feeble ray,
 In ever blooming prospect rise,
    Unconscious of decay.

3 Lord, send a beam of light divine,
    To guide our upward aim!
 With one reviving touch of Thine
    Our languid hearts inflame.

4 Then shall, on faith's sublimest wing,
    Our ardent wishes rise
 To those bright scenes, where pleasures spring,
    Immortal in the skies.
                        Anne Steele

494   *"Great is your reward in heaven."*   [ARIEL

There is a dwelling-place above;
Thither to meet the God of love,
    The poor in spirit go:
There is a paradise of rest;
For contrite hearts and souls distrest
    Its streams of comfort flow.

2 There is a voice to mercy true;
 To them who mercy's path pursue
    That voice shall bliss impart:
 There is a sight from man concealed;
 That sight, the face of God revealed,
    Shall bless the pure in heart.

3 There is a name in heaven bestowed;
 That name, which hails them sons of God,
    The friends of peace shall know:
 There is a kingdom in the sky,
 Where they shall reign with God on high,
    Who serve Him here below.
                        Richard Mant

Heaven

[O GOTT, DU FROMMER GOTT

495 *"There remaineth therefore a rest to the people of God."*

THERE is a blessed home
  Beyond this land of woe,
Where trials never come,
  Nor tears of sorrow flow;
Where faith is lost in sight,
  And patient hope is crowned,
And everlasting light
  Its glory throws around.

2 There is a land of peace,
    Good angels know it well;
  Glad songs that never cease
    Within its portals swell;
  Around its glorious throne
    Ten thousand saints adore
  Christ, with the Father One
    And Spirit, evermore.

3 O joy all joys beyond,
    To see the Lamb who died,
  And count each sacred wound
    In hands, and feet, and side;
  To give to Him the praise
    Of every triumph won,
  And sing through endless days
    The great things He hath done.

4 Look up, ye saints of God,
    Nor fear to tread below
  The path your Saviour trod
    Of daily toil and woe;
  Wait but a little while
    In uncomplaining love,
  His own most gracious smile
    Shall welcome you above.

Sir Henry Williams Baker

496 *"God hath given to us eternal life,* [JUDGMENT HYMN
and this life is in His Son."

Eternity! eternity!
O bright, O blest eternity!
Which Jesus hath obtained for those
Who seek in Him their sure repose;
A little while they suffer here,
But lo! eternity is near!

2 Eternity! eternity!
Soon shall these eyes thy wonders see;
O may I now the world despise,
And upward raise my thankful eyes,
And seek the joys that shall abide,
From sin and sorrow purified!

3 Eternity! eternity!
Prepare me for eternity!
Now grant me, Lord, Thy humble mind,
To all my Father's will resigned:
Now give me faith that rests on Thee;
Lord, in Thy love remember me!
Arthur Tozer Russell

497 *"And I saw heaven opened."* [NEW JERUSALEM

WE are on our journey home,
  Where Christ our Lord is gone;
We shall meet around His throne,
  When He makes His people one
    In the new Jerusalem.

2 We can see that distant home,
    Though clouds arise dark between;
  Faith views the radiant dome,
    And a luster flashes keen
      From the new Jerusalem.

3 O glory shining far
   From the never-setting Sun!
 O trembling morning-star!
   Our journey 's almost done
     To the new Jerusalem!

4 Our hearts are breaking now
   Those mansions fair to see;
 O Lord, Thy heavens bow,
   And raise us up with Thee
     To the new Jerusalem!
                    Charles Beecher

498 [GERMAN TE DEUM
      "Lord, if he sleep, he shall do well."

THE saints of God! their conflict past,
And life's long battle won at last,
No more they need the shield or sword,
They cast them down before their Lord:
  O happy saints! for ever blest,
  At Jesus' feet how safe you rest!

2 The saints of God! their wanderings done,
 No more their weary course they run,
 No more they faint, no more they fall,
 No foes oppress, no fears appal:
   O happy saints! for ever blest,
   In that dear home how sweet your rest!

3 O God of saints! to Thee we cry;
 O Saviour! plead for us on high;
 O Holy Ghost! our Guide and Friend,
 Grant us Thy grace till life shall end:
   That with all saints our rest may be
   In that bright Paradise with Thee!

499 *"Our conversation is in heaven."* [THREE ANGELS

EARTH has engrossed my love too long!
'Tis time I lift mine eyes
Upward, dear Father, to Thy throne,
And to my native skies.

2 There the blest Man, my Saviour, sits:
The God! how bright He shines!
And scatters infinite delights
On all the happy minds.

3 Seraphs, with elevated strains,
Circle the throne around;
And move, and charm the starry plains
With an immortal sound.

4 Jesus, the Lord, their harps employs;
Jesus, Thy love they sing!
Jesus, the life of all our joys,
Sounds sweet from every string.

5 Now let me rise and join their song,
And be an angel too;
My heart, my hand, my ear, my tongue,—
Here's joyful work for you.

6 I would begin the music here,
And so my soul should rise:
O for some heavenly notes to bear
My spirit to the skies!

7 There ye that love my Saviour sit,
There I would fain have place,
Among your thrones, or at your feet,
So I might see His face!

Isaac Watts

500   *"He that overcometh, the same shall be clothed in white raiment."*   [GOSPEL

WHAT are these in bright array,
  This innumerable throng,
Round the altar, night and day,
  Hymning one triumphant song?—
'Worthy is the Lamb once slain,
  Blessing, honor, glory, power,
Wisdom, riches, to obtain,
  New dominion every hour.'

2 These through fiery trials trod!—
  These from great affliction came:
Now before the throne of God,
  Sealed with His almighty name,
Clad in raiment pure and white,
  Victor palms in every hand,
Through their dear Redeemer's might,
  More than conquerors they stand.

3 Hunger, thirst, disease, unknown,
  On immortal fruits they feed;
Them the Lamb amid the throne
  Shall to living fountains lead:
Joy and gladness banish sighs;
  Perfect love dispels all fear;
And for ever from their eyes
  God shall wipe away the tear.
                James Montgomery

501   *"There the weary be at rest."*   [LANDSTUHL

THERE is an hour of peaceful rest,
  To mourning wanderers given:
There is a joy for souls distrest,
A balm for every wounded breast,
  'Tis found above—in heaven.

Heaven

2 There is a home for weary souls
  By sin and sorrow driven;
When tost on life's tempestuous shoals,
Where storms arise and ocean rolls,
  And all is drear but heaven.

3 There, faith lifts up her cheerful eye,
  To brighter prospects given;
And views the tempest passing by,
The evening shadows quickly fly,
  And all serene in heaven.

4 There, fragrant flowers immortal bloom,
  And joys supreme are given;
There, rays divine disperse the gloom;—
Beyond the confines of the tomb
  Appears the dawn of heaven.
            William Bingham Tappan

[CHRISTMAS
502 *"To me to live is Christ, and to die is gain."*

Lord, it belongs not to my care
  Whether I die or live;
To love and serve Thee is my share,
  And this Thy grace must give.

2 If life be long, I will be glad,
    That I may long obey;
  If short, yet why should I be sad,
    To soar to endless day?

3 Christ leads me through no darker rooms
    Than He went through before;
  He that unto God's kingdom comes
    Must enter by this door.

4 Come, Lord, when grace hath made me meet
    Thy blessed face to see;
  For if Thy work on earth be sweet,
    What will Thy glory be!

5 Then shall I end my sad complaints
    And weary sinful days,
  And join with all triumphant saints
    To sing Jehovah's praise.

6 My knowledge of that life is small;
    The eye of faith is dim;
  But 'tis enough that Christ knows all,
    And I shall be with Him.
                              Richard Baxter

503   [THREE ANGELS
      *"Thine eyes shall see the King in His beauty: they shall
      behold the land that is very far off."*

  THERE is a land of pure delight,
    Where saints immortal reign;
  Infinite day excludes the night,
    And pleasures banish pain.

2 There everlasting spring abides,
    And never-withering flowers:
  Death, like a narrow sea, divides
    This heavenly land from ours.

3 Sweet fields beyond the swelling flood
    Stand drest in living green;
  So to the Jews old Canaan stood,
    While Jordan rolled between.

4 But timorous mortals start and shrink
    To cross the narrow sea,
  And linger, shivering on the brink,
    And fear to launch away.

5 O could we make our doubts remove,
  These gloomy doubts that rise,
And see the Canaan that we love,
  With unbeclouded eyes:—

6 Could we but climb where Moses stood,
  And view the landscape o'er,—
Not Jordan's stream, nor death's cold flood,
  Should fright us from the shore.
                    Isaac Watts

[VOM HIMMEL
504 "*The spirit shall return unto God who gave it.*"

Now let our souls, on wings sublime,
Rise from the vanities of time,
Draw back the parting veil, and see
The glories of eternity.

2 Born by a new celestial birth,
Why should we grovel here on earth?
Why grasp at vain and fleeting toys,
So near to heaven's eternal joys?

3 Shall aught beguile us on the road
While we are walking back to God?
For strangers into life we come,
And dying is but going home.

4 Welcome, sweet hour of full discharge,
That sets our longing souls at large;
Unbinds our chains, breaks up our cell;
And gives us with our God to dwell.

5 To dwell with God, to feel His love,
Is the full heaven enjoyed above;
And the sweet expectation now,
Is the young dawn of heaven below.
                    Thomas Gibbons

Heaven

505 [VOM HIMMEL
"I shall be satisfied, when I awake with Thy likeness."

What sinners value I resign;
Lord, 'tis enough that Thou art mine:
I shall behold Thy blissful face,
And stand complete in righteousness.

2 This life's a dream, an empty show;
But the bright world, to which I go,
Hath joys substantial and sincere;
When shall I wake and find me there?

3 O glorious hour! O blest abode!
I shall be near and like my God!
And flesh and sin no more control
The sacred pleasures of the soul.

4 My flesh shall slumber in the ground,
Till the last trumpet's joyful sound;
Then burst the chains with sweet surprise,
And in my Saviour's image rise.
Isaac Watts

506 *"And there shall be no more death."* [REDHEAD

How vain is all beneath the skies,
How transient every earthly bliss;
How slender all the fondest ties,
That bind us to a world like this.

2 The evening cloud, the morning dew,
The withering grass, the fading flower,
Of earthly hopes are emblems true,
The glory of a passing hour.

3 But though earth's fairest blossoms die,
And all beneath the sky is vain,
There is a land whose confines lie
Beyond the reach of care and pain.

4 Then let the hope of joys to come
    Dispel our cares and chase our fears:
  If God be ours, we're traveling home,
    Though passing through a vale of tears.

[CHRISTMAS

507 *"Behold, the tabernacle of God is with men."*
  Lo! what a glorious sight appears
    To our believing eyes!
  The earth and seas are past away,
    And the old rolling skies.

2 From the third heaven, where God resides,
    That holy, happy place,
  The new Jerusalem comes down,
    Adorned with shining grace.

  Attending angels shout for joy,
    And the bright armies sing,—
  'Mortals, behold the sacred seat
    Of your descending King.

4 'The God of glory down to men
    Removes His blest abode;
  Men, the dear objects of His grace,
    And He the loving God.

5 'His own kind hand shall wipe the tears
    From every weeping eye;
  And pains, and groans, and griefs, and fears,
    And death itself, shall die.'

6 How long, dear Saviour, O how long
    Shall this bright hour delay?
  Fly swifter round, ye wheels of time,
    And bring the welcome day!
                      Isaac Watts

508 *"Behold, I make all things new."* [HEAVENLY BLISS

There is no night in heaven;
   In that blest world above
Work never can bring weariness,
   For work itself is love.
There is no grief in heaven;
   For life is one glad day,
And tears are of those former things
   Which all have past away.

2 There is no sin in heaven;
   Behold that blessed throng;
All holy in their spotless robe,
   All holy in their song.
There is no sin in heaven;
   Here, who from sin is free?
Yet angels aid us in our strife
   For Christ's true liberty.

3 There is no death in heaven;
   For they who gain that shore
Have won their immortality
   And they can die no more.
There is no death in heaven;
   But when the Christian dies,
The angels wait his parted soul,
   And waft it to the skies.

509 *"O that I had wings like a dove! for then* [HEXHAM
would I fly away, and be at rest."

I would not live alway: I ask not to stay
Where storm after storm rises dark o'er the way;
The few lurid mornings that dawn on us here,
Are enough for life's woes, full enough for its cheer.

2 I would not live alway, thus fettered by sin,
Temptation without and corruption within:
E'en the rapture of pardon is mingled with fears,
And the cup of thanksgiving with penitent tears.

3 I would not live alway; no—welcome the tomb;
Since Jesus hath lain there, I dread not its gloom;
There, sweet be my rest, till He bid me arise
To hail Him in triumph descending the skies.

4 Who, who would live alway, away from his God;
Away from yon heaven, that blissful abode,
Where the rivers of pleasure flow o'er the bright plains,
And the noontide of glory eternally reigns:—

5 Where the saints of all ages in harmony meet,
Their Saviour and brethren transported to greet;
While the anthems of rapture unceasingly roll,
And the smile of the Lord is the feast of the soul.
                William Augustus Muhlenberg

[PILGRIM

510 *"In My Father's house are many mansions."*

I'M but a stranger here;
Earth is a desert drear,
    Heaven is my home.
Danger and sorrow stand
Round me on every hand;
Heaven is my fatherland,
    Heaven is my home.

2 What though the tempest rage?
  Short is my pilgrimage,
    Heaven is my home:
  And time's wild wintry blast
  Soon will be overpast;
  I shall reach home at last,
    Heaven is my home.

3 There, at my Saviour's side,
  I shall be glorified;
    Heaven is my home;
  There with the good and blest,
  Those I love most and best,
  I shall for ever rest;
    Heaven is my home.

4 Grant me to murmur not,
  Whate'er my earthly lot;
    Heaven is my home;
  Grant me to surely stand
  There at my Lord's right hand;
  Heaven is my fatherland,
    Heaven is my home.
            Thomas Rawson Taylor

511   "*Death is swallowed up in victory.*"   [REQUIEM

FRIEND after friend departs;
  Who hath not lost a friend?
There is no union here of hearts,
  That finds not here an end:
Were this frail world our only rest,
Living or dying, none were blest.

2 Beyond the flight of time,
    Beyond this vale of death,
  There surely is some blessed clime,
    Where life is not a breath,

Nor life's affections transient fire,
Whose sparks fly upward to expire.

3 There is a world above,
   Where parting is unknown;
A whole eternity of love,
   Formed for the good alone;
And faith beholds the dying here -
Translated to that happier sphere.

4 Thus star by star declines
   Till all are past away,
As morning high and higher shines
   To pure and perfect day;
Nor sink those stars in empty night;
They hide themselves in heaven's own light.
James Montgomery

Topical Index

Activity, Christian, 401-413
Advent. See CHRIST.
Afflictions, 421-447
Ascension of Christ, 151-155, 158-160
Ashamed of Christ, 134, 394, 417
Atonement, 117, 118, 127, 128, 139, 140, 180-209
Beatitudes, 337, 494
Bible, 17, 21, 33, 40, 58, 211
Burial hymns, 301, 302, 453-461, 501, 504, 506
Christ ascended, 151-155, 158-160
  birth of, 109-120
  cross of, 140-144, 189, 190, 276
  example of, 135-139, 275, 398
  faith in, 186, 192, 203-209, 241, 246, 247, 258, 262-276, 353-377
  future kingdom of, 212-224, 234, 284
  joy in, 225, 282-327
  the Judge, 462-470, 479-481
  a King, 117, 120, 121, 133, 150, 158, 217, 219-224, 284, 293
  interceding, 151-155, 157, 204, 262, 440
  the Light of life, 54, 125, 180, 181, 369, 375

Christ, love of to us, 113, 130, 131, 138-140, 151, 152, 194, 201, 209, 266, 273, 274, 305, 307, 318, 319, 324
  not ashamed of, 134, 394, 417
  praise to, 9, 14, 37, 38, 112, 113, 116-133, 138-155, 159, 160, 180-196, 205-209, 226, 227, 238, 239, 282, 284, 285, 288, 305-307, 315, 316, 341
  redemption by, 117, 118, 127, 128, 139, 1.0, 180-209
  rest in, 182, 197-199, 203, 256, 267, 279, 280, 329-333, 361, 487, 488, 501
  resurrection of, 14, 34, 145-148, 161
  a Sacrifice, 139-144, 189-194. 205, 251, 259
  second coming of, 464-482
  sufferings of, 139-144, 158
  union with, 136, 238. 336
  the Way, the Truth, the Life, 132, 206
Church, delight in the, 226-240
  militant, 228, 235
  triumphant, 159, 217. 219-224, 231, 234, 239, 491-500
  unity of the, 232, 235, 238-240

Index

Close of worship, 41-44
Communion hymns, 241-255
Confession of sin, 181, 188, 256-280, 372, 373
Conversion, 128-133, 152, 166, 178-210, 256-280
    of the world, 212-225, 234
Cross, bearing the, 406-447
    Christ on the, 140-144, 189, 190, 276
Daily worship, 45-67
Death, 453-463, 475, 506, 511
Easter, 14, 34, 145-148, 161
Eternity, 77, 451, 453, 459, 473, 483-511
Evening hymns, 60-66
Faith, 186, 192, 203-209, 241, 246, 247, 258, 262-276, 353-377
Forgiveness, 181-210, 256-281, 373
Funeral hymns, 301, 302, 453-461, 501, 504, 506
God, adoration of, 1-43, 68-108, 193, 196, 283, 286, 287, 291-300, 303, 304, 308-314, 317-328
    dependence on, 77, 83, 85, 87, 350-352, 354, 356, 422-447
    house of, 6-13, 18, 19, 22-29
    presence of, 24, 28, 97-99
    providence of, 46, 63, 67, 83, 85, 88, 96, 102, 291, 292, 311, 349-352, 354, 366
    a Refuge, 22, 46, 83, 182, 198, 236, 280, 344-349, 377, 447
    a Sovereign, 81, 101, 104-106, 312, 424-427, 435, 436
Grace, saving, 184-196, 208, 209, 259
Heaven, 22, 23, 483-511

Holy Spirit invoked, 5, 162-178, 215, 216, 242, 290
Hope, Christian, 11, 180-209, 256-280, 329-344
House of God, 6-13, 18, 19, 22-29
Invitations of the Gospel, 33, 181-187, 191-203, 208, 210, 225
Invocations, 2-5, 7-13, 16, 19, 25, 26, 28, 29, 31, 35, 213
Joy, Christian, 225, 282-327
Judgment day, 269, 461-482
Life, uncertainty of, 448-453, 461, 475, 478, 502, 505, 506
Lord's day, 1-44
Lord's Supper, 241-255
Love of God to us, 100, 113, 130, 131, 138-140, 151, 152, 192-196, 201, 209, 266, 273, 274, 287, 306, 307, 318, 319, 322, 324-326, 346
Love to God, 87, 166, 201, 246, 288, 289, 295, 310, 313-319, 324-327
Missions, 213-225, 234
Morning hymns, 45-59, 67
Mortality, 448-453, 461, 475, 478, 506
New Year, 448-451
Omnipotence, 96, 104-106, 312
Omnipresence, 97-99
Omniscience, 97, 99
Opening of worship, 1-40
Peace, Christian, 198, 199, 203, 205, 267, 280, 336, 345-349
Penitence, 181, 256-281, 372, 373
Pentecost, 162, 167
Pilgrimage, 287, 333, 354, 366, 475, 478, 484, 485, 495, 497
Prayer, 10-12, 29, 183, 262, 377-391, 440
Preaching of the word, 16, 165
Providence of God, 46, 63, 67, 83, 85, 88, 96, 102, 291, 292, 311, 349-352, 354, 366

Punishment, future, 461-471, 473, 477
Purity of heart, 97, 310, 334, 342, 343
Redemption, 117, 118, 127, 128, 139, 140, 180-209
Repentance, 181, 256-281, 372, 373
Resignation, 421-447
Rest in Christ, 182, 197-199, 203, 256, 267, 279, 280, 329-333, 361, 487, 488, 501
Resurrection of Christ, 14, 34, 145-148, 161
Sabbath, 1-44
Salvation, 116-118, 127, 128, 139, 140, 180-209
Sanctuary, 6-13, 18, 19, 22-29
Scriptures, Holy, 17, 21, 33, 40, 58, 211
Service, Christian, 396-439

Sin, confession of, 181, 188, 256-280, 372, 373
Sovereignty of God, 81, 101, 104-106, 312, 424-427, 435, 436
Star of Bethlehem, 109-111, 180
Submission, 421-447
Supper, Lord's, 241-255
Temptations, 405, 409, 414, 445
Time, 448-453, 478, 504
Trials, 405-447
Trinity, praise to the, 2, 3, 69, 74, 76, 196, 213, 214
Union with Christ, 136, 238, 336
Unity of the Church, 232, 235, 238-240
Warfare, Christian, 401-412
Watchfulness, 411-414
Worship, daily, 45-67
   Sabbath, 1-44
Year, old and new, 448-451

Index of First Lines

[A broken heart, my God, my King] ----------- 271
A charge to keep I have --------------------- 401
A few more years shall roll ----------------- 478
[A glory gilds the sacred page] -------------- 40
A mighty fortress is our God ---------------- 445
A sinner, Lord, behold I stand -------------- 262
Abide with me! fast falls the even-tide ------ 63
According to Thy gracious word -------------- 255
Again the daylight fills the sky ------------- 52
Again the Lord of life and light ------------- 37
Ah, how shall fallen man -------------------- 188
All glory, laud, and honor ------------------ 121
All hail the power of Jesus' name ----------- 117
All people that on earth do dwell ------------ 75
All praise to Thee, Eternal Lord ------------ 113
All praise to Thee, my God, this night ------- 64
Almighty God, Thy piercing eye -------------- 269
Alway in the Lord rejoice ------------------- 314
Am I a soldier of the cross ----------------- 406
Amazing grace,—how sweet the sound --------- 195
And dost Thou say, Ask what thou wilt ------- 388
And must I part with all I have ------------- 421
And will the Judge descend ------------------ 468
And wilt Thou pardon, Lord ------------------ 268
Angels, from the realms of glory ------------ 110
Approach, my soul, the mercy-seat ----------- 385
Arise, O King of grace! arise ---------------- 20
As pants the hart for cooling streams ------- 323
As the sun doth daily rise ------------------- 48
As when the weary traveler gains ------------ 359
As with gladness men of old ----------------- 111
Asleep in Jesus! blessed sleep -------------- 458
Author of good! to Thee we turn ------------- 384
Awake, and sing the song -------------------- 227

Index

Awake, my soul, and with the sun 49
Awake, my soul! in joyful lays 306
Awake, my soul! lift up thine eyes 411
Awake, my soul, stretch every nerve 408
Awake our souls, away our fears 407
Awake, ye saints, and raise your eyes 451

Be Thou exalted, O my God 71
Be with me, Lord, where'er I go 397
Before Jehovah's awful throne 79
Behold, a Stranger's at the door 200
Behold the glories of the Lamb 159
Behold the morning sun 58
Behold the path that mortals tread 461
Behold the throne of grace 389
Behold Thy servant drawing near 247
Behold what wondrous grace 328
Bless, O my soul, the living God 93
Blessed are they whose hearts are pure 342
Blessed fountain, full of grace 320
Blessing, honor, thanks, and praise 455
Blest are the humble souls that see 337
Blest are the pure in heart 343
Blest are the souls that hear and know 225
Blest be the tie that binds 240
Blest be Thou, O God of Israel 90
Blest be Thy love, dear Lord 429
Blest day of God, most calm, most bright 19
Blot out our sins of old 260
Bread of heaven! on Thee we feed 245
Brief life is here our portion 484
Brightest and best of the sons of the morning .. 109
Broad is the road that leads to death 444
Brother, though from yonder sky 457
By Christ redeemed, in Christ restored 249

Call Jehovah Thy salvation 351
Christ is made the sure foundation 25
Christ, of all my hopes the ground 420
Christ the Lord is risen to-day 34
Christ, whose glory fills the skies 54
Christ will gather in His own 460
Church of the Ever-living God 231
Come, blessed Spirit! Source of light 173

Come, dearest Lord, descend and dwell.......... 4
Come, Ever-blessed Spirit, come 290
[Come, Gracious Spirit, Heavenly Dove]........169
Come hither, all ye weary souls................203
Come, Holy Ghost, who ever One..............163
Come, Holy Spirit, come 164
Come, Holy Spirit, Heavenly Dove, My sinful..172
Come, Holy Spirit, Heavenly Dove, With all Thy 169
[Come, humble sinner, in whose breast].........258
Come, kingdom of our God...................234
Come, let us join our cheerful songs............315
Come, let us join our songs of praise............151
Come, let us sing the song of songs.............155
Come, my soul, thy suit prepare 387
Come, O Creator Spirit blest..................170
Come! said Jesus' sacred voice................199
Come, Thou Almighty King................... 74
Come, Thou desire of all Thy saints............ 11
Come, Thou Everlasting Spirit.................242
Come, Thou Fount of every blessing...........341
Come, trembling sinner, in whose breast........258
Come unto Me, ye weary.....................197
Come, ye disconsolate, where'er ye languish....182
Come, ye sinners, poor and wretched 265
[Come, ye weary, heavy-laden]................265
Command Thy blessing from above............. 2
Commit thou all thy griefs....................435
Crown Him with crowns of gold...............150

Day of judgment, day of wonders..............464
[Dear Father, to Thy mercy-seat]..............386
Dear Refuge of my weary soul.................447
Depth of mercy! can there be 273
Descend from heaven, Immortal Dove..........490
Did Christ o'er sinners weep..................281
Didst Thou, my Saviour, suffer shame..........417
Dismiss us with Thy blessing, Lord 44
Do not I love Thee, O my Lord...............327
Does the gospel word proclaim 256

Early, my God, without delay.................. 27
Earth has engrossed my love too long 499
Enthroned on high, Almighty Lord............177
Eternal God! Eternal King....................467

Index

Eternal Spirit! we confess	176
Eternal Sun of righteousness	371
Eternity! eternity	496

Faith adds new charms to earthly bliss	355
Faith is the dawning of the day	356
Faith is the polar star	353
Far from the world, O Lord, I flee	347
Father, hear our humble claim	382
Father!—if I may call Thee so	473
Father of glory! to Thy name	196
Father of mercies, God of love	311
Father! whate'er of earthly bliss	437
For all Thy saints, O Lord	301
For ever blessed be the Lord	392
For ever with the Lord	488
For mercies, countless as the sands	305
For thee, O dear, dear country	485
For Thy mercy and Thy grace	450
Forth in Thy name, O Lord, I go	51
Fountain of grace, rich, full, and free	126
Friend after friend departs	511
From all that dwell below the skies	286
From all Thy saints in warfare	302
From every stormy wind that blows	377
From Greenland's icy mountains	218
From the cross uplifted high	140
From the recesses of a lowly spirit	378

Gird on Thy conquering sword	133
Give me the wings of faith, to rise	491
[Give to the winds thy fears]	435
Glorious things of thee are spoken	230
Glory to God on high	149
[Glory to Thee, my God, this night]	64
Go, labor on; spend and be spent	410
God calling yet! shall I not hear	277
God, in the gospel of His Son	33
God is love; His mercy brightens	322
God is my strong salvation	393
God is the refuge of His saints	236
God moves in a mysterious way	441
God of mercy, God of grace	303
God of the morning, at whose voice	59

Index

God, the everlasting God 175
Grace! 'tis a charming sound 187
Gracious Spirit, Dove divine 178
Great God! how infinite art Thou 77
Great God, we sing that mighty hand 449
Great God! what do I see and hear 480
Great God, whose universal sway 219
Guide me, O Thou great Jehovah 354

Hail, Thou once despised Jesus 123
Hail to the Lord's Anointed 222
Hail tranquil hour of closing day 61
Hark, my soul! it is the Lord 201
Hark! ten thousand harps and voices 284
Hark, the glad sound, the Saviour comes 118
Hark, the herald angels sing 112
Hark! the song of jubilee 223
Hark! what mean those holy voices 115
Hast thou sinned? Sin no more 264
Hasten, Lord, the glorious time 217
He lives, the great Redeemer lives 157
He who on earth as man was known 154
He who once in righteous vengeance 144
He's come! let every knee be bent 179
High in the heavens, Eternal God 103
Holy and reverend is the name 86
Holy, holy, holy Lord! Be Thy glorious name 89
Holy, holy, holy Lord, God of Hosts, when heaven . 78
Holy, holy, holy Lord God almighty 69
Holy Jesus, Saviour blest 132
Hosanna to the living Lord 9
How are Thy servants blest, O Lord 350
How calm and beautiful the morn 147
How firm a foundation, ye saints of the Lord 446
How gentle God's commands 434
How heavy is the night 181
How pleasant, how divinely fair 18
How shall a contrite spirit pray 183
How sweet the name of Jesus sounds 288
How sweetly flowed the gospel's sound 137
How vain is all beneath the skies 506

I heard the voice of Jesus say 376
I know that my Redeemer lives 368

Index

I love the volume of Thy word 17
I love Thy kingdom, Lord 226
I saw One hanging on a tree 259
I worship Thee, sweet Will of God 433
I would not live alway; I ask not to stay 509
If human kindness meets return 250
If, through unruffled seas 424
I'm but a stranger here 510
I'm not ashamed to own my Lord 394
In all my vast concerns with Thee 99
[In evil long I took delight] 259
In heavenly love abiding 349
In the cross of Christ I glory 142
In Thy name O Lord! assembling 31
In true and patient hope 335
In vain we seek for peace with God 205
Infinite excellence is Thine 125
It came upon the midnight clear 114
It is not death to die 459

Jehovah, God! Thy gracious power 96
Jerusalem, my happy home 483
Jerusalem the golden 486
Jesus! and shall it ever be 134
Jesus calls us, o'er the tumult 398
Jesus Christ is risen to-day 161
Jesus, I my cross have taken 415
Jesus, if still Thou art to-day 263
Jesus, Lover of my soul 418
Jesus, my Strength, my Hope 414
Jesus! Name of wondrous love 128
Jesus! our best beloved Friend 391
Jesus shall reign where'er the sun 224
Jesus! the very thought of Thee 130
Jesus, Thine all-victorious love 166
Jesus, Thou Joy of loving hearts 248
Jesus, Thy blood and righteousness 186
Jesus, we look to Thee 28
Jesus, where'er Thy people meet 29
Join all the glorious names 124
Joy to the world! the Lord is come 120
Just as I am, without one plea 373

[Know, my soul, thy full salvation] 415

Lead, kindly Light, amid the encircling gloom..366
Let me be with Thee where Thou art............332
Let saints below in concert sing................232
Let songs of praises fill the sky................162
Life is the time to serve the Lord..............278
Lift up, lift up your voices now................160
Lift up to God the voice of praise.............. 84
Lift up your heads, eternal gates...............293
Lift up your heads, ye mighty gates............282
Light of those whose dreary dwelling...........369
Lo! God is here! let us adore 24
Lo! He comes, with clouds descending..........482
Lo! on a narrow neck of land...................469
Lo! what a glorious sight appears..............507
Lord, as to Thy dear cross we flee..............275
Lord, at this closing hour...................... 41
Lord, dismiss us with Thy blessing............. 43
Lord God of Hosts, by all adored.............. 72
Lord God of morning and of night.............. 57
Lord, I am come! Thy promise is my plea......280
[Lord, I am Thine; but Thou wilt prove]......505
Lord, I believe a rest remains..................361
Lord I believe; Thy power I own...............357
Lord, in the morning Thou shalt hear.......... 8
Lord, it belongs not to my care................502
Lord Jesus, are we one with Thee...............238
Lord Jesus, when we stand afar.................276
Lord of all being! throned afar................ 80
Lord of the Sabbath! hear our vows............ 23
Lord of the worlds above....................... 6
Lord, show Thy glory, as of old................167
Lord, teach us how to pray aright..............380
Lord, Thou hast been Thy people's rest........108
Lord, Thou hast searched and seen me through.. 97
Lord, Thou hast won—at length I yield.........266
Lord! we come before Thee now................. 12
Lord! when before Thy throne we meet..........252
Love Divine, all love excelling.................318

Majestic sweetness sits enthroned...............307
Many centuries have fled.......................253
Morn of morns, and day of days................. 13
Most surely at the appointed time..............481
My dear Redeemer and my Lord..................135

Index

My faith looks up to Thee 362
My faith shall triumph o'er the grave 474
[My Father, to Thy mercy-seat] 386
My God, accept my heart this day 270
My God and Father, while I stray 432
My God, how endless is Thy love 47
My God, how wonderful Thou art 295
My God, I love Thee; not because 324
[My God, my Father, while I stray] 432
My God, the Spring of all my joys 313
My God, 'tis to Thy mercy-seat 386
My Maker and my King 87
My Shepherd is the living Lord 292
My Shepherd will supply my need 291
My soul, be on thy guard 405
My soul, repeat His praise 309
My spirit on Thy care 443

Nature with open volume stands 209
Nearer, my God to Thee 423
[New every morning is the love] 55
No more, my God! I boast no more 370
Not all the blood of beasts 251
Not to condemn the sons of men 192
Not to the terrors of the Lord 233
Now let our souls, on wings sublime 504
Now may He who from the dead 42
Now thank we all our God 283
[Now that the daylight fills the sky] 52
Now that the day-star glimmers bright 53
Now to the Lord a noble song 193

O bless the Lord, my soul 308
O bread to pilgrims given 254
O cease, my wandering soul 198
O Christ! our Hope, our heart's Desire 152
O Christ! our King, Creator, Lord 143
O Christ, who hast prepared a place 330
O could I speak the matchless worth 127
O could our thoughts and wishes fly 493
O day of rest and gladness 15
O draw me, Father, after Thee 321
O for a closer walk with God 372
O for a heart to praise my God 310

Index

O for a thousand tongues to sing	316
O for the death of those	454
O gift of gifts! O grace of faith	358
O God! by whom the seed is given	16
O God of Hosts, the mighty Lord	304
O God of truth, O Lord of might	56
[O God, our Help in ages past]	83
O God, Thou art my God alone	287
O God, whose presence glows in all	7
O happy soul, that lives on high	326
O heavenly Jerusalem	492
O heavenly Word, Eternal Light	122
O help us, Lord! each hour of need	340
O holy Saviour, Friend unseen	395
O how could I forget Him	246
O it is hard to work for God	409
O Jesus, bruised and wounded more	244
O Jesus, Lord of heavenly grace	50
O Jesus, Saviour of the lost	267
O Lamb of God, still keep me	422
O Lord, I would delight in Thee	317
O Lord, in perfect bliss above	237
O Lord most high, Eternal King	153
O Lord of life, and truth, and grace	229
O Lord our God, arise	214
O Love Divine, how sweet Thou art	319
O Love Divine, that stooped to share	431
O Love, how deep! how broad! how high	139
O mean may seem this house of clay	136
O mother dear, Jerusalem	489
O One with God the Father	375
O Paradise! O Paradise	487
O Sacred Head! once wounded	141
O Saviour! is Thy promise fled	212
[O Son of God, in glory crowned]	465
O Spirit of the living God	216
O stay thy tears, for they are blest	456
O that my load of sin were gone	272
O that the Lord would guide my ways	399
O Thou, in whom our love doth find	325
O Thou that hearest prayer	165
O Thou that hear'st the prayer of faith	364
O Thou, that hear'st when sinners cry	271
O Thou, the contrite sinners' Friend	438

O Thou, to whom, in ancient time	39
O Thou, to whose all-searching sight	419
O Thou, who by a star didst guide	334
O Thou, who didst with love untold	360
[O Thou, who hear'st the prayer or faith]	364
O Thou whom neither time nor space	76
O Thou whose tender mercy hears	257
O timely happy, timely wise	55
O where are kings and empires now	228
O where shall rest be found	279
O worship the King, all glorious above	82
O'er the distant mountains breaking	476
On God the race of man depends	452
On this day, the first of days	32
One sweetly solemn thought	475
One there is above all others	181
Our God, our Help in ages past	83
Our Heavenly Father calls	390
Pleasant are Thy courts above	22
Plunged in a gulf of dark despair	194
Praise, my soul, the King of heaven	91
Praise the Lord, His glories show	73
Praise the Lord! ye heavens, adore Him	92
Praise to the Holiest in the hight	138
Praise waits in Zion, Lord, for Thee	10
Prayer is the soul's sincere desire	379
Quiet, Lord, my froward heart	428
Redeemed from guilt, redeemed from fears	289
Remember Me, the Saviour said	241
Rise, my soul, and stretch thy wings	333
Rock of ages! cleft for me	344
Round the Lord in glory seated	300
Safely through another week	26
Salvation! O the joyful sound	185
[Saviour, Source of every blessing]	341
Shine on our souls, Eternal God	67
Show pity, Lord; O Lord, forgive	274
Since all the coming scenes of time	425
Sing praise to God who reigns above	94
Sing to the Lord a joyful song	30

Index

Sing we the song of those who stand............239
So let our lips and lives express...............416
Softly, now, the light of day................... 62
Soldiers of Christ, arise 404
Soldiers who to Christ belong..................402
Songs of praise the angels sang................299
Songs of thankfulness and praise...............119
Sovereign and transforming Grace............... 35
Sovereign Ruler of the skies...................427
Speak, for Thy servant heareth.................400
Spirit Divine, attend our prayers..............168
Spirit of God, that moved of old...............171
Spirit of power and might, behold..............215
Spirit of truth! on this Thy day............... 5
Stand up, my soul, shake off thy fears.........412
Stand up, stand up for Jesus...................403
Sun of my soul, Thou Saviour dear.............. 66

That day of wrath! that dreadful day...........477
The abyss of many a former sin.................261
The Church's one foundation....................235
The day is past and over....................... 60
The day of resurrection........................ 14
[The day of wrath! that dreadful day]..........477
The floods, O Lord, lift up their voice........106
The golden gates are lifted up.................331
The harvest dawn is near.......................472
The Head that once was crowned with thorns....158
The heavens declare Thy glory, Lord............211
The last loud trumpet's wondrous sound.........462
The Lord descended from above..................105
The Lord is King! lift up Thy voice............312
The Lord is my Shepherd, no want shall I know.102
The Lord is risen indeed 148
The Lord Jehovah reigns, And royal state.......101
The Lord Jehovah reigns, His throne is built... 81
The Lord my Shepherd is........................ 88
The Lord on high proclaims.....................208
The Lord our God is full of might..............104
The Lord will come! the earth shall quake......470
The promise of My Father's love................243
The race that long in darkness walked..........116
The saints of God! their conflict past.........498
[The Saviour hanging on the tree]..............259

The shade and gloom of life are fled ---------- 145
The spacious firmament on high -------------- 107
The Spirit breathes upon the word ------------ 40
The Spirit, in our hearts -------------------- 202
The starry firmament on high ---------------- 21
Thee we adore, Eternal Lord ----------------- 63
Thee we adore, Eternal Name ---------------- 453
There is a blessed home -------------------- 495
There is a dwelling-place above -------------- 494
There is a fountain filled with blood ---------- 184
There is a land of pure delight -------------- 503
There is a safe and secret place -------------- 345
There is an hour of peaceful rest ------------ 501
There is an hour when I must part ---------- 463
There is no night in heaven ----------------- 508
They who seek the throne of grace ---------- 381
[Thine earthly Sabbaths, Lord, we love] ------ 23
This day, at Thy creating word -------------- 3
This is the day of light --------------------- 36
This is the day the Lord hath made ---------- 38
Thou art gone up on high ------------------- 329
Thou art my hiding-place, O Lord ----------- 348
Thou art the Way—to Thee alone ----------- 206
Thou blessed Spirit, by whose aid ------------ 174
Thou blest Creator of the world ------------- 207
Thou Grace Divine, encircling all ------------ 326
Thou Judge of quick and dead -------------- 466
Thou, Lord, of all the parent art ------------ 95
Thou who didst leave Thy Father's breast ---- 129
Thou, whose Almighty word ---------------- 213
Thrice happy he whose tranquil mind -------- 439
Thrice happy souls, who born of heaven ----- 45
Through all the changing scenes of life ------ 294
Thus far the Lord has led me on ------------ 65
Thy holy will, my God, be mine ------------- 426
Thy praise alone, O Lord, doth reign -------- 296
Thy way, not mine, O Lord ----------------- 430
'Tis by the faith of joys to come ------------- 365
To God be glory, peace on earth ------------- 70
To God in whom I trust -------------------- 339
Trembling before Thine awful throne -------- 298

Unite, my roving thoughts, unite ------------ 346
Up to the hills I lift mine eyes -------------- 46

Up to the Lord that reigns on high............297
Upward I lift mine eyes....................... 85

Wake the song of jubilee......................220
Walk in the light! so shalt thou know..........374
Watchman! tell us of the night................221
We are on our journey home....................497
We sing the praise of Him who died............189
We walk by faith, and not by sight............367
We would see Jesus!—for the shadows lengthen.156
What are these in bright array................500
What equal honors shall we bring..............285
What sinners value I resign...................505
Whate'er my God ordains is right..............436
When all Thy mercies, O my God................100
When at Thy footstool, Lord, I bend...........383
When gathering clouds around I view...........442
When I can read my title clear................363
When I survey the wondrous cross..............190
When Jesus came to earth of old...............465
When marshaled on the nightly plain...........180
When my last hour is close at hand............471
When sins and fears prevailing rise...........338
When Thou, my righteous Judge, shalt come... 479
Where high the heavenly temple stands.........440
Wherewith, O Lord, shall I draw near..........204
While Thee I seek, protecting Power...........352
While, with ceaseless course, the sun.........148
Whither shall a creature run.................. 98
[Who are these in bright array]...............500
Who, O Lord, when life is o'er................396
Why will ye waste on trifling cares...........210
With one consent, let all the earth...........   1

Ye servants of the Lord.......................413
Ye that in His courts are found...............191
Yes, the Redeemer rose........................146

www.ingramcontent.com/pod-product-compliance
Lightning Source LLC
Chambersburg PA
CBHW032031220426
43664CB00006B/432